THE SHAKESPEARE PARALLEL TEXT SERIES, THIRD EDITION

W9-AJY-552

Othello

by William Shakespeare

Perfection Learning® Corporation
Logan, Iowa 51546-0500

Editorial Director	Julie A. Schumacher
Senior Editor	Rebecca Christian
Series Editor	Rebecca Burke
Editorial Assistant	Kate Winzenburg
Writer, Modern Version	Wim Coleman
Design Director	Randy Messer
Design	Mark Hagenberg
Production	PerfecType
Art Research	Laura Wells
Cover Art	Brad Holland

© 2004 **Perfection Learning® Corporation**
1000 North Second Avenue, P.O. Box 500
Logan, Iowa 51546-0500
Tel: 1-800-831-4190 • Fax: 1-800-543-2745

Printed in the United States of America.

PB ISBN-13: 978-0-7891-6082-9
PB ISBN-10: 0-7891-6082-X

RLB ISBN-13: 978-0-7569-1485-1
RLB ISBN-10: 0-7569-1485-X
  10 11 12 13 14 QW 14 13 12 11 10

Table of Contents

Othello
Fatal Jealousy

During the 1560s, an Italian diplomat in France heard rumors that his wife was being unfaithful to him. When he hurried back home to Italy to confront her, she protested her innocence, and he believed her. But with apologies, he strangled her anyway. Because his honor had been tainted, she could not be allowed to live.

The Italian author Giraldi Cinthio probably had this true event in mind when he first told the story of Othello. The hero of Cinthio's tale is a Moor (a dark-skinned northern African) who serves Venice as a military general. Like the real-life Italian diplomat, the fictional Othello is driven by jealousy to murder his innocent wife, Desdemona.

Shakespeare read Cinthio's version of the Othello story in a French translation and rewrote it as a stage tragedy, first presented in 1604.

Audiences Then and Now

Of all Shakespeare's greatest tragedies, *Othello* presents the most problems for today's audiences and readers. Now that domestic violence is recognized as a grave issue, how are we supposed to feel about this tale of murderous male jealousy?

In Shakespeare's England, a wife was considered a man's property. Wife-beating was routine and, for the most part, socially acceptable. Female adultery was grounds for marital separation—and for a short time in the mid-1500s, punishable by death. Of course, men were largely exempt from such penalties.

If Desdemona had really been guilty of adultery, many of Shakespeare's playgoers would have considered her murder justifiable. They found Desdemona's death tragic only because she was innocent. And they found it easy to sympathize with her deluded husband. Today's audiences are not quite so sure how to respond to Othello.

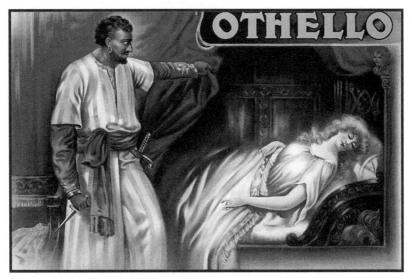

Lithograph printed between 1920 and 1930

A Valiant Warrior

On the one hand, we find much to sympathize with in the Moor. We are keenly aware that he is a racial and cultural outsider in Venice. Shakespeare himself probably thought little about race one way or the other. But during the centuries since his time, we have become keenly aware of the wages of prejudice. We grow uneasy when characters like Brabantio and Roderigo spout racial slurs against Othello.

And of course, Othello possesses genuine nobility and talents. In addition to being of royal descent, he is a valiant leader whose martial skills are essential to Venice's government. His integrity as a soldier is impeccable.

But his relationship with Desdemona is troubling. After he has killed Desdemona and discovered her innocence, Othello claims to have loved her "not wisely, but too well . . . ." While this line might have rung true in Shakespeare's time, it often makes today's readers and playgoers cringe.

Surely, we assume, Othello wouldn't have suspected Desdemona of infidelity if he had really known her. And how can he claim to have loved someone he never really knew? We can't help suspecting that Othello loved an ideal, not a flesh-and-blood human being.

Julienne Marie and James Earl Jones as Desdemona and Othello, 1964 production at the Delacorte Theatre, Central Park

Desdemona begging

Spirited Innocence

Our reactions to Desdemona are likely to be less complicated. We may even be surprised at how much we like her. These days, we tend to scoff at female characters who are celebrated for their innocence and purity. But Desdemona is more than a stereotype of passive femininity.

Othello himself admits that she wooed him aggressively. She is also more openly eager than her husband to consummate their marriage. And she is bold about pleading to Othello on behalf of his disgraced lieutenant, Cassio; she refuses to think of military matters as off-limits to her.

In fact, the play's characters speak of her as something of a soldier. "Our general's wife is now the general," Iago says of her. Cassio calls her "our great captain's captain." Even Othello greets her as "my fair warrior." And Desdemona herself wishes she had been born a man so she could have experienced her husband's adventures.

Her spirited assertiveness fills us with admiration and affection. Some critics have scarcely been able to forgive Shakespeare (let alone Othello) for her violent, pathetic death.

A Demi-Devil

In a more unsettling way, we cannot help but feel attracted to Othello's evil nemesis, Iago. We dread the consequences of his plots and deceptions. But his delight in his own cunning is somehow contagious. For one thing, he addresses the audience far more frequently than Othello, making us feel like unwitting accomplices.

We always know what he's up to—and yet he remains a mystery. Why is he so vengeful? Is it because Othello promoted Cassio and not him to the rank of lieutenant? Or because he mistakenly believes that Othello and Cassio have slept with his wife?

Some critics believe these motives are sufficient to explain Iago's actions. Others wonder if Iago has any real motives at all. Might he love doing evil purely for evil's sake?

Frederick Warde as Iago

In creating him, Shakespeare probably remembered outdoor religious plays he'd seen as a boy. These plays often featured an allegorical character known as "Vice," who represented wickedness. Vice was an entertaining and amusing character who, like Iago, took the audience into his confidence.

Iago's resemblance to the allegorical Vice gives him an outsized grandeur; he is also so vividly human that he chills us with familiarity. He is one of Shakespeare's most unforgettable characters.

A Voice for Today

Much ink has been spilt analyzing the characters of Othello, Desdemona, Iago, and even the rather colorless Cassio. Less has been written about Iago's sharp-tongued wife, Emilia.

Emilia is worldly and cynical—seemingly Desdemona's opposite. Most unlike Desdemona, she has few illusions about her marriage to Iago. True, she doesn't recognize her husband's capacity for villainy for some time. But once she does, she is a tower of moral outrage, and she does more than any other character in the play to destroy him.

In a much-ignored speech tucked away in Act IV, Emilia rails against what we call today the double standard. According to this now-waning code, women are expected to conform more strictly to sexual morality than men. Emilia makes short work of this concept:

Let husbands know
Their wives have sense like them; they see and smell
And have their palates both for sweet and sour
As husbands have.

Today, this speech impresses us with its eloquent common sense. But it wasn't so in Shakespeare's time, at least not for male readers and playgoers.

Emilia's words remind us to always be on the lookout for rare little gems in Shakespeare. Certainly, he was a master of grand effects. Othello's final "not wisely but too well" speech is stunning theater. But it's often in smaller, quieter moments like Emilia's speech that Shakespeare truly transcends his age.

※ ※ ※

Timeline

1564   Shakespeare is baptized.

1568   Elizabeth I becomes Queen of England.

1572   Shakespeare begins grammar school.

1576   Opening of The Theatre, the first permanent playhouse in England.

1580   Drake sails around the world.

1582   Shakespeare marries Anne Hathaway.

1583   Shakespeare's daughter Susanna is baptized.

1585   Shakespeare's twins are baptized.

1588   Spanish Armada is defeated.

1592–94   Plague closes all of London's theaters.

1594   *Titus Andronicus* becomes first printed Shakespeare play.

1594   Shakespeare joins the Lord Chamberlain's Men.

1599   Lord Chamberlain's Men build the Globe Theatre; Shakespeare is part-owner of the building.

1609   Shakespeare's *Sonnets* published for the first time.

1610   Shakespeare retires to Stratford.

1613   Globe Theatre burns to the ground.

1616   William Shakespeare dies at the age of 52.

1623   Shakespeare's wife dies.
First Folio published.

Reading *Othello*

Using This Parallel Text

This edition of *Othello* is especially designed for readers who aren't familiar with Shakespeare. If you're fairly comfortable with his language, simply read the original text on the left-hand page. When you come to a confusing word or passage, refer to the modern English version on the right or the footnotes at the bottom.

If you think Elizabethan English doesn't even sound like English, read a passage of the modern version silently. Then read the same passage of the original. You'll find that Shakespeare's language begins to come alive for you. You may choose to work your way through the entire play this way.

As you read more, you'll probably find yourself using the modern version less and less. Remember, the parallel version is meant to be an aid, not a substitute for the original. If you read only the modern version, you'll cheat yourself out of Shakespeare's language—his quick-witted puns, sharp-tongued insults, and evocative images.

Keep in mind that language is a living thing, constantly growing and changing. New words are invented and new definitions for old words are added. Since Shakespeare wrote over four hundred years ago, it is not surprising that his work seems challenging to today's readers.

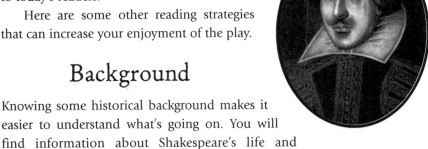

Here are some other reading strategies that can increase your enjoyment of the play.

Background

Knowing some historical background makes it easier to understand what's going on. You will find information about Shakespeare's life and Elizabethan theater at the back of the book. Reading the summaries that precede each act will also help you to follow the action of the play.

Getting the Beat

Like most dramatists of his time, Shakespeare frequently used **blank verse** in his plays. In blank verse, the text is written in measured lines that do not rhyme. Look at the following example from *Othello*.

> She lov'd me for the dangers I had pass'd,
> And I lov'd her that she did pity them.
> This only is the witchcraft I have us'd.
> Here comes the lady. Let her witness it.

You can see that the four lines above are approximately equal in length, but they do not cover the whole width of the page as the lines in a story or essay might. They are, in fact, unrhymed verse with each line containing ten or eleven syllables. Furthermore, the ten syllables can be divided into five sections, called **iambs**, or feet. Each iamb contains one unstressed (**U**) and one stressed (**/**) syllable. Try reading the lines below, giving emphasis to the capitalized syllable in each iamb.

U	/	U	/	U	/	U	/	U	/
She LOVED		me FOR		the DAN		gers I		had PASS'D,	

U	/	U	/	U	/	U	/	U	/
And I		loved HER		that SHE		did PI		ty THEM.	

The length of a line of verse is measured by counting the stresses. This length is known as the **meter.** When there are five stresses and the rhythm follows an unstressed/stressed pattern, it is known as **iambic pentameter**. Much of Shakespeare's work is written in iambic pentameter.

Of course, Shakespeare was not rigid about this format. He sometimes varied the lines by putting accents in unusual places, by having lines with more or fewer than ten syllables, and by varying where pauses occur. An actor's interpretation can also add variety. (Only a terrible actor would deliver lines in a way that makes the rhythm sound singsong!)

Prose

In addition to verse, Shakespeare wrote speeches in **prose**, or language without rhythmic structure. Look at the dialogue between Roderigo and Iago on pages 68–74 (Act I, Scene iii, lines 329–402). If you try beating out an iambic rhythm to these lines, you'll find it doesn't work because the characters are speaking in prose. Not until Roderigo leaves and Iago speaks in soliloquy ("Thus do I ever make my fool my purse . . . ") will you be able to find the rhythm of iambic pentameter again. Shakespeare often uses prose for comic speeches, to show madness, and for characters of lower social rank such as servants. His upper-class characters generally do not speak in prose. But these weren't hard and fast rules as far as Shakespeare was concerned. Whether characters speak in verse or prose is often a function of the situation and whom they're addressing, as well as their social status.

Contractions

As you know, contractions are words that have been combined by substituting an apostrophe for a letter or letters that have been removed. Contractions were as common in Shakespeare's time as they are today. For example, we use *it's* as a contraction for the words *it is*. In Shakespeare's writing you will discover that *'tis* means the same thing. Shakespeare often used the apostrophe to shorten words so that they would fit into the rhythmic pattern of a line. This is especially true of verbs ending in *-ed*. Note that in Shakespeare's plays, the *-ed* at the end of a verb is usually pronounced as a separate syllable. Therefore, *walked* would be pronounced as two syllables, *walk*ed*, while *walk'd* would be only one.

Speak and Listen

Remember that plays are written to be acted, not read silently. Reading out loud—whether in a group or alone—helps you to "hear" the meaning. Listening to another reader will also help. You might also enjoy listening to a recording of the play by professional actors.

Clues and Cues

Shakespeare was sparing in his use of stage directions. In fact, many of those in modern editions were added by later editors. Added stage directions are usually indicated by brackets. For example, [*aside*] tells the actor to give the audience information that the other characters can't hear.

Sometimes a character's actions are suggested by the lines themselves.

The Play's the Thing

Finally, if you can't figure out every word in the play, don't get discouraged. The people in Shakespeare's audience couldn't either. At that time, language was changing rapidly and standardized spelling, punctuation, grammar, and even dictionaries did not exist. Besides, Shakespeare loved to play with words. He made up new combinations, like *fat-guts* and *mumble-news*. To make matters worse, the actors probably spoke very rapidly. But the audience didn't strain to catch every word. They went to a Shakespeare play for the same reasons we go to a movie—to get caught up in the story and the acting, to have a great laugh or a good cry.

❉ ❉ ❉

Cast of Characters

OTHELLO a Moorish general in the Venetian army

DESDEMONA a Venetian lady

BRABANTIO a Venetian senator, father to Desdemona

IAGO Othello's standard-bearer, or "ancient"

EMILIA Iago's wife and Desdemona's attendant

CASSIO Othello's second-in-command, or lieutenant

RODERIGO a Venetian gentleman

DUKE OF VENICE

LODOVICO
GRATIANO } Venetian gentlemen, kinsmen to Brabantio

VENETIAN SENATORS

MONTANO an official in Cyprus

BIANCA a woman in Cyprus in love with Cassio

CLOWN a comic servant to Othello and Desdemona

GENTLEMEN OF CYPRUS

SAILORS

SERVANTS, ATTENDANTS, OFFICERS, MESSENGERS, HERALD, MUSICIANS, TORCHBEARERS

Othello

ACT I

Spanish opera singer Placido Domingo as Othello in Verdi's opera *Otello*, directed by
Franco Zeffirelli, 1985

"A fellow almost damned in a fair wife . . ."

❊ ❊ ❊

Before You Read

1. This play will present a marriage between two people of different cultural and racial backgrounds. What kind of conflicts might develop in such a play?

2. Think of a time when you were lied to by someone you trusted. How did this experience make you feel?

3. Have you ever felt like an outsider? Describe the situation and your reaction to it.

Literary Elements

1. **Exposition** is the background information needed to understand the action of a story. Early in Act I, Iago has two long speeches that tell how he has been overlooked for a promotion and why he is plotting revenge. While they give important information, they also provide insights into Iago's character and foreshadow the deceit to come.

2. **Imagery** refers to language that appeals to the five senses. A storm at sea is described this way in *Othello*: ". . . the chidden billow seems to pelt the clouds; / The wind-shak'd surge, with high and monstrous mane, / Seems to cast water on the burning Bear / And quench the guards of th' ever-fixed Pole."

3. A **monologue** is a speech delivered to other characters in the play. In Act I, Scene i, Iago tells Roderigo in a monologue about his plans to seek revenge on Othello. A **soliloquy** is a speech delivered by a character when he or she is alone; Act I ends with Iago on stage alone, calling Roderigo a fool and revealing that he is only using him.

Words to Know

The following vocabulary words appear in Act I in the original text of Shakespeare's play. However, they are words that are still used today. Read the definitions here and pay attention to the words as you read the play (they will be in boldfaced type).

abhor	hate; detest
equivocal	open to two interpretations; undecided
facile	easy; simplistic
gall	annoy; irritate
imminent	upcoming; threatening
incur	earn; acquire
iniquity	wickedness; evil
insolent	rude; disrespectful
lascivious	lustful; lewd
obsequious	excessively courteous; flattering
palpable	obvious; clear
promulgate	proclaim; declare
timorous	fearful; terrified
usurped [usurp'd]	took without permission; appropriated
vexation	anger; annoyance

Act Summary

One night in Venice, Roderigo is stunned by what his friend Iago tells him. He says that the beautiful Desdemona has eloped with Othello, a Moorish general. As Desdemona's rejected suitor, Roderigo is wild with jealousy.

Iago assures Roderigo that he, too, hates Othello. Othello's longtime ensign, Iago had expected to be promoted to lieutenant. Instead, Othello chose Cassio, who has never even seen battle.

Iago and Roderigo go to the house of Brabantio, Desdemona's father, to tell him about the elopement. Furious, Brabantio seeks out Othello, who has been summoned by the Duke of Venice on other business.

Douglass Campbell as Othello, Nicholas Hannen as Brabantio, and Irene Worth as Desdemona, 1951 production by the Old Vic Theatre Company

To the Duke, Brabantio accuses Othello of having bewitched Desdemona. How else, Brabantio asks, could she have fallen in love with the black, fearsome Moor?

But Othello tells the Duke a very different story. He was a frequent guest at Brabantio's house, where he told many tales of his adventures. These stories—not witchcraft—won Desdemona's love.

Desdemona herself arrives at the Duke's palace and declares her devotion to Othello. The Duke rejects Brabantio's accusation and moves on to more pressing matters.

A Turkish fleet is on its way to attack the island of Cyprus. The Duke names Othello the new governor of Cyprus, and orders him to leave immediately to defend the island. Desdemona will join her husband there.

Iago promises to help Roderigo become Desdemona's lover. But Iago is really only tricking Roderigo out of his money and using him for revenge. Rumor has it that Othello has slept with Iago's wife. Whether this rumor is true or not, Iago is determined to ruin the Moor.

ACT I, SCENE I

[*Venice. A street.*] *Enter* RODERIGO *and* IAGO.

RODERIGO

Tush! Never tell me! I take it much unkindly
That thou, Iago, who hast had my purse
As if the strings were thine, shouldst know of this.

IAGO

'Sblood,* but you'll not hear me.
5   If ever I did dream of such a matter,
Abhor me.

RODERIGO

Thou told'st me thou didst hold him in thy hate.

IAGO

Despise me if I do not. Three great ones of the city,
In personal suit to make me his lieutenant,
10   Off-capp'd to him; and, by the faith of man,
I know my price; I am worth no worse a place.
But he, as loving his own pride and purposes,
Evades them with a bombast circumstance
Horribly stuff'd with epithets of war,
15   And, in conclusion,
Nonsuits my mediators; for "Certes," says he,
"I have already chose my officer."
And what was he?
Forsooth, a great arithmetician,
20   One Michael Cassio, a Florentine,
(A fellow almost damn'd in a fair wife)*
That never set a squadron in the field,
Nor the division of a battle knows
More than a spinster, unless the bookish theoric,
25   Wherein the togged consuls can propose
As masterly as he. Mere prattle without practice
Is all his soldiership. But he, sir, had th' election;

---

4   *'Sblood* an oath meaning "God's blood"

21 (*A fellow . . . fair wife*) Shakespeare may have originally intended for Cassio to
be married and forgot to correct this reference when he changed Cassio to a
bachelor.

ACT 1, SCENE 1

A street in Venice. RODERIGO *and* IAGO *enter.*

RODERIGO

What! Not tell me! I take it very badly
that you, Iago, who have had my money
as if it were your own, would know about this.

IAGO

By God, you just won't listen to me!
If I ever dreamed up such a thing,   5
you can hate me for it.

RODERIGO

You told me you hated him.

IAGO

Despise me if I don't. Three great men in the city
personally asked him to make me his lieutenant
and took off their hats to him; and, by God,   10
I know what I'm worth; I deserve no lower rank.
But he, in love with his own pride and purposes,
evades my friends with roundabout puffery,
overblown with lots of war talk;
and, to sum up,   15
he denies my mediators. "Certainly," he says,
"I've already picked my officer."
And who is he?
No one but a great tactician,
a certain Michael Cassio, a Florentine   20
(a man whose good-looking wife spells trouble for him),
who never led a squadron on the field,
and doesn't know the first thing about war—
no more than a spinster does—unless you mean book learning,
in which elderly statesmen are   25
just as learned as he is. Just talk and no experience:
that's the kind of soldier he is. But he, sir, was chosen;

And I, of whom his eyes had seen the proof
At Rhodes, at Cyprus, and on other grounds
30 Christen'd and heathen, must be be-lee'd and calm'd
By debitor and creditor; this counter-caster,
He, in good time, must his lieutenant be,
And I—God bless the mark!—his Moorship's ancient.

RODERIGO

By heaven, I rather would have been his hangman.

IAGO

35 Why, there's no remedy. 'Tis the curse of service,
Preferment goes by letter and affection,
And not by old gradation, where each second
Stood heir to th' first. Now, sir, be judge yourself
Whether I in any just term am affin'd
40 To love the Moor.

RODERIGO

I would not follow him then.

IAGO

                              O, sir, content you;
I follow him to serve my turn upon him.
We cannot all be masters, nor all masters
45 Cannot be truly follow'd. You shall mark
Many a duteous and knee-crooking knave
That, doting on his own **obsequious** bondage,
Wears out his time, much like his master's ass,
For naught but provender, and when he's old, cashier'd.
50 Whip me such honest knaves. Others there are
Who, trimm'd in forms and visages of duty,
Keep yet their hearts attending on themselves,
And, throwing but shows of service on their lords,
Do well thrive by them and, when they have lin'd
55   their coats,
Do themselves homage. These fellows have some soul;
And such a one do I profess myself. For, sir,
It is as sure as you are Roderigo,
Were I the Moor, I would not be Iago.
60 In following him, I follow but myself;

and I (whose abilities he has seen
at Rhodes, Cyprus, and in other countries
both Christian and heathen) must be stopped head-on   30
by this accountant, this bookkeeper.
He, to be sure, will be his lieutenant,
and I (God help us all!), the noble Moor's ensign.

RODERIGO

By heaven, I would rather be his hangman.

IAGO

Well, there's nothing to be done; this is what comes of good   35
    service.
Promotion comes from influence and personal liking
and not from good old seniority, where a man second in line
is heir to the one in first place. Now, sir, judge for yourself
if I am bound by any good reason
to love the Moor.   40

RODERIGO

I wouldn't follow him, then.

IAGO

Oh, sir, rest assured.
I'll follow him to get back at him.
We can't all be in charge, and some who are in charge
can't be honestly followed. You will notice   45
many a dutiful, bowing rascal
who, delighting in his own subservience,
uses up his time much like his master's donkey does,
for nothing except his feed. And when he's old, he's dismissed.
You can whip those honest rascals for all I care! There are others 50
who, putting on a good show of duty,
are really looking out for their own interest;
and, giving their lords just a hollow show of duty,
they get along quite well. When they've stuffed their pockets,   55
they serve themselves and no one else. These fellows have
    some spirit,
and I consider myself to be one of their sort. Because, sir,
as sure as your name is Roderigo,
if I were the Moor, I wouldn't be Iago.
In following him, I'm really following my own desires.   60

Heaven is my judge, not I for love and duty,
But seeming so, for my peculiar end;
For when my outward action doth demonstrate
The native act and figure of my heart
65 In complement extern, 'tis not long after
But I will wear my heart upon my sleeve
For daws* to peck at. I am not what I am.

RODERIGO

What a full fortune does the thick-lips* owe,
If he can carry 't thus!

IAGO

70   Call up her father,
Rouse him. Make after him, poison his delight,
Proclaim him in the streets. Incense her kinsmen,
And, though he in a fertile climate dwell,
Plague him with flies. Though that his joy be joy,
75 Yet throw such chances of **vexation** on 't,
As it may lose some colour.

RODERIGO

Here is her father's house; I'll call aloud.

IAGO

Do, with like **timorous** accent and dire yell
As when, by night and negligence, the fire
80 Is spied in populous cities.

RODERIGO

What, ho, Brabantio! Signior Brabantio, ho!

IAGO

Awake! What, ho, Brabantio! Thieves! Thieves!
Look to your house, your daughter, and your bags!
Thieves! Thieves!

    BRABANTIO *appears above, at a window.*

---

67 *daws* or jackdaws, are birds of the crow family found in Europe

68 *thick-lips* a reference to Othello's supposedly Negroid appearance. References
such as Roderigo's here, as well as later remarks about Othello's "sooty" and
"black" coloring, seem to indicate that Shakespeare pictured Othello as black.

As heaven is my judge, I'll not act with sincere love and duty,
but I'll seem to, for my own personal ends;
for when my behavior truly reflects
the real motives of my heart
in outward appearance, it won't be long   65
before I wear my heart on my sleeve
for jackdaws to peck at. I'm never what I seem to be.

RODERIGO

What good luck the thick-lips has
if he can get away with this!

IAGO

Wake up her father: 70
get him riled. Chase after Othello and ruin his joy,
mock him in the streets, outrage her relatives,
and though he lives in a pleasant climate,
annoy him with flies. If we can't stop his joy from being joy,
we can at least cause him enough trouble   75
to make it lose some of its flavor.

RODERIGO

Here's her father's house. I'll call out.

IAGO

Do so, and with a terrifying voice and a desperate yell,
as when, because of some carelessness at night, a fire
has been spotted in a populous city.   80

RODERIGO

Hello! Brabantio! Signior Brabantio! Hello!

IAGO

Wake up! Hello, Brabantio! Thieves! Thieves! Thieves!
Check your house, your daughter, and your money!
Thieves! Thieves!

> BRABANTIO *enters at an upstairs window.*

BRABANTIO

85   What is the reason of this terrible summons?
      What is the matter there?

RODERIGO

      Signior, is all your family within?

IAGO

      Are your doors lock'd?

BRABANTIO

                          Why, wherefore ask you this?

IAGO

90   'Zounds,* sir, you're robb'd! For shame, put on your gown.
      Your heart is burst, you have lost half your soul.
      Even now, now, very now, an old black ram
      Is tupping your white ewe. Arise, arise!
      Awake the snorting citizens with the bell,
95   Or else the devil will make a grandsire of you.
      Arise, I say!

BRABANTIO

                          What, have you lost your wits?

RODERIGO

      Most reverend signior, do you know my voice?

BRABANTIO

      Not I. What are you?

RODERIGO

100   My name is Roderigo.

BRABANTIO

                          The worser welcome;
      I have charg'd thee not to haunt about my doors.
      In honest plainness thou hast heard me say
      My daughter is not for thee; and now, in madness,
105   Being full of supper and distemp'ring draughts,
      Upon malicious bravery dost thou come
      To start my quiet.

RODERIGO

                          Sir, sir, sir—

---

90   *'Zounds* a curse meaning "God's wounds"

BRABANTIO

What's the reason for this awful racket?   85
What's the matter here?

RODERIGO

Signior, is all your family indoors?

IAGO

Are your doors locked?

BRABANTIO

Why? What's your reason for asking?

IAGO

Heavens, sir, you've been robbed! For shame, put on your gown!   90
Your heart has been burst, you've lost half your soul.
Even now, now, right now, an old black ram
is mating with your white ewe. Get up, get up!
Wake up your snoring neighbors with the bell,
or else the devil will make you a grandfather.   95
Get up, I tell you!

BRABANTIO

What, are you out of your mind?

RODERIGO

Most honored gentleman, don't you know my voice?

BRABANTIO

No. Who are you?

RODERIGO

My name is Roderigo.   100

BRABANTIO

You're not welcome here!
I've told you not to hang around my door!
You've heard me say quite plainly
that my daughter is not for you. And now, like a crazy man
full of supper and intoxicating drink,   105
you come here with dangerous mischief
to disrupt my peace.

RODERIGO

Sir, sir, sir—

BRABANTIO

But thou must needs be sure
110 My spirits and my place have in their power
To make this bitter to thee.

RODERIGO

Patience, good sir.

BRABANTIO

What tell'st thou me of robbing?
This is Venice; my house is not a grange.

RODERIGO

115 Most grave Brabantio
In simple and pure soul I come to you.

IAGO

'Zounds, sir, you are one of those that will not serve God,
if the devil bid you. Because we come to do you service
and you think we are ruffians, you'll have your daughter
120 cover'd with a Barbary horse; you'll have your nephews
neigh to you; you'll have coursers for cousins, and jennets
for germans.

BRABANTIO

What profane wretch art thou?

IAGO

I am one, sir, that comes to tell you your daughter and the
125 Moor are now making the beast with two backs.

BRABANTIO

Thou art a villain.

IAGO

You are a senator.

BRABANTIO

This thou shalt answer; I know thee, Roderigo.

RODERIGO

Sir, I will answer anything. But, I beseech you,
130 If 't be your pleasure and most wise consent,
As partly I find it is, that your fair daughter,
At this odd-even and dull watch o' th' night,
Transported, with no worse nor better guard

BRABANTIO

But you should be told
that, with my temper and my position, I have it in my power   110
to make you pay for this.

RODERIGO

Be patient, good sir.

BRABANTIO

Why do you talk to me of robbing? This is Venice,
not some out-of-the-way farmhouse.

RODERIGO

Most reverend Brabantio,   115
I have come here with pure and simple motives.

IAGO

Heavens, sir, you're one of those who wouldn't serve God if
the devil told you to. Because we have come to help you, and
you think we are ruffians, you'll let your daughter be mated
with a Moorish horse. You'll have your grandsons neigh at you.   120
You'll have chargers for relations and Spanish horses for your
nearest family.

BRABANTIO

What kind of foul-mouthed creature are you?

IAGO

I am a man, sir, who has come to tell you that your daughter
and the Moor are now making the beast with two backs.   125

BRABANTIO

You are a villain.

IAGO

You are a senator.

BRABANTIO

You'll answer for this. I know who you are, Roderigo.

RODERIGO

Sir, I'll answer everything. But I beg you,
if it is with your desire and your wise consent   130
(as I'm starting to think it is) that your lovely daughter,
at this strange hour between night and morning,
has been carried off with no worse or better a guard

But with a knave of common hire, a gondolier,
135 To the gross clasps of a **lascivious** Moor—
If this be known to you and your allowance,
We then have done you bold and saucy wrongs;
But if you know not this, my manners tell me
We have your wrong rebuke. Do not believe
140 That, from the sense of all civility,
I thus would play and trifle with your reverence.
Your daughter, if you have not given her leave,
I say again, hath made a gross revolt,
Tying her duty, beauty, wit, and fortunes
145 In an extravagant and wheeling stranger
Of here and everywhere. Straight satisfy yourself.
If she be in her chamber or your house,
Let loose on me the justice of the state
For thus deluding you.

BRABANTIO
150 Strike on the tinder, ho!
Give me a taper! Call up all my people!
This accident is not unlike my dream;
Belief of it oppresses me already.
Light, I say! Light!

[*Exit above.*]

IAGO
155 Farewell; for I must leave you.
It seems not meet, nor wholesome to my place,
To be produc'd—as, if I stay, I shall—
Against the Moor; for, I do know, the state,
However this may **gall** him with some check,
160 Cannot with safety cast him, for he's embark'd
With such loud reason to the Cyprus wars,
Which even now stands in act, that, for their souls,
Another of his fathom they have none
To lead their business; in which regard,
165 Though I do hate him as I do hell-pains,
Yet for necessity of present life,
I must show out a flag and sign of love,
Which is indeed but sign. That you shall surely find him,

than a lowly, hired rascal, a gondolier,
and delivered to the repulsive embraces of a lustful Moor—   135
if you know this already, and you allow it,
we then have done you a bold and insolent wrong.
But if you do not know this, my sense of fair play tells me
that you rebuke us wrongly. Don't believe
that, from a feeling of propriety alone,   140
I would come like this to tease and play games with a
    respectable man like you.
Your daughter, if you haven't given her permission,
I tell you again, has rebelled outrageously,
tying her duty, beauty, intelligence, and fortunes
to a wandering and vagrant stranger   145
who lives here and everywhere. Go see for yourself at once.
If she is in her room, or your house,
bring the justice of the state against me
for deceiving you like this.

BRABANTIO

Light the kindling, now!   150
Give me a candle! Wake up the household!
What you've said is not unlike my dream;
I'm already disturbed by my belief in it.
Light, I say! Light!

    He exits from above.

IAGO

Good-bye, for I must leave you.   155
It doesn't seem proper or beneficial to my position
to be a witness (as I will be if I stay)
against the Moor. For I know that the state,
though it might give him a slight reprimand,
can't dismiss him safely. For I know he's on his way,   160
with a great to-do, to the Cyprus wars,
which are going on right now. And to save their souls,
they don't have another man with his abilities
to take charge of their business. Therefore,
though I hate him as much as I hate the pains of hell,   165
still, the present circumstances make it necessary
for me to put on an outward appearance of love—
which is really just a show. To be sure that you'll find him,

170   Lead to the Sagittary* the raised search;
And there will I be with him. So, farewell.

> [*Exit.*]

> Enter below, BRABANTIO *in his night-gown, and*
> SERVANTS *with torches.*

BRABANTIO
It is too true an evil; gone she is;
And what's to come of my despised time
Is naught but bitterness.— Now, Roderigo,
Where didst thou see her?— O unhappy girl!—

175   With the Moor, say'st thou?— Who would be a father!
How didst thou know 'twas she?— O, she deceives me
Past thought!— What said she to you?— Get more tapers;
Raise all my kindred.— Are they married, think you?

RODERIGO
Truly, I think they are.

BRABANTIO
180   O heaven! How got she out? O treason of the blood!
Fathers, from hence trust not your daughters' minds
By what you see them act.—Is there not charms
By which the property of youth and maidhood
May be abus'd? Have you not read, Roderigo,

185   Of some such thing?

RODERIGO
               Yes, sir, I have indeed.

BRABANTIO
Call up my brother.—O, would you had had her!—
Some one way, some another.—Do you know
Where we may apprehend her and the Moor?

---

169   *Sagittary* probably the name of an inn

bring your search party to the Sagittary,
and I'll be with him there. So, good-bye.   170

> *He exits.*

> BRABANTIO *enters below in his nightgown, with* SERVANTS
> *carrying torches.*

BRABANTIO
This evil thing is all too true. She's gone;
and what's left of my wretched life
will be nothing but bitterness. Now, Roderigo,
where did you see her?—Oh, the unfortunate girl!—
With the Moor, you said?—Who would want to be a father?— 175
How did you know it was her?—Oh, she deceives me
beyond imagining!—What did she say to you?—Get more
    candles!
Wake up my family!—Are they already married, do you think?

RODERIGO
Indeed, I think they are.

BRABANTIO
Oh, heavens! How did she get out? Oh, to have my own flesh   180
    and blood rebel like this!
Fathers, from now on, never trust your daughters' minds
on the basis of what you see them do. Aren't there magical
    spells
by which the nature of youth and virginity
can be deluded? Haven't you heard, Roderigo,
about this sort of thing?   185

RODERIGO
Yes, sir, I certainly have.

BRABANTIO
Wake up my brother.—Oh, if only she had been yours!—
(*to his* SERVANTS) Some of you go one way, and some of you
    go another. (*to* RODERIGO) Do you know
where we may apprehend her and the Moor?

RODERIGO

190   I think I can discover him, if you please
To get good guard and go along with me.

BRABANTIO

Pray you, lead on. At every house I'll call;
I may command at most.— Get weapons, ho!
And raise some special officers of night.—
195   On, good Roderigo; I'll deserve your pains.

[*Exeunt.*]

RODERIGO

 I think I can find him if you will   190
 get a good escort and come along with me.

BRABANTIO

 Please lead on. I'll call out at every house;
 I'm influential enough to get help from most of them. (*to his*
  SERVANTS) Get weapons at once,
 and wake up the special night guards!
 Let's go, good Roderigo. I'll reward your efforts.   195

  They exit.

ACT I, SCENE II

[*Another street.*] *Enter* OTHELLO, IAGO, *and*
ATTENDANTS *with torches.*

IAGO

Though in the trade of war I have slain men,
Yet do I hold it very stuff o' th' conscience
To do no contriv'd murder. I lack **iniquity**
Sometimes to do me service. Nine or ten times
5   I'd thought to have yerk'd him here under the ribs.

OTHELLO

'Tis better as it is.

IAGO

                Nay, but he prated,
And spoke such scurvy and provoking terms
Against your Honour
10   That, with the little godliness I have,
I did full hard forbear him. But, I pray you, sir,
Are you fast married? Be assur'd of this,
That the magnifico is much belov'd,
And hath in his effect a voice potential
15   As double as the Duke's. He will divorce you,
Or put upon you what restraint or grievance
The law, with all his might to enforce it on,
Will give him cable.

OTHELLO

                Let him do his spite;
20   My services which I have done the signiory*
Shall out-tongue his complaints. 'Tis yet to know—
Which, when I know that boasting is an honour,
I shall **promulgate**—I fetch my life and being
From men of royal siege, and my demerits
25   May speak unbonneted to as proud a fortune
As this that I have reach'd. For know, Iago,
But that I love the gentle Desdemona,

---

20   *signiory* the rulers of Venice

ACT 1, SCENE 2

Another street. OTHELLO, IAGO, *and* ATTENDANTS *enter with torches.*

IAGO

Though in the practice of war I have killed men,
still, I consider it the very essence of principle
to not commit premeditated murder. Sometimes I don't have
    enough wickedness
to serve my own needs. Nine or ten times
I considered jabbing him right here, under the ribs.   5

OTHELLO

It's better as it is.

IAGO

No, but he spoke rudely
and said such insulting and provoking things
against your Honor
that, with what little patience I have,   10
I could scarcely stop from attacking him. But I ask you, sir,
are you securely married? You can be sure of this:
Brabantio is much loved
and has enough of a voice in things
to match the Duke. He'll see to it that you're divorced,   15
or bring whatever restraints and charges against you
which the law, with all his power to enforce it,
will allow him.

OTHELLO

Let him do his worst.
The services which I have performed for the state   20
will speak louder than his complaints. It's not yet known—
but when I find out it's honorable to boast,
I will proclaim it—that I am descended
from men of royal rank. And for my just desserts,
I have the right to claim (without apology) as fine a fortune 25
as the one I have gained by marriage. Be sure of this, Iago:
if I didn't love the gentle Desdemona so much,

I would not my unhoused free condition
Put into circumscription and confine
30   For the sea's worth. But, look! What lights come yond?

Enter CASSIO, *with* OFFICERS *and torches.*

IAGO

Those are the raised father and his friends.
You were best go in.

OTHELLO

Not I; I must be found.
My parts, my title, and my perfect soul
35   Shall manifest me rightly. Is it they?

IAGO

By Janus,* I think no.

OTHELLO

The servants of the Duke and my lieutenant.
The goodness of the night upon you, friends!
What is the news?

CASSIO

40   The Duke does greet you, General,
And he requires your haste-post-haste appearance,
Even on the instant.

OTHELLO

               What is the matter, think you?

CASSIO

Something from Cyprus, as I may divine;
45   It is a business of some heat. The galleys
Have sent a dozen sequent messengers
This very night at one another's heels,
And many of the Consuls, rais'd and met,
Are at the Duke's already. You have been hotly call'd for;
50   When, being not at your lodging to be found,
The Senate hath sent about three several quests
To search you out.

---

36   *Janus* a Roman god with two faces

I wouldn't have my unconfined, free condition
put into boundaries and confines
for all the treasure in the sea. But look; some torchbearers 30
are coming.

CASSIO and OFFICERS enter with torches.

IAGO

They are the awakened father and his friends.
You'd better get inside.

OTHELLO

Not I. I must be found.
My talents, my title, and my clean conscience
will speak well of me. Is it them? 35

IAGO

By Janus, I don't think so.

OTHELLO

The Duke's servants? And my lieutenant?
Best wishes of the night to you, friends!
What's the news?

CASSIO

The Duke sends his greetings, General; 40
and he asks that you immediately appear before him
this very instant.

OTHELLO

What do you think is the matter?

CASSIO

Some news from Cyprus, I imagine.
It's urgent business. The officers of the galleys 45
have sent a dozen messengers consecutively,
this very night, at one another's heels.
And many of the Consuls, awake and gathered,
are already at the Duke's. You have been urgently called for.
When you were not to be found at your home, 50
the Senate sent out three separate parties
to search for you.

OTHELLO

               'Tis well I am found by you.
I will but spend a word here in the house.
55   And go with you.

     [*Exit.*]

CASSIO

            Ancient, what makes he here?

IAGO

Faith, he tonight hath boarded a land carrack.
If it prove lawful prize, he's made forever.

CASSIO

I do not understand.

IAGO

60   He's married.

CASSIO

                     To who?

IAGO

Marry,* to—

     Reenter OTHELLO.

           Come, captain, will you go?

OTHELLO

Have with you.

CASSIO

65   Here comes another troop to seek for you.

     Enter BRABANTIO, RODERIGO, *and* OFFICERS *with
torches and weapons.*

IAGO

It is Brabantio. General, be advis'd;
He comes to bad intent.

OTHELLO

            Holla! Stand there!

---

62 *Marry* an oath taken from the phrase "by the Virgin Mary," which came to mean
"indeed" or "really"

OTHELLO
It's good that you have found me.
I have just a word to say inside,
and then I'll go with you.   55

      Exit.

CASSIO
Ensign, what's he doing here?

IAGO
To tell the truth, he has boarded a rich vessel tonight.
If it proves a lawful prize, he's set for life.

CASSIO
I don't understand.

IAGO
He's married.   60

CASSIO
To whom?

IAGO
Why, to—

      OTHELLO *reenters.*

Come, captain, are you ready to go?

OTHELLO
Let's be gone.

CASSIO
Here comes another group of searchers.   65

      BRABANTIO, RODERIGO, *and* OFFICERS *enter with torches and*
      weapons.

IAGO
It's Brabantio. General, be warned;
he comes with bad intentions.

OTHELLO
Hello! Stand right there!

RODERIGO

Signior, it is the Moor.

BRABANTIO

70   Down with him, thief!

[They draw their swords.]

IAGO

You, Roderigo! Come, sir, I am for you.

OTHELLO

Keep up your bright swords, for the dew will rust them.
Good signior, you shall more command with years
Than with your weapons.

BRABANTIO

75   O thou foul thief, where hast thou stow'd my daughter?
Damn'd as thou art, thou hast enchanted her;
For I'll refer me to all things of sense,
If she in chains of magic were not bound,
Whether a maid so tender, fair, and happy,
80   So opposite to marriage that she shunn'd
The wealthy curled darlings of our nation,
Would ever have, t' **incur** a general mock,
Run from her guardage to the sooty bosom
Of such a thing as thou—to fear, not to delight.
85   Judge me the world, if 'tis not gross in sense
That thou hast practis'd on her with foul charms,
Abus'd her delicate youth with drugs or minerals
That weakens motion. I'll have 't disputed on;
'Tis probable, and **palpable**, to thinking.
90   I therefore apprehend and do attach thee
For an abuser of the world, a practiser
Of arts inhibited and out of warrant.
Lay hold upon him; if he do resist,
Subdue him at his peril.

OTHELLO

95   Hold your hands,
Both you of my inclining and the rest.
Were it my cue to fight, I should have known it

RODERIGO

Signior, it is the Moor.

BRABANTIO

Down with him, the thief! 70

Both groups of men draw their swords.

IAGO

You, Roderigo! Come, sir, I'll fight you.

OTHELLO

Put away your shining swords; the dew will rust them.
Good signior, you'll do better to command on the authority
     of your age
than with your weapons.

BRABANTIO

Oh, you foul thief, where have you hidden my daughter? 75
Damned as you are, you've put a spell on her!
For I ask you in the name of common sense,
if she weren't bound in the chains of magic,
would a girl so tender, lovely, and happy,
so opposed to marriage that she shunned 80
the wealthiest young beaus of our nation,
would she have ever (at the threat of public shame)
run from her safety to the sooty bosom
of such a thing as you—worthy of fear, not delight?
Let the world judge for me if it isn't grossly obvious 85
that you have practiced foul spells on her,
deceiving her delicate youth with drugs or minerals
that weaken the will. I'll have it argued legally.
It's probable and all too clear to see.
Therefore, I arrest and charge you 90
as a deceiver of the world, a practitioner
of forbidden and illegal arts.
Lay hold of him. If he resists,
let it be at his own risk.

OTHELLO

Leave your swords alone— 95
both those of you on my side and the rest.
If it were my cue to fight, I would have known it

Without a prompter.—Whither will you that I go
To answer this your charge?

BRABANTIO

100   To prison, till fit time
Of law and course of direct session
Call thee to answer.

OTHELLO

What if I do obey?
How may the Duke be therewith satisfi'd,
105   Whose messengers are here about my side,
Upon some present business of the state,
To bring me to him?

OFFICER

'Tis true, most worthy signior.
The Duke's in council; and your noble self,
110   I am sure, is sent for.

BRABANTIO

How? The Duke? In council?
In this time of the night? Bring him away;
Mine's not an idle cause. The Duke himself,
Or any of my brothers of the state,
115   Cannot but feel this wrong as 'twere their own;
For if such actions may have passage free,
Bondslaves and pagans shall our statesmen be.

[*Exeunt.*]

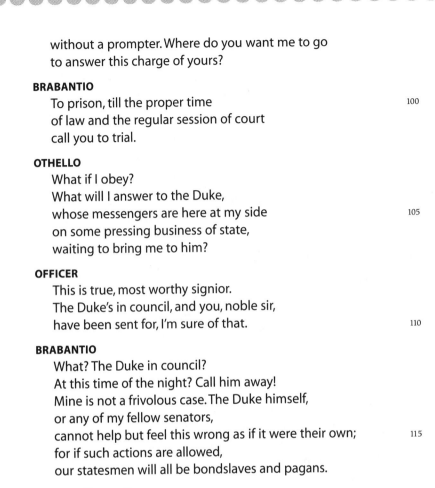

without a prompter. Where do you want me to go
to answer this charge of yours?

BRABANTIO

To prison, till the proper time   100
of law and the regular session of court
call you to trial.

OTHELLO

What if I obey?
What will I answer to the Duke,
whose messengers are here at my side   105
on some pressing business of state,
waiting to bring me to him?

OFFICER

This is true, most worthy signior.
The Duke's in council, and you, noble sir,
have been sent for, I'm sure of that.   110

BRABANTIO

What? The Duke in council?
At this time of the night? Call him away!
Mine is not a frivolous case. The Duke himself,
or any of my fellow senators,
cannot help but feel this wrong as if it were their own;   115
for if such actions are allowed,
our statesmen will all be bondslaves and pagans.

> *They exit.*

ACT I, SCENE III

[A council-chamber.] The DUKE *and* SENATORS *sit at a table, with lights;* OFFICERS *attending.*

DUKE

There is no composition in these news
That gives them credit.

1. SENATOR

Indeed, they are disproportion'd;
My letters say a hundred and seven galleys.

DUKE

5   And mine, a hundred forty.

2. SENATOR

And mine, two hundred!
But though they jump not on a just account—
As in these cases, where the aim reports,
'Tis oft with difference—yet do they all confirm

10   A Turkish fleet, and bearing up to Cyprus.

DUKE

Nay, it is possible enough to judgment.
I do not so secure me in the error
But the main article I do approve
In fearful sense.

SAILOR [*within*]

15   What, ho! What, ho! What, ho!

Enter a SAILOR.

OFFICER

A messenger from the galleys.

DUKE

Now, what's the business?

SAILOR

The Turkish preparation makes for Rhodes.
So was I bid report here to the state

20   By Signior Angelo.

ACT 1, SCENE 3

A council chamber. The DUKE *and* SENATORS *sit at a table with lights,* OFFICERS *in attendance.*

DUKE
There is not enough consistency to these reports
to give them credibility.

FIRST SENATOR
Indeed, they are quite different.
My letters say a hundred and seven galleys.

DUKE
And mine a hundred and forty.   5

SECOND SENATOR
And mine two hundred.
But although they don't agree on a certain number
(since in cases where approximation is relied on,
there are often inconsistencies), still, they all confirm
that a Turkish fleet is approaching Cyprus.   10

DUKE
Yes, that seems likely enough upon consideration.
I'm not so comforted by the fact that these estimates differ
that I fail to see the news
as alarming.

SAILOR (*calling from offstage*)
Hello! Hello! Hello!   15

        A SAILOR *enters.*

OFFICER
It's a messenger from the galleys.

DUKE
What's happened?

SAILOR
The Turkish fleet is headed for Rhodes.
I was sent to report this to the leaders of the state
by Signior Angelo.   20

DUKE

How say you by this change?

1. SENATOR

                                    This cannot be,
By no assay of reason; 'tis a pageant,
To keep us in false gaze. When we consider
25   Th' importancy of Cyprus to the Turk,
And let ourselves again but understand
That, as it more concerns the Turk than Rhodes,
So may he with more **facile** question bear it,
For that it stands not in such warlike brace,
30   But altogether lacks th' abilities
That Rhodes is dress'd in; if we make thought of this,
We must not think the Turk is so unskillful
To leave that latest which concerns him first,
Neglecting an attempt of ease and gain
35   To wake and wage a danger profitless.

DUKE

Nay, in all confidence, he's not for Rhodes.

OFFICER

Here is more news.

            Enter a MESSENGER.

MESSENGER

The Ottomites,* Reverend and Gracious,
Steering with due course towards the isle of Rhodes,
40   Have there injointed them with an after fleet.

1. SENATOR

Ay, so I thought. How many, as you guess?

MESSENGER

Of thirty sail; and now they do restem
Their backward course, bearing with frank appearance
Their purposes toward Cyprus. Signior Montano,
45   Your trusty and most valiant servitor,
With his free duty recommends you thus,
And prays you to believe him.

---

38   *Ottomites* another name for the Turks

DUKE
What do you say about this change?

FIRST SENATOR
This makes
no sense at all. It's just a pretense
to keep us looking the wrong way. If we consider
the importance of Cyprus to the Turk   25
and remind ourselves again
that, not only is it of greater concern to the Turk than Rhodes,
but also that the Turk may take Cyprus more easily
because it is not militarily prepared
and altogether lacks the warlike capabilities   30
that Rhodes has—If we think about this,
we cannot believe that the Turk is inept enough
to leave for the last the thing which concerns him first,
neglecting an enterprise which is easy and worthwhile
in order to pursue a profitless danger.   35

DUKE
No, we can be sure he's not headed for Rhodes.

OFFICER
Here's more news.

     A MESSENGER *enters.*

MESSENGER
The Ottomites, you reverend gentlemen,
steering with due course toward the island of Rhodes,
have joined up there with an approaching fleet.   40

FIRST SENATOR
Yes, just as I thought. How many, do you guess?

MESSENGER
About thirty sails; and now they are sailing
in the opposite direction, very obviously
headed for Cyprus. Signior Montano,
your most worthy and most valiant servant,   45
sends word of this out of his unbounded duty to you
and begs you to believe him.

DUKE

'Tis certain, then, for Cyprus.
Marcus Luccicos, is not he in town?

1. SENATOR

50   He's now in Florence.

DUKE

Write from us to him;
Post-post-haste. Dispatch.

1. SENATOR

Here comes Brabantio and the valiant Moor.

Enter BRABANTIO, OTHELLO, CASSIO, IAGO,
RODERIGO, *and* OFFICERS.

DUKE

Valiant Othello, we must straight employ you
55   Against the general enemy Ottoman.
[*to* BRABANTIO] I did not see you. Welcome, gentle
    signior.
We lack'd your counsel and your help tonight.

BRABANTIO

So did I yours. Good your Grace, pardon me;
60   Neither my place nor aught I heard of business
Hath rais'd me from my bed, nor doth the general care
Take hold on me; for my particular grief
Is of so flood-gate and o'erbearing nature
That it engluts and swallows other sorrows
65   And it is still itself.

DUKE

Why, what's the matter?

BRABANTIO

My daughter! O, my daughter!

SENATOR

Dead?

BRABANTIO

Ay, to me;
70   She is abus'd, stol'n from me, and corrupted

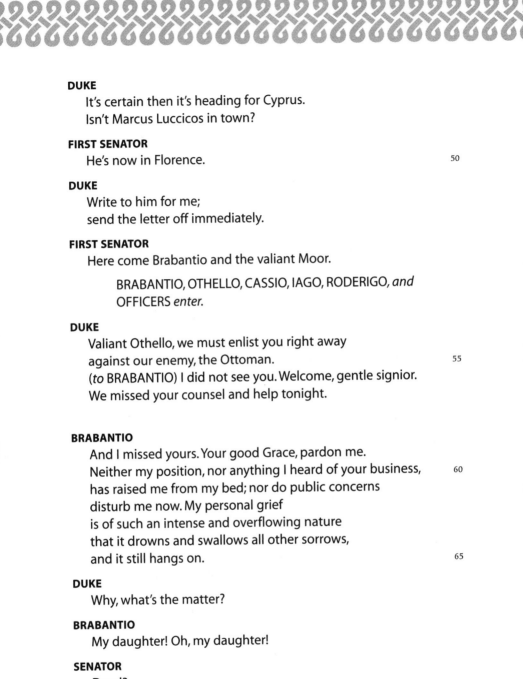

DUKE
It's certain then it's heading for Cyprus.
Isn't Marcus Luccicos in town?

FIRST SENATOR
He's now in Florence.   50

DUKE
Write to him for me;
send the letter off immediately.

FIRST SENATOR
Here come Brabantio and the valiant Moor.

> BRABANTIO, OTHELLO, CASSIO, IAGO, RODERIGO, *and*
> OFFICERS *enter.*

DUKE
Valiant Othello, we must enlist you right away
against our enemy, the Ottoman.   55
(*to* BRABANTIO) I did not see you. Welcome, gentle signior.
We missed your counsel and help tonight.

BRABANTIO
And I missed yours. Your good Grace, pardon me.
Neither my position, nor anything I heard of your business,   60
has raised me from my bed; nor do public concerns
disturb me now. My personal grief
is of such an intense and overflowing nature
that it drowns and swallows all other sorrows,
and it still hangs on.   65

DUKE
Why, what's the matter?

BRABANTIO
My daughter! Oh, my daughter!

SENATOR
Dead?

BRABANTIO
Yes, to me!
She has been deceived, stolen from me, and corrupted   70

By spells and medicines bought of mountebanks;*
For nature so prepost'rously to err—
Being not deficient, blind, or lame of sense—
Sans witchcraft could not.

DUKE

75   Whoe'er he be that in this foul proceeding
Hath thus beguil'd your daughter of herself
And you of her, the bloody book of law
You shall yourself read in the bitter letter,
After your own sense, yea, though our proper son
80   Stood in your action.

BRABANTIO

                Humbly I thank your Grace.
Here is the man—this Moor, whom now it seems
Your special mandate for the state affairs
Hath hither brought.

ALL

85   We are very sorry for 't.

DUKE [*to* OTHELLO]
What, in your own part, can you say to this?

BRABANTIO
Nothing, but this is so.

OTHELLO
Most potent, grave, and reverend signiors,
My very noble and approv'd good masters,
90   That I have ta'en away this old man's daughter,
It is most true; true, I have married her.
The very head and front of my offending
Hath this extent, no more. Rude am I in my speech,
And little bless'd with the soft phrase of peace;
95   For since these arms of mine had seven years' pith
Till now, some nine moons wasted, they have us'd
Their dearest action in the tented field,
And little of this great world can I speak
More than pertains to feats of broil and battle,

---

71 *mountebanks* traveling peddlers, often seen at fairs or carnivals

by spells and medicines bought from wandering quacks.
It's not in her nature to behave so outrageously—
when she's not deficient, blind, or half-witted—
without the influence of witchcraft.

DUKE

Whoever he is that, with this foul action,   75
has tricked your daughter out of her self-possession,
and you of her, the severe book of our laws
shall be read to him by you yourself to the strictest letter
according to your own interpretation—yes, even if it were my
    own son
who stood accused by you.   80

BRABANTIO

I humbly thank you, your grace.
Here is the man—this Moor, whom now, it seems,
your special command for state business
has brought here.

ALL

We are very sorry for it.   85

DUKE (*to* OTHELLO)

What can you say for yourself about this?

BRABANTIO

Nothing, except that it's true.

OTHELLO

Most powerful, grave, and reverend signiors,
my very noble and proven good masters:
that I have taken away this old man's daughter   90
is very true; it is true that I have married her.
The extent of my offense
amounts to no more than this. I am not articulate
and not very gifted with the soft-spokenness of peace
because between the time my arms had seven years of strength   95
until about nine months ago, they have done
their most important work in the battlefield.
I can speak very little of this great world
that doesn't pertain to deeds of battle and struggle.

100 And therefore little shall I grace my cause
In speaking for myself. Yet, by your gracious patience,
I will a round unvarnish'd tale deliver
Of my whole course of love—what drugs, what charms,
What conjuration, and what mighty magic,
105 (For such proceeding I am charg'd withal)
I won his daughter.

BRABANTIO

A maiden never bold;
Of spirit so still and quiet that her motion
Blush'd at herself. And she, in spite of nature,
110 Of years, of country, credit, everything,
To fall in love with what she fear'd to look on!
It is a judgment maim'd and most imperfect
That will confess perfection so could err
Against all rules of nature, and must be driven
115 To find out practices of cunning hell,
Why this should be. I therefore vouch again
That with some mixtures powerful o'er the blood,
Or with some dram conjur'd to this effect,
He wrought upon her.

DUKE

120 To vouch this is no proof,
Without more wider and more overt test
Than these thin habits and poor likelihoods
Of modern seeming do prefer against him.

1. SENATOR

But, Othello, speak:
125 Did you by indirect and forced courses
Subdue and poison this young maid's affections?
Or came it by request, and such fair question
As soul to soul affordeth?

OTHELLO

I do beseech you,
130 Send for the lady to the Sagittary
And let her speak of me before her father.
If you do find me foul in her report,

For that reason, I won't much help my cause 100
by speaking for myself. Still, if your gracious patience allows it,
I will tell a plain and honest story
of the whole course of my love—what drugs, what charms,
what conjurations, and what mighty magic
(for these are the things I'm charged with) 105
I used to win his daughter.

BRABANTIO
This girl was never bold.
She was of a temper so quiet and modest that she
blushed at every impulse. And she—in spite of her nature,
of her age, of country, reputation, everything— 110
has fallen in love with what she was afraid to look at!
It is a foolish and inaccurate assumption
to suggest perfection could go wrong
against all the rules of nature, and one is driven
to find out what tricks of cunning hell 115
could have led this to happen. So I insist again
that, with some potion that controls the blood,
Or with some drink brewed for this purpose,
he has worked his will on her.

DUKE
To swear this is not proof. 120
Without more sure and extensive tests
than these frail assumptions and slight possibilities
of ordinary appearance, you can hardly speak against him.

FIRST SENATOR
But speak up, Othello.
Did you, by dishonest and deceptive methods, 125
control and poison this young girl's affection?
Or did it come at your request and with the proper kind of
   discussion
that one person should have with another?

OTHELLO
I ask you
to send to the Sagittary for the lady 130
and let her speak about me in front of her father.
If you find that her report of me is evil,

The trust, the office I do hold of you,
Not only take away, but let your sentence
135   Even fall upon my life.

DUKE
Fetch Desdemona hither.

[*Exeunt two or three.*]

OTHELLO
Ancient, conduct them; you best know the place.

[*Exit* IAGO *and* ATTENDANTS.]

And, till she come, as truly as to heaven
I do confess the vices of my blood,
140   So justly to your grave ears I'll present
How I did thrive in this fair lady's love,
And she in mine.

DUKE
Say it, Othello.

OTHELLO
Her father lov'd me, oft invited me,
145   Still question'd me the story of my life
From year to year— the battles, sieges, fortunes,
That I have pass'd.
I ran it through, even from my boyish days
To the very moment that he bade me tell it;
150   Wherein I spoke of most disastrous chances
Of moving accidents by flood and field,
Of hair-breadth scapes i' th' **imminent** deadly breach,
Of being taken by the **insolent** foe
And sold to slavery, of my redemption thence
155   And portance in my traveler's history;
Wherein of antres vast and deserts idle,
Rough quarries, rocks, and hills whose heads touch heaven,
It was my hint to speak—such was my process—
And of the Cannibals that each other eat,
160   The Anthropophagi,* and men whose heads
Do grow beneath their shoulders. These things to hear
Would Desdemona seriously incline.

---

160   *Anthropophagi* Scythians, who were rumored to be cannibals

then let not only the trust and title you have given me
be taken away, but let your sentence
be passed against my life. 135

DUKE

Bring Desdemona here.

Two or three ATTENDANTS *exit.*

OTHELLO

Ensign, lead them; you know the place best.

IAGO *and* ATTENDANTS *exit.*

And until she comes, as sincerely as if to heaven
I will confess to you all the wickedness of my blood,
and speak honestly to your serious ears 140
of how I succeeded in gaining this fair lady's love,
and she mine.

DUKE

Tell us, Othello.

OTHELLO

Her father loved me and often invited me over.
He always asked me for the story of my life 145
from year to year—the battles, sieges, and fortunes
I've experienced.
I told it all, starting with my childhood days and continuing
up to the moment that he asked me to tell it.
I told of very dangerous situations; 150
of terrible accidents in floods or on the field;
of hairbreadth escapes in threatening and deadly battle;
of being taken prisoner by my insolent enemy
and sold into slavery; of my escape from that
and my behavior throughout my travels. 155
Vast caves and desolate deserts,
rough quarries, rocks and hills whose peaks reach to heaven—
all these were spoken of—that's how it went—
and of cannibals who eat each other,
the Anthropophagi, and men whose heads 160
grow below their shoulders. To hear all this,
Desdemona would lean forward intently;

But still the house affairs would draw her thence,
Which ever as she could with haste dispatch
165 She'd come again, and with a greedy ear
Devour up my discourse. Which, I observing,
Took once a pliant hour, and found good means
To draw from her a prayer of earnest heart
That I would all my pilgrimage dilate,
170 Whereof by parcels she had something heard,
But not intentively. I did consent,
And often did beguile her of tears
When I did speak of some distressful stroke
That my youth suffer'd. My story being done,
175 She gave me for my pains a world of sighs.
She swore, in faith, 'twas strange, 'twas passing strange,
'Twas pitiful, 'twas wondrous pitiful.
She wish'd she had not heard it; yet she wish'd
That heaven had made her such a man. She thank'd me,
180 And bade me, if I had a friend that lov'd her,
I should but teach him how to tell my story,
And that would woo her. Upon this hint I spake.
She lov'd me for the dangers I had pass'd,
And I lov'd her that she did pity them.
185 This only is the witchcraft I have us'd.
Here comes the lady; let her witness it.

Enter DESDEMONA, IAGO, *and* ATTENDANTS.

DUKE
I think this tale would win my daughter too.
Good Brabantio,
Take up this mangled matter at the best;
190 Men do their broken weapons rather use
Than their bare hands.*

BRABANTIO
              I pray you, hear her speak.
If she confess that she was half the wooer,
Destruction on my head if my bad blame
195 Light on the man!— Come hither, gentle mistress.

190-91 *Men do their broken . . . hands.* The Duke means that like any civilized man,
Othello would likely have used civilized means to accomplish his goals.

but still, the business of the house would call her away.
She'd finish her work as quickly as she could
and come back again, and with a greedy ear,   165
devour my story. I noticed this,
found a convenient time, and managed
to elicit from her an earnest request
that, at one sitting, I would tell her all my travels,
which she had heard something of piecemeal   170
but not without interruptions. I consented
and often brought tears from her
when I spoke of some serious danger
I suffered in my youth. When my story was over,
she gave me a world of sighs for my trouble.   175
She swore, in truth, that it was strange, that it was very strange,
that it was sad, that it was terribly sad.
She wished she hadn't heard it; and yet she wished
that heaven had made such a man for her. She thanked me
and told me that if I had a friend who loved her,   180
I should just teach him how to tell my story,
and he could woo her with it. I took this opportunity to speak.
She loved me because of the dangers I had experienced,
and I loved her because she was moved by them.
This is the only witchcraft I have used.   185
Here comes the lady; let her confirm it.

    DESDEMONA, IAGO, *and* ATTENDANTS *enter.*

DUKE

I think this story would win my daughter, too.
Good Brabantio,
make the best of this difficult situation.
Men prefer to use their broken weapons   190
rather than their bare hands.

BRABANTIO

I ask you to hear her speak.
If she admits that she was half the wooer,
may I be damned for bringing my unjust accusation
against this man! Come here, gentle lady.   195

Do you perceive in all this noble company
Where most you owe obedience?

DESDEMONA

                           My noble father,
I do perceive here a divided duty.
200   To you I am bound for life and education;
My life and education both do learn me
How to respect you; you are the lord of duty;
I am hitherto your daughter. But here's my husband;
And so much duty as my mother show'd
205   To you, preferring you before her father,
So much I challenge that I may profess
Due to the Moor, my lord.

BRABANTIO

God be with you! I have done.
Please it your Grace, on to the state affairs.
210   I had rather to adopt a child than get it.—
Come hither, Moor.
I here do give thee that with all my heart
[Which, but thou hast already, with all my heart]
I would keep from thee.—For your sake, jewel,
215   I am glad at soul I have no other child;
For thy escape would teach me tyranny,
To hang clogs on them.—I have done, my lord.

DUKE

Let me speak like yourself and lay a sentence
Which as a grise or step, may help these lovers
220   Into your favour.
When remedies are past, the griefs are ended
By seeing the worst, which late on hopes depended.
To mourn a mischief that is past and gone
Is the next way to draw new mischief on.
225   What cannot be preserv'd when fortune takes,
Patience her injury a mock'ry makes.
The robb'd that smiles steals something from the thief;
He robs himself that spends a bootless grief.

Do you know, in all this noble gathering,
to whom you owe the most obedience?

DESDEMONA

My noble father,
I see that I have a divided obligation here.
I am indebted to you for my life and education;   200
my life and education both teach me
to respect you: you are the lord of my duty;
before now, I was only your daughter. But here's my husband;
and as much obedience as my mother showed
to you, offering more to you than to her father,   205
the same, I insist, I now consider
due to the Moor, my lord.

BRABANTIO

God be with you! I'm done with it.
If it please you, your Grace, let's get on with state business.
I'd rather adopt a child than beget one.   210
Come here, Moor.
I now give to you with all my heart
that which, if you didn't already have her, with all my heart
I would keep from you. (*to* DESDEMONA) Because of you, my
    jewel,
I am glad in my heart that I have no other children,   215
since your escape would make me tyrannical
and lead me to put shackles on them—I am finished, my lord.

DUKE

Let me speak as you should and repeat a proverb
which, one way or another, might help these lovers
find your favor.   220
When remedies are useless, grief is killed
by seeing the worst—a grief which was kept alive by hope.
To complain of a misfortune that is done and over with
is the best way to bring on more misfortunes.
When fortune takes something and one can't get it back,   225
one makes a mockery of the injury by enduring it patiently.
A person who's been robbed and smiles steals something
    from the thief.
A person robs himself who persists in grieving pointlessly.

BRABANTIO

So let the Turk of Cyprus us beguile;

230   We lose it not, so long as we can smile.

He bears the sentence well that nothing bears

But the free comfort which from thence he hears,

But he bears both the sentence and the sorrow

That, to pay grief, must of poor patience borrow.

235   These sentences, to sugar or to gall,

Being strong on both sides, are **equivocal**.

But words are words; I never yet did hear

That the bruis'd heart was pierced through the ear.

I humbly beseech you, proceed to the affairs of state.

DUKE

240   The Turk with a most mighty preparation makes for

Cyprus. Othello, the fortitude of the place is best known

to you; and though we have there a substitute of most

allowed sufficiency, yet opinion, a sovereign mistress of

effects, throws a more safer voice on you. You must

245   therefore be content to slubber the gloss of your new

fortunes with this more stubborn and boist'rous

expedition.

OTHELLO

The tyrant custom, most grave senators,

Hath made the flinty and steel couch of war

250   My thrice-driven bed of down. I do agnize

A natural and prompt alacrity

I find in hardness, and do undertake

These present wars against the Ottomites.

Most humbly therefore bending to your state,

255   I crave fit disposition for my wife,

Due reference of place and exhibition,

With such accommodation and besort

As levels with her breeding.

DUKE

Why at her father's.

BRABANTIO

260   I will not have it so.

BRABANTIO

So let the Turks trick us out of Cyprus;
we won't lose it, as long as we can smile about it. 230
He endures the sentence well who doesn't suffer anything
except the comfort of freedom when he hears it.
But he endures both the sentence and the suffering
when he has to pay his grief by borrowing from poor patience.
This advice contains sweetness and bitterness, 235
both very strong, in equal amounts.
But words are only words: I haven't yet heard of a
bruised heart being treated through the ear.
I humbly beg you, get on with the business of state.

DUKE

The Turks with a very mighty force are heading for Cyprus. 240
Othello, you best know the strength of the place; and though
I have a very capable viceroy in power there, yet public
opinion—the final word on how matters will be decided—
declares you are the best man for the job. So you'll have to
content yourself to dull the shine on your newfound luck 245
with this rough and violent expedition.

OTHELLO

That tyrant, Habit, most serious senators,
has made the flinty and steel couch of war
a carefully prepared feather bed to me. I recognize in myself 250
a natural and eager willingness
to suffer hardship. I will take part
in this current war against the Ottomites.
And so, most humbly bowing before your majesty,
I ask for proper treatment of my wife; 255
appropriate regard for her rank, and an allowance of money,
with the kind of residence and company
that fits with her breeding.

DUKE

If it please you, let it be at her father's.

BRABANTIO

I won't have that. 260

OTHELLO
Nor I.

DESDEMONA
Nor would I there reside
To put my father in impatient thoughts
By being in his eye. Most gracious Duke,
265   To my unfolding lend your prosperous ear;
And let me find a charter in your voice
T' assist my simpleness.

DUKE
What would you, Desdemona?

DESDEMONA
That I did love the Moor to live with him,
270   My downright violence and storm of fortunes
May trumpet to the world. My heart's subdu'd
Even to the very quality of my lord.
I saw Othello's visage in his mind,
And to his honours and his valiant parts
275   Did I my soul and fortunes consecrate.
So that, dear lords, if I be left behind,
A moth of peace, and he go to the war,
The rites for which I love him are bereft me,
And I a heavy interim shall support
280   By his dear absence. Let me go with him.

OTHELLO
Let her have your voice.
Vouch with me, Heaven, I therefore beg it not
To please the palate of my appetite,
Nor to comply with heat, the young affects
285   In me defunct and proper satisfaction,
But to be free and bounteous to her mind;
And heaven defend your good souls that you think
I will your serious and great business scant
When she is with me. No, when light-wing'd toys
290   Of feather'd Cupid* seel* with wanton dullness

---

290   *Cupid* the Roman god of love, depicted as a winged youth

290   *seel* sew up; in falconry, the eyelids of hawks were often sewn shut in order to tame them.

OTHELLO
Nor I.

DESDEMONA
And I won't stay there
and make my father impatient
by being in his sight. Most gracious Duke,
listen to my appeal with favor   265
and use your voice to give me permission,
smoothing out my inept pleading.

DUKE
What do you want, Desdemona?

DESDEMONA
That I have loved the Moor enough to live with him,
my violent behavior and reckless chance-taking   270
declares to all the world. My heart has been won and converted
even to my lord's soldiering profession.
I saw Othello's qualities beyond his appearance,
and to his reputation and military abilities,
I have dedicated my fortunes and my soul.   275
And so, dear lords, if I am left behind,
an idle creature of peace, and he goes to the war,
the rights I have as his wife will be taken away from me,
and I will suffer a sad time
during his absence. Let me go with him.   280

OTHELLO
Let her have your permission.
I assure you by heaven, I am not asking this
out of my longing for her
or to suit my lust—this new passion
which has not been consummated—   285
but to give her freely and generously what she wants.
And heaven forbid that you good men should think
I will neglect your great and serious business
if she is with me. No, when light-winged toys
of feathered Cupid close up with lustful blindness   290

My speculative and offic'd instruments
That my disports corrupt and taint my business,
Let housewives make a skillet of my helm,
And all indign and base adversities
295 Make head against my estimation!

DUKE

Be it as you shall privately determine,
Either for her stay or going. Th' affair cries haste,
And speed must answer it.

1. SENATOR

You must away tonight.

DESDEMONA

300 Tonight, my lord?

DUKE

This night.

OTHELLO

With all my heart.

DUKE

At nine i' th' morning here we'll meet again.
Othello, leave some officer behind
305 And he shall our commission bring to you,
With such things else of quality and respect
As doth import you.

OTHELLO

So please your Grace, my ancient;
A man he is of honesty and trust.
310 To his conveyance I assign my wife,
With what else needful your good Grace shall think
To be sent after me.

DUKE

Let it be so.
Good night to everyone. [*to* BRABANTIO] And, noble
315 signior,
If virtue no delighted beauty lack,
Your son-in-law is far more fair* than black.

---

317 *fair* here means both "white" and "lovely"

my alert and dutiful eyes,
and my pastimes corrupt and interfere with my business,
let housewives make a skillet of my helmet
and all kinds of unworthy and evil adversities
attack my reputation!   295

DUKE

You may decide for yourselves
whether she goes or stays. This business demands haste,
and speed is necessary.

FIRST SENATOR

You must leave tonight.

DESDEMONA

Tonight, my lord?   300

DUKE

This night.

OTHELLO

With all my heart.

DUKE

At nine in the morning we'll meet here again.
Othello, leave some officer behind,
and he will bring our commission to you   305
and other things which are proper
for you to have.

OTHELLO

If it please you, your Grace, use my ensign.
He is a trustworthy and honest man.
I give my wife over to his escort,   310
along with whatever else you think, your good Grace, it is
    necessary
to be sent to me.

DUKE

It's settled, then.
Good night to everyone. (*to* BRABANTIO) And, noble Signior,   315
if virtue is a sign of beauty,
your son-in-law is far lighter than he is black.

1. SENATOR

Adieu, brave Moor; use Desdemona well.

BRABANTIO

Look to her, Moor, if thou hast eyes to see;
320   She has deceiv'd her father, and may thee.   *He exits.*

OTHELLO

My life upon her faith!

[*Exuent* DUKE, SENATORS, CASSIO, *and* OFFICERS.]

Honest Iago,
My Desdemona must I leave to thee.
I prithee, let thy wife attend on her;
325   And bring them after in the best advantage.
Come, Desdemona, I have but an hour
Of love, of worldly matters and direction,
To spend with thee. We must obey the time.

[*Exeunt* OTHELLO *and* DESDEMONA.]

RODERIGO

Iago—

IAGO

330   What say'st thou, noble heart?

RODERIGO

What will I do, think'st thou?

IAGO

Why, go to bed and sleep.

RODERIGO

I will incontinently drown myself.

IAGO

If thou dost, I shall never love thee after. Why,
335   thou silly gentleman!

RODERIGO

It is silliness to live, when to live is torment, and then
have we a prescription to die when death is our physician.

FIRST SENATOR
Good-bye, brave Moor. Take care of Desdemona.

BRABANTIO
Watch her, Moor, if you have eyes to see.
She has deceived her father and might deceive you too.   320
    [*He exits.*]

OTHELLO
I'll stake my life on her fidelity!

       The DUKE, SENATORS, CASSIO, *and* OFFICERS *exit.*

Honest Iago,
I must leave my Desdemona to your care.
I ask you to please let your wife attend to her
and bring them along when the time is best.   325
Come along, Desdemona. I have just an hour left
for love, and for practical business and instructions,
to spend with you. We must obey time.

       OTHELLO *and* DESDEMONA *exit.*

RODERIGO
Iago—

IAGO
What do you say, noble fellow?   330

RODERIGO
What do you think I should do?

IAGO
Why, go to bed and sleep.

RODERIGO
I'll go drown myself at once.

IAGO
If you do, I'll not love you anymore.
Why, what a foolish gentleman you are!   335

RODERIGO
It is foolish to live when living torments me. And we have a
prescription to die when Death is our doctor.

IAGO

O villainous! I have look'd upon the world for four times
seven years, and since I could distinguish betwixt a benefit
340 and an injury, I never found man that knew how to love
himself. Ere I would say I would drown myself for the love
of a guinea hen, I would change my humanity with a
baboon.

RODERIGO

What should I do? I confess it is my shame to be so fond,
345 but it is not in my virtue to amend it.

IAGO

Virtue? A fig!* 'Tis in ourselves that we are thus or thus.
Our bodies are our gardens, to the which our wills are
gardeners; so that if we will plant nettles or sow lettuce,
set hyssop* and weed up thyme, supply it with one gender
350 of herbs or distract it with many, either to have it sterile
with idleness or manured with industry, why the power
and corrigible authority of this lies in our wills. If the
balance of our lives had not one scale of reason to poise
another of sensuality, the blood and baseness of our
355 natures would conduct us to most preposterous
conclusions. But we have reason to cool our raging
motions, our carnal stings, our unbitted lusts—whereof I
take this that you call love to be a sect, or scion.

RODERIGO

It cannot be.

IAGO

360 It is merely a lust of the blood and a permission of the
will. Come, be a man! Drown thyself? Drown cats and
blind puppies! I have profess'd me thy friend, and I
confess me knit to thy deserving with cables of perdurable
toughness. I could never better stead thee than now. Put
365 money in thy purse; follow thou the wars; defeat thy
favour with an **usurp'd** beard. I say, put money in thy
purse. It cannot be long that Desdemona should continue
her love to the Moor—put money in thy purse—nor he

---

346 *fig* here means "a worthless thing"

349 *hyssop* a fragrant herb

IAGO

How villainous! I have lived in this world for twenty-eight
years; and ever since I could distinguish between a benefit
and an injury, I've never met a man who knew how to love   340
himself. Before I'd say I'd drown myself for the love of a guinea
hen, I'd change places with a baboon.

RODERIGO

What should I do? I confess it is to my shame to be so foolish,
but I don't have the strength to change it.   345

IAGO

Strength? A fig! It is in our own natures that we are who we
are. Our bodies are our gardens, to which our wills are
gardeners. So, if we want to plant nettles or sow lettuce, put in
spices and harvest thyme, grow one kind of herb or grow   350
many, either have it barren because of laziness or rich through
hard work—why, the power and corrective authority to do so
lies in our wills. If the balance of our lives didn't have one scale
of reason to counterbalance the other scale of sensuality, the
basic savagery of our natures would lead us into the most   355
outrageous situations. But we have reason to cool our raging
appetites, our carnal desires, and our unchecked lusts. Therefore,
I conclude that what you call love is a cutting or offshoot.

RODERIGO

It can't be.

IAGO

It is just lust of the blood and permission of the will. Come on, 360
be a man! Drown yourself? Drown cats and blind puppies! I've
called myself your friend, and I assure you, I'm bound to you by
cords of enduring toughness. I could never serve you better
than right now. Put money in your purse. Go to the wars;   365
disguise your good looks by wearing a beard. I tell you, put
money in your purse. It isn't possible that Desdemona will
continue to love the Moor for long—put money in your purse—
nor he her. It had an explosive beginning for her, and you'll

his to her. It was a violent commencement in her, and
370 thou shalt see an answerable sequestration— Put but
money in thy purse. These Moors are changeable in their
wills—fill thy purse with money. The food that to him
now is as luscious as locusts,* shall be to him shortly as
bitter as coloquintida.* She must change for youth; when
375 she is sated with his body, she will find the error of her
choice; she must have change, she must; therefore, put
money in thy purse. If thou wilt needs damn thyself, do it
a more delicate way than drowning. Make all the money
thou canst. If sanctimony and a frail vow betwixt an erring
380 barbarian and a super-subtle Venetian be not too hard for
my wits and all the tribe of hell, thou shalt enjoy her;
therefore make money. A pox of drowning thyself! It is
clean out of the way. Seek thou rather to be hang'd in
compassing thy joy than to be drown'd and go without her.

RODERIGO

385 Wilt thou be fast to my hopes if I depend on the issue?

IAGO

Thou art sure of me. Go, make money. I have told thee
often, and I retell thee again and again, I hate the Moor.
My cause is hearted; thine hath no less reason. Let us be
conjunctive in our revenge against him. If thou canst
390 cuckold him,* thou dost thyself a pleasure, me a sport.
There are many events in the womb of time which will be
delivered. Traverse! Go, provide thy money. We will have
more of this tomorrow. Adieu.

RODERIGO

Where shall we meet i' th' morning?

IAGO

395 At my lodging.

RODERIGO

I'll be with thee betimes.

IAGO

Go to, farewell. Do you hear, Roderigo?

---

373 *locusts* probably the sweet fruit of the carob tree

374 *coloquintida* a bitter apple used to produce a laxative

390 *cuckold him* commit adultery with his wife

see it end much the same way. Just put money in your purse. 370
These Moors are changeable in their lusts. Fill your purse with
money. The food that now seems as sweet as fruit to him will
soon seem as bitter as a sour apple. She must grow to prefer
someone younger. When she is wearied with his body, she'll 375
see the error of her choice. She'll need a change, that's certain.
So put money in your purse. If you have to damn yourself, do
it in a more delicate way than drowning. Make all the money
you can. If sacred bonds and a frail vow made between a
wandering barbarian and a very subtle Venetian is not too 380
much for me and all the devils in hell, she will be yours. So get
money. Forget about drowning yourself! It's completely
ridiculous. Take your chances on being hanged for trying to
get what you want instead of drowning and going without her.

RODERIGO

Will you steadfastly support my hopes if I rely on the outcome? 385

IAGO

You can count on me. Go, get money. I've often told you, and
I'll say it again and again, I hate the Moor. I hate him from the
bottom of my heart, and you have cause to as well. Let us work
together to get revenge on him. If you can cuckold him, you'll
give yourself pleasure and me amusement. There are many 390
things just waiting to be born which will come to pass soon.
Move! Go! Get yourself money! We'll talk more about this
tomorrow. Good-bye.

RODERIGO

Where will we meet in the morning?

IAGO

At my lodging. 395

RODERIGO

I'll meet you early.

IAGO

Go on, good-bye. Wait, do you hear me, Roderigo?

RODERIGO

What say you?

IAGO

No more of drowning, do you hear?

RODERIGO

400   I am chang'd.

IAGO

Go to, farewell. Put money enough in your purse.

RODERIGO

I'll sell all my land.   *He exits.*

IAGO

Thus do I ever make my fool my purse;
For I mine own gain'd knowledge should profane
405   If I would time expend with such a snipe*
But for my sport and profit. I hate the Moor,
And it is thought abroad that 'twixt my sheets
He has done my office. I know not if 't be true,
But I, for mere suspicion in that kind,
410   Will do as if for surety. He holds me well;
The better shall my purpose work on him.
Cassio's a proper man. Let me see now:
To get his place and to plume up my will
In double knavery—How, how?—Let's see.
415   After some time, to abuse Othello's ear
That he is too familiar with his wife.
He hath a person and a smooth dispose
To be suspected, fram'd to make women false.
The Moor is of a free and open nature
420   That thinks men honest that but seem to be so,
And will as tenderly be led by th' nose
As asses are.
I have 't. It is engender'd. Hell and night
Must bring this monstrous birth to the world's light.

    [*Exit.*]

---

405   *snipe* a bird also known as a woodcock and a synonym for "fool" because it was
so easily captured

RODERIGO

What is it?

IAGO

No more talk of drowning, do you hear?

RODERIGO

I've changed my mind. 400

IAGO

Good-bye. Take enough money with you.

RODERIGO

I'll go sell all my land. (RODERIGO *exits.*)

IAGO

This is how I always make my living off some fool;
for I would insult my own practical wisdom
if I spent my time with such a fool 405
just for my amusement and profit. I hate the Moor;
and it is rumored around that, in my own bed,
he has taken my place. I don't know if it is true;
but just out of sheer suspicion, I
will act as if I were sure of it. He esteems me highly; 410
that will make it easier to work my purpose against him.
Cassio's a handsome man. Let me see now;
to get his position and gratify myself
by double villainy—How, how? Let's see.
After a while, I'll deceive Othello by telling him 415
that Cassio is too familiar with his wife.
His good looks and fine manners
make it seem possible—he's built to make women turn
      unfaithful.
The Moor is free and open-minded
and thinks men are honest when they only seem to be, 420
so he will be as easily led by the nose
as asses are.
I have it! It's planned! Hell and night
must bring this wicked plot to the light of day.

      Exit.

Act I Review

Discussion Questions

1. What kind of relationship do you think Iago and Roderigo had before the play's outset?

2. What is Brabantio's reaction to the news brought by Iago and Roderigo?

3. When Brabantio and his followers make their threatening entrance in Scene ii, Othello's first words to them are, "Keep up your bright swords, for the dew will rust them." What does this line tell you about Othello's character?

4. What impending crisis do the Duke and his senators face at the beginning of Scene iii?

5. Why does Brabantio believe that Othello could have won Desdemona's love only through witchcraft?

6. How did Brabantio feel about Othello before the outset of the play?

7. Why do you think the Duke so readily dismisses Brabantio's suit against Othello?

8. How does Iago raise Roderigo's spirits at the end of Act I?

Literary Elements

1. **Exposition** is background information. Shakespeare throws the audience off guard at the opening of *Othello* by beginning his scene in mid-conversation. The audience pays close attention in order to catch up. What important pieces of information do you learn during Scene i?

2. **Imagery** refers to language that appeals to the senses. There are many images of animals in *Othello*. Note Iago's references to horses,

birds, donkeys, and other beasts in the first scene—as when he tells Brabantio, "an old black ram / Is tupping your white ewe." Look for further animal images as you read the play. Which characters use animal images most? What do such images contribute to the ideas of the play?

3. A **monologue** is a speech delivered to other characters in the play; Othello's speech to the Duke and senators in Scene iii ("Her father lov'd me, oft invited me") is a monologue. A **soliloquy** is a speech delivered by a character when he or she is alone; Act I ends with a soliloquy by Iago—"Thus do I ever make my fool my purse . . ." As you continue reading the play, decide whether long speeches are monologues or soliloquies.

Writing Prompts

1. The action of *Othello* begins in mid-conversation. Write a dialogue between Iago and Roderigo that might have come before the play's opening lines. Consider Roderigo's words, "Tush! Never tell me!" What has Iago just said to provoke this exclamation?

2. In Scene i, we learn that Roderigo unsuccessfully courted Desdemona. Write a love letter from him to her. Give a strong sense of his personality.

3. Write some entries in Desdemona's diary describing her early impressions of Othello.

4. Write a story for a Venice newspaper describing events of Act I. Emphasize either Othello's elopement with Desdemona or the Turkish threat to Cyprus.

5. Write a description of Othello based on what you have learned about him so far. Start by listing words and phrases that describe his character. Then include specific quotes from the play to support your writing.

Othello

ACT II

Irene Jacob and Laurence Fishburne as Desdemona and Othello, 1995 film directed by Oliver Parker

"O my soul's joy!"

❈ ❈ ❈

Before You Read

1. At this point in the play, do you find Othello a sympathetic or unsympathetic character? Explain your response.

2. What is your assessment of Desdemona's character, based on what you know about her so far? Name what you think are her strengths, weaknesses, virtues, and faults.

3. Why do you think Othello and Desdemona fell in love? Explain whether you think their love is the basis of a good marriage.

4. How do you expect Othello's outsider status in Venice society to contribute to his tragic downfall?

Literary Elements

1. **Foreshadowing** refers to hints in the text about what will occur later in the plot. In Act I, when Iago says "I am not what I am," we know he is two-faced and will probably betray others as well as Othello, whom he's already plotting against.

2. Since there was little scenery in Shakespeare's theater, he depended on language to establish **settings**. In scenes at the Cyprus harbor, vivid language about ships coming into port conveys mental images that the stage technology of Shakespeare's day could not provide.

3. Although most of *Othello* is written in **verse**, Shakespeare often uses **prose** (language without rhythmic structure). In Act I, Scene ii, lines 7–18, when Iago is warning Othello about Brabantio's anger, he speaks in verse. Yet in Scene iii, lines 360–384, when he is convincing Roderigo to join him in a plot and ranting against Othello, he speaks in prose.

Words to Know

The following vocabulary words appear in Act II in the original text of Shakespeare's play. However, they are words that are still used today. Read the definitions here and pay attention to the words as you read the play (they will be in boldfaced type).

assails	attacks; assaults
egregiously	conspicuously; flagrantly
eminent	well-known; famous
imperious	arrogant; domineering
indiscreet	careless; reckless
infirmity	illness; sickness
inordinate	excessive; extravagant
nuptial	marriage; wedding
paradoxes	contradictions; puzzles
peevish	irritable; bad-tempered
provocation	stimulation; encouragement
rebuke	reproach; reprimand
renounce	reject; give up
requisites	basics; fundamentals

Act Summary

Cyprus's current governor, Montano, awaits both the Venetian and Turkish fleets. Good news arrives—the Turkish fleet has been destroyed in a storm. But the Venetian ships have been scattered. Will they reach Cyprus safely?

Ships arrive carrying Cassio, Desdemona, Roderigo, Iago, and Iago's wife, Emilia—but not Othello. This doesn't stop Iago from plotting against the Moor. He notices Cassio's gallant treatment of Desdemona and realizes that it should be easy to arouse Othello's jealousy toward Cassio.

Othello finally arrives, and Montano respectfully turns command of Cyprus over to its new governor. Othello proclaims a night of celebration.

Iago tells Roderigo that Desdemona is in love with Cassio. He also urges Roderigo to start a fight with Cassio at the first opportunity. Then Iago meets with Cassio, who is supposed to stand watch that night.

Iago offers the lieutenant wine. Cassio refuses at first, protesting that he becomes drunk easily. But Iago insists, and Cassio drinks. Soon, Cassio is extremely drunk, and Roderigo provokes him to a violent quarrel. When Montano tries to break them up, Cassio wounds the former governor.

Othello arrives, demanding an explanation for the fray. With pretended reluctance, Iago puts the blame on Cassio. Othello dismisses the lieutenant from his service.

Cassio is distraught and perplexed. But Iago assures him that no lasting damage is done. Cassio can appeal to Desdemona for help, Iago says. She will influence her husband to reinstate the lieutenant.

Nathaniel Parker as Cassio and Kenneth Branagh as Iago, 1995 film directed by Oliver Parker

ACT II, SCENE I

[A sea-port in Cyprus. An open place near the quay.]
Enter MONTANO *and two* GENTLEMEN. *

MONTANO

What from the cape can you discern at sea?

1. GENTLEMAN

Nothing at all; it is a high-wrought flood.
I cannot, 'twixt the heaven and the main,
Descry a sail.

MONTANO

5   Methinks the wind hath spoke aloud at land;
A fuller blast ne'er shook our battlements.
If it hath ruffian'd so upon the sea,
What ribs of oak, when mountains melt on them,
Can hold the mortise? What shall we hear of this?

2. GENTLEMAN

10   A segregation of the Turkish fleet.
For do but stand upon the foaming shore,
The chidden billow seems to pelt the clouds;
The wind-shak'd surge, with high and monstrous mane,
Seems to cast water on the burning Bear*

15   And quench the guards* of th' ever-fixed Pole.
I never did like molestation view
On the enchafed flood.

MONTANO

If that the Turkish fleet
Be not enshelter'd and embay'd, they are drown'd;

20   It is impossible to bear it out.

Enter a third GENTLEMAN.

---

s.d.   *two Gentlemen* The First Gentleman is generally positioned on a platform above the other characters to act as lookout.

14   *burning Bear* the constellation of Ursa Minor

15   *guards* stars in the constellation of the Little Bear; companion stars of the Pole Star (North Star)

ACT 2, SCENE 1

A seaport in Cyprus. An open place near the harbor.
MONTANO and two GENTLEMEN enter.

MONTANO
What can you view of the sea from the cape?

FIRST GENTLEMAN
Nothing at all; it is a wild and terrible downpour.
I cannot, between the sky and the water,
make out a sail.

MONTANO
I think the wind has spoken aloud to the land.   5
A storm like this has never before shaken our battlements.
If it has caused as much turbulence upon the sea,
what oak hulls—when mountains are melted by the rain—
could hold together? What can we expect to happen?

SECOND GENTLEMAN
The Turkish fleet will be scattered.   10
If you just stand on the storm-washed shore,
the beaten waves themselves seem to strike the clouds.
The wind-shaken tide, with high and huge crests,
seems to throw water on the shining Bear
and drown the guardian stars of the Pole Star.   15
I have never seen such turmoil
on the angry water.

MONTANO
If the Turkish fleet
is not protected or at bay, they have been drowned.
It's impossible that they could survive this.   20

A third GENTLEMAN enters.

3. GENTLEMAN

News, lads! Our wars are done.
The desperate tempest hath so bang'd the Turks,
That their designment halts. A noble ship of Venice
Hath seen a grievous wreck and sufferance
25   On most part of their fleet.

MONTANO

How? Is this true?

3. GENTLEMAN

                    The ship is here put in.
A Veronese, Michael Cassio,
Lieutenant to the warlike Moor Othello,
30   Is come on shore; the Moor himself at sea,
And is in full commission here for Cyprus.

MONTANO

I am glad on 't; 'tis a worthy governor.

3. GENTLEMAN

But this same Cassio, though he speak of comfort
Touching the Turkish loss, yet he looks sadly
35   And prays the Moor be safe, for they were parted
With foul and violent tempest.

MONTANO

                       Pray heavens he be;
For I have serv'd him, and the man commands
Like a full soldier. Let's to the seaside, ho!
40   As well to see the vessel that's come in
As to throw out our eyes for brave Othello,
Even till we make the main and th' aerial blue
An indistinct regard.

3. GENTLEMAN

                  Come, let's do so;
45   For every minute is expectancy
Of more arrivance.

      Enter CASSIO.

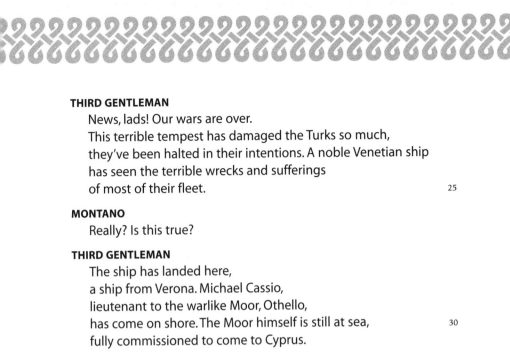

THIRD GENTLEMAN
   News, lads! Our wars are over.
   This terrible tempest has damaged the Turks so much,
   they've been halted in their intentions. A noble Venetian ship
   has seen the terrible wrecks and sufferings
   of most of their fleet.   25

MONTANO
   Really? Is this true?

THIRD GENTLEMAN
   The ship has landed here,
   a ship from Verona. Michael Cassio,
   lieutenant to the warlike Moor, Othello,
   has come on shore. The Moor himself is still at sea,   30
   fully commissioned to come to Cyprus.

MONTANO
   I'm glad to hear it. He'll make a worthy governor.

THIRD GENTLEMAN
   But the same Cassio I mentioned, although he tells good news
   about the Turkish loss, is very worried
   and prays that the Moor is safe, for they were separated   35
   by a terrible and violent storm.

MONTANO
   Let's pray heaven that he is;
   for I have served under him, and the man commands
   like a real soldier. Let's go to the seaside, come!
   Not only to meet the vessel that's come in,   40
   but also to look for the brave Othello,
   and watch until we can't tell the sea and the blue sky
   apart from one another.

THIRD GENTLEMAN
   Come, let's do so;
   for every minute we are expecting   45
   more arrivals.

      CASSIO *enters.*

CASSIO

    Thanks, you the valiant of this warlike isle,
    That so approve the Moor! O, let the heavens
    Give him defence against the elements,
50   For I have lost him on a dangerous sea.

MONTANO

    Is he well shipp'd?

CASSIO

    His bark is stoutly timber'd, and his pilot
    Of very expert and approv'd allowance;
    Therefore my hopes, not surfeited to death,
55   Stand in bold cure.

        [*Voices cry within, "A sail, a sail, a sail!"*]

        Enter a fourth GENTLEMAN.

CASSIO

    What noise?

MESSENGER

    The town is empty; on the brow o' th' sea
    Stand ranks of people, and they cry, "A sail!"

CASSIO

    My hopes do shape him for the governor.

        [*A shot.*]

2. GENTLEMAN

60   They do discharge their shot of courtesy.
    Our friends at least.

CASSIO

                I pray you, sir, go forth,
    And give us truth who 'tis that is arriv'd.

2. GENTLEMAN

    I shall.

        [*Exit.*]

MONTANO

65   But, good lieutenant, is your general wiv'd?

CASSIO
Thanks, you valiant men of this war-torn island,
who so honor the Moor! Oh, let heaven
give him defense against the elements,
for I have lost him on a dangerous sea! 50

MONTANO
Is he in a good ship?

CASSIO
His ship has strong timbers, and his pilot
has very expert and proven abilities.
And so my hopes, not dead yet,
may well be restored. 55

Offstage a voice cries, "A sail, a sail, a sail!"

A fourth GENTLEMAN *enters.*

CASSIO
What's this noise?

FOURTH GENTLEMAN
The town is empty. At the edge of the sea,
ranks of people are standing, and they cry, "A sail!"

CASSIO
My hopes for the governor grow stronger.

A shot is heard offstage.

SECOND GENTLEMAN
They fire a shot of greeting. 60
At least we know they are friends.

CASSIO
I ask you to go there, sir,
and truly report back to us who has arrived.

SECOND GENTLEMAN
I will.

He exits.

MONTANO
But, good lieutenant, is your general married? 65

CASSIO

    Most fortunately. He hath achiev'd a maid
    That paragons description and wild fame;
    One that excels the quirks of blazoning pens,
    And in th' essential vesture of creation
70   Does tire the ingener.

        Reenter second GENTLEMAN.

                How now? Who has put in?

2. GENTLEMAN

    'Tis one Iago, ancient to the General.

CASSIO

    He has had most favourable and happy speed.
    Tempests themselves, high seas, and howling winds,
75   The gutter'd rocks and congregated sands,
    Traitors ensteep'd to clog the guiltless keel,
    As having sense of beauty, do omit
    Their mortal natures, letting go safely by
    The divine Desdemona.

MONTANO

80   What is she?

CASSIO

    She that I spake of, our great captain's captain,
    Left in the conduct of the bold Iago,
    Whose footing here anticipates our thoughts
    A se'nnight's speed. Great Jove,* Othello guard,
85   And swell his sail with thine own powerful breath,
    That he may bless this bay with his tall ship,
    Make love's quick pants in Desdemona's arms,
    Give renew'd fire to our extinct spirits,
    And bring all Cyprus comfort!

       Enter DESDEMONA, IAGO, RODERIGO, *and* EMILIA.

90   O, behold,
    The riches of the ship is come on shore!
    You men of Cyprus, let her have your knees.
    Hail to thee, lady, and the grace of heaven,

---

84 *Jove* the head god in the Roman pantheon; he dispensed justice and ruled over
the gods and men

CASSIO

Well-married. He has won a girl
who surpasses description and exaggerated gossip;
one who exceeds the fancy descriptions of praising pens.
In her basic qualities,
she defies the imagination of an ingenuous praiser. 70

The SECOND GENTLEMAN *enters.*

What now? Who has landed?

SECOND GENTLEMAN

It's a certain Iago, ensign to the general.

CASSIO

He's had a most favorable and fortunate arrival.
The tempests themselves, the high seas and howling winds,
the jagged rocks and gathered sand— 75
hidden traitors to ensnare the innocent keel—
as if they had a sense of beauty, have forgotten
their deadly natures and let safely pass
the divine Desdemona.

MONTANO

Who is she? 80

CASSIO

She's the one I spoke of, our great captain's captain,
left in the protection of the bold Iago,
whose arrival here comes at least
a week earlier than expected. Great Jove, guard Othello,
and fill his sail with your powerful breath, 85
so he might bless this bay with his brave ship,
gasp his love in Desdemona's arms,
renew the fire of our exhausted spirits,
and bring all Cyprus comfort!

DESDEMONA, IAGO, RODERIGO, *and* EMILIA *enter.*

Oh, look! 90
The riches of the ship are now on shore!
You men of Cyprus, bow down before her.
Greetings to you, lady! And may the grace of heaven

Before, behind thee, and on every hand
95   Enwheel thee round.

DESDEMONA

                    I thank you, valiant Cassio.
What tidings can you tell me of my lord?

CASSIO

He is not yet arriv'd; nor know I aught
But that he's well and will be shortly here.

DESDEMONA

100   O, but I fear—How lost you company?

CASSIO

The great contention of sea and skies
Parted our fellowship.—But, hark! A sail.

Within "A sail, a sail!" [*Guns heard.*]

2. GENTLEMAN

They give their greeting to the citadel.
This likewise is a friend.

CASSIO

105   See for the news.

[*Exit* GENTLEMAN.]

Good ancient, you are welcome. [*to* EMILIA] Welcome,
    mistress.
Let it not gall your patience, good Iago,
That I extend my manners; 'tis my breeding
110   That gives me this bold show of courtesy. [*kissing her*]

IAGO

Sir, would she give you so much of her lips
As of her tongue she oft bestows on me,
You'd have enough.

DESDEMONA

Alas, she has no speech.

IAGO

115   In faith, too much;
I find it still, when I have list to sleep.
Marry, before your Ladyship, I grant,

be in front of you, behind you, and on both sides of you,
and utterly surround you!   95

DESDEMONA

Thank you, valiant Cassio.
What news can you give me of my husband?

CASSIO

He's not yet arrived; I know nothing
except that he's well and will be here shortly.

DESDEMONA

Oh, but I'm afraid! How did you get separated?   100

CASSIO

The great quarrel between the sea and the sky
parted us from one another.—But listen. A sail!

Offstage a voice cries, "A sail, a sail!" A shot is also heard.

SECOND GENTLEMAN

They give their greeting to the fortress.
This is a friend, too.

CASSIO

Go see what's the news.   105

GENTLEMAN exits.

Good ensign, you are welcome. (*to* EMILIA) Welcome, madam.
I hope it doesn't try your patience, good Iago,
if I stretch my manners. It's my upbringing
that teaches me to make such a bold display of courtesy.   110

He kisses her.

IAGO

Sir, if she gave you as much of her lips
as she often gives me of her tongue
you'd have plenty.

DESDEMONA

But really, she doesn't chatter at all!

IAGO

I tell you, she talks too much.   115
Even when I want to sleep, she's still talking.
Though, indeed, in front of your Ladyship, I'll admit

She puts her tongue a little in her heart
And chides with thinking.

EMILIA

120   You have little cause to say so.

IAGO

Come on, come on! You are pictures out of door, bells in
your parlours, wild-cats in your kitchens, saints in your
injuries, devils being offended, players in your huswifery,
and huswives* in your beds.

DESDEMONA

125   O, fie upon thee, slanderer!

IAGO

Nay, it is true, or else I am a Turk.
You rise to play and go to bed to work.

EMILIA

You shall not write my praise.

IAGO

                        No, let me not.

DESDEMONA

130   What wouldst thou write of me, if thou shouldst praise me?

IAGO

O gentle lady, do not put me to 't;
For I am nothing if not critical.

DESDEMONA

Come on, assay.—There's one gone to the harbour?

IAGO

Ay, madam.

DESDEMONA [*aside*]

135   I am not merry; but I do beguile
The thing I am by seeming otherwise.—
Come, how wouldst thou praise me?

---

124   *huswives* also means "hussies"

that she hides her tongue in her heart a little
and scolds me only in her thoughts.

EMILIA

You have little reason to say that. 120

IAGO

Come, come! You women are the picture of virtue away from
home, merry when playing the hostess, wildcats in your
kitchen, saints when you criticize, devils when you're offended,
slack in your household duties, but really earnest in bed.

DESDEMONA

Oh, shame on you, slanderer! 125

IAGO

No, it's true, or else I am a Turk.
You get up in the morning to play and go to bed to work.

EMILIA

I won't let you write my praises.

IAGO

No, I won't.

DESDEMONA

What would you write about me, if you were to praise me? 130

IAGO

Oh, gentle lady, don't ask me to do it,
for I am nothing if not critical.

DESDEMONA

Come on, try it.—Has someone gone to the harbor?

IAGO

Yes, madam.

DESDEMONA (*to herself*)

I am not merry; but I'll forget 135
the way I really feel by seeming to be otherwise.
(*to* IAGO) Come now, how would you praise me?

IAGO

I am about it; but indeed my invention comes from my
pate as birdlime* does from frieze; it plucks out brains
140 and all. But my Muse* labours, and thus she is deliver'd:
"If she be fair and wise, fairness and wit,
The one's for use, the other useth it."

DESDEMONA

Well prais'd! How if she be black* and witty?

IAGO

"If she be black, and thereto have a wit,
145 She'll find a white* that shall her blackness hit."

DESDEMONA

Worse and worse.

EMILIA

How if fair and foolish?

IAGO

"She never yet was foolish that was fair;
For even her folly help'd her to an heir."

DESDEMONA

150 These are old fond **paradoxes** to make fools laugh i' th'
alehouse. What miserable praise hast thou for her that's
foul and foolish?

IAGO

"There's none so foul and foolish thereunto,
But does foul pranks which fair and wise ones do."

DESDEMONA

155 O heavy ignorance! Thou praisest the worst best. But what
praise couldst thou bestow on a deserving woman indeed,
one that in the authority of her merit did justly put on the
vouch of very malice itself?

---

139 *birdlime* a sticky substance used to trap birds

140 *Muse* one of the nine goddesses of classical mythology; patronesses of learning
and the arts

IAGO

I'm thinking about it, but really, my ideas are as ha~~
out of my head as birdlime from a heavy cloth—they pu~~
my brains and everything. But my Muse is in labor, and here is .
what she gives birth to:
If she is pretty and clever, beauty and cleverness;
The beauty is to be used, the cleverness is for using it.

DESDEMONA

Well-praised! What if she is ugly and clever?

IAGO

If she is ugly but clever too,
She'll find a man who will be happy with her.   145

DESDEMONA

Worse and worse.

EMILIA

What if she's pretty and foolish?

IAGO

No woman has ever been foolish who was also pretty,
For even her foolishness helped her to have an heir.

DESDEMONA

These are old, silly sayings to make fools laugh in the bar.   150
What miserable praise do you have for a woman who's ugly
and foolish?

IAGO

There's no one who is so ugly and so foolish as well,
Who doesn't do the same naughty things that pretty and wise
     women do.

DESDEMONA

What terrible ignorance! You've praised the worst the most   155
highly. But what praise would you give to a woman who really
deserves it—one who, by virtue of all her good qualities, can
justifiably claim the praise of even the most malicious?

---

143   *black* here means "unattractive"; light-skinned women were considered more
      beautiful than dark-skinned women in Shakespeare's day (see Shakespeare's
      Sonnet CXXX).

145   *white* puns on the word "wight," which meant "person"

IAGO

"She that was ever fair and never proud,
160   Had tongue at will and yet was never loud,
Never lack'd gold and yet went never gay,
Fled from her wish and yet said, 'Now I may,'
She that being anger'd, her revenge being nigh,
Bade her wrong stay and her displeasure fly,
165   She that in wisdom never was so frail
To change the cod's head for the salmon's tail,
She that could think and ne'er disclose her mind,
See suitors following and not look behind,
She was a wight, if ever wight were—"

DESDEMONA

170   To do what?

IAGO

"To suckle fools and chronicle small beer."*

DESDEMONA

O, most lame and impotent conclusion!—Do not learn
of him, Emilia, though he be thy husband.—How say
you, Cassio? Is he not a most profane and liberal
175   counselor?

CASSIO

He speaks home, madam. You may relish him more in the
soldier than in the scholar.

IAGO [*aside*]

He takes her by the palm. Ay, well said, whisper.
With as little a web as this will I gyve as great a fly as
180   Cassio. Ay, smile upon her, do. I will give thee in thine
own courtship. You say true; 'tis so, indeed. If such tricks
as these strip you out of your lieutenantry, it had been
better you had not kiss'd your three fingers so oft, which
now again you are most apt to play the sir in. Very good;
185   well kiss'd! An excellent courtesy! 'Tis so, indeed. Yet again
your fingers to your lips? Would they were clyster pipes for
your sake! (*Trumpets within.*) The Moor! I know his
trumpet.*

---

171   *"To . . . beer."* These are obviously meaningless chores to Iago's mind.

188   *his trumpet* Men of Othello's standing often had an individual trumpet call.

IAGO

> She who was always pretty, but never boastful;
> could speak well, but never talked too much;   160
> never lacked gold and yet never was extravagantly dressed;
> denied her desires, but yet said, "Now I may have this";
> she who being angered and her opportunity for revenge at
>   hand
> made herself hold her temper and forget her anger;
> she who in her wisdom never made the mistake   165
> of trading something good for something bad;
> she who could think, but never let her thoughts be known;
> see suitors following her and not look behind her;
> she was a person (if there ever was such a person)—

DESDEMONA

> To do what?   170

IAGO

> —to coddle fools and keep household accounts.

DESDEMONA

> Oh, what a flat and pointless conclusion! Don't believe him,
> Emilia, even though he is your husband. What do you think,
> Cassio? Isn't he a most worldly and lewd advisor?   175

CASSIO

> He does talk some common sense, madam. He's easier to
> appreciate as a soldier than as a scholar.

IAGO (*to himself*)

> He takes her by the hand. Yes, very good, whisper to her! With
> this little web, I'll catch a fly as big as Cassio. Yes, smile at her,
> go ahead! I'll catch you in your own flirtation. You agreed with   180
> me; and I was right indeed! If this behavior of yours causes
> you to lose your lieutenancy, you'll wish you hadn't acted the
> gallant so much. And even now you're acting like the courtly
> gentleman. Very good! Well-kissed! What lovely manners! I
> really mean it! What, are you blowing her another kiss? Better   185
> that your fingers were an enema tube! (*A trumpet blows
> offstage.*) It's the Moor! I know his trumpet.

CASSIO

'Tis truly so.

DESDEMONA

190   Let's meet him and receive him.

CASSIO

Lo, where he comes!

Enter OTHELLO *and* ATTENDANTS.

OTHELLO

O my fair warrior!

DESDEMONA

My dear Othello!

OTHELLO

It gives me wonder great as my content

195   To see you here before me. O my soul's joy!
If after every tempest come such calms,
May the winds blow till they have waken'd death,
And let the labouring bark climb hills of seas
Olympus high, and duck again as low

200   As hell's from heaven! If it were now to die,
'Twere now to be most happy, for I fear
My soul hath her content so absolute
That not another comfort like to this
Succeeds in unknown fate.

DESDEMONA

205   The heavens forbid
But that our loves and comforts should increase,
Even as our days do grow!

OTHELLO

Amen to that, sweet powers!
I cannot speak enough of this content;

210   It stops me here; it is too much of joy.
And this, and this, the greatest discords be [*kissing her*]
That e'er our hearts shall make!

IAGO [*aside*]

O, you are well tun'd now!
But I'll set down the pegs that make this music,

215   As honest as I am.

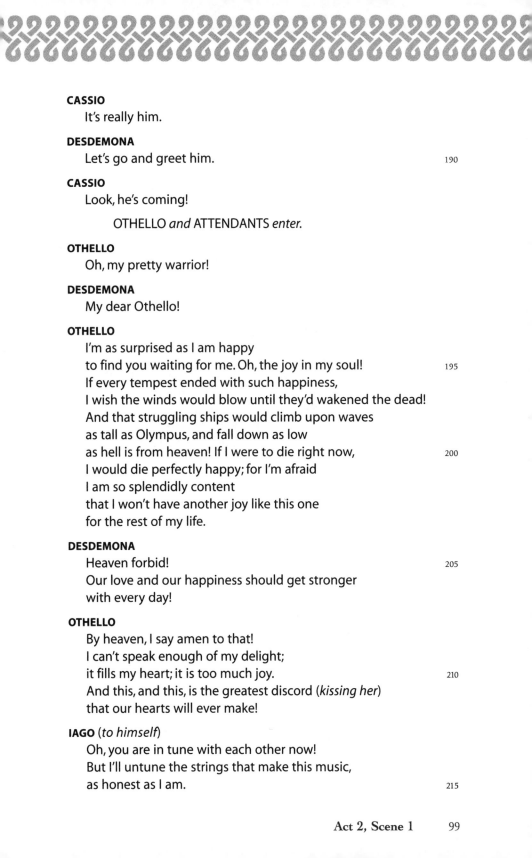

CASSIO

    It's really him.

DESDEMONA

    Let's go and greet him. 190

CASSIO

    Look, he's coming!

        OTHELLO *and* ATTENDANTS *enter.*

OTHELLO

    Oh, my pretty warrior!

DESDEMONA

    My dear Othello!

OTHELLO

    I'm as surprised as I am happy
    to find you waiting for me. Oh, the joy in my soul! 195
    If every tempest ended with such happiness,
    I wish the winds would blow until they'd wakened the dead!
    And that struggling ships would climb upon waves
    as tall as Olympus, and fall down as low
    as hell is from heaven! If I were to die right now, 200
    I would die perfectly happy; for I'm afraid
    I am so splendidly content
    that I won't have another joy like this one
    for the rest of my life.

DESDEMONA

    Heaven forbid! 205
    Our love and our happiness should get stronger
    with every day!

OTHELLO

    By heaven, I say amen to that!
    I can't speak enough of my delight;
    it fills my heart; it is too much joy. 210
    And this, and this, is the greatest discord (*kissing her*)
    that our hearts will ever make!

IAGO (*to himself*)

    Oh, you are in tune with each other now!
    But I'll untune the strings that make this music,
    as honest as I am. 215

OTHELLO

Come, let us to the castle.—
News, friends: our wars are done, the Turks are drown'd.
How does my old acquaintance of this isle?
Honey, you shall be well desir'd in Cyprus;
220   I have found great love amongst them. O my sweet,
I prattle out of fashion, and I dote
In mine own comforts. I prithee, good Iago,
Go to the bay and disembark my coffers.
Bring thou the master to the citadel;
225   He is a good one, and his worthiness
Does challenge much respect. Come, Desdemona,
Once more, well met at Cyprus.

      [*Exeunt* OTHELLO, DESDEMONA, *and* ATTENDANTS.]

IAGO [*to* RODERIGO]

Do thou meet me presently at the harbour. Come hither.
If thou be'st valiant—as they say base men being in love
230   have then a nobility in their natures more than is
native to them—list me. The lieutenant tonight watches
on the court of guard. First, I must tell thee this:
Desdemona is directly in love with him.

RODERIGO

With him? Why, 'tis not possible.

IAGO

235   Lay thy finger this, and let thy soul be instructed. Mark me
with what violence she first lov'd the Moor, but for
bragging and telling her fantastical lies. And will she love
him still for prating? Let not thy discreet heart think it.
Her eye must be fed; and what delight shall she have to
240   look on the devil? When the blood is made dull with the
act of sport, there should be, again to inflame it and to
give satiety a fresh appetite, loveliness in favour, sympathy
in years, manners, and beauties, all which the Moor is
defective in. Now, for want of these requir'd conveniences,
245   her delicate tenderness will find itself abus'd, begin to
heave the gorge, disrelish and abhor the Moor. Very nature
will instruct her in it and compel her to some second

OTHELLO

    Come, let's go to the castle.

    News, friends! Our wars are over; the Turks have been drowned.

    How are all my old friends here on this island?—

    (*to* DESDEMONA) My dear, you'll be well-beloved in Cyprus;

    I've found great love here. Oh, my sweet,   220

    I ramble on unsuitably, and I act foolishly

    because of my delight. Good Iago, I ask you

    to go to the bay and get my money from the ship.

    And bring the master to the castle.

    He's a good man, and his fine qualities   225

    command much respect. Come, Desdemona.

    Oh, it is good to see you here in Cyprus.

        Everyone exits except IAGO *and* RODERIGO.

IAGO (*to* RODERIGO)

    Meet me soon at the harbor. Be sure to come. If you are

    brave—and they say cowardly men who are in love have

    more nobility in their natures than usual—listen to me. The   230

    lieutenant keeps watch on the guardhouse tonight. First, I'd

    better tell you this: Desdemona is madly in love with him.

RODERIGO

    With him? Why, it isn't possible.

IAGO

    Keep mum, and just listen. Remember how violently she first   235

    loved the Moor, and just because he bragged and told her

    fantastic lies? Will she keep loving him just because he

    continues to babble? Don't you believe it. She needs a handsome

    man; and what joy will she have to look at the devil? When the

    appetite tires of love-making, one needs something to spark it   240

    again and renew one's appetite—like good looks, and sameness

    of age, manners, and appearances. The Moor has none of

    these. Now because she lacks these desirable advantages, her

    delicate sensibilities will feel abused and reject, hate, and   245

    despise the Moor. Nature itself will teach her to act this way

    and force her to seek out someone else. Now, sir, if you'll admit

choice. Now, sir, this granted—as it is a most pregnant and
unforc'd position—who stands so **eminent** in the degree

250 of this fortune as Cassio does? A knave very voluble, no
further conscionable than in putting on the mere form of
civil and humane seeming for the better compassing of his
salt and most hidden loose affection. Why, none, why,
none! A slipper and subtle knave, a finder-out of

255 occasions that has an eye can stamp and counterfeit
advantages, though true advantage never present itself; a
devilish knave! Besides, the knave is handsome, young,
and hath all those **requisites** in him that folly and green
minds look after; a pestilent complete knave, and the

260 woman hath found him already.

RODERIGO

I cannot believe that in her; she's full of most bless'd
condition.

IAGO

Bless'd fig's end! The wine she drinks is made of grapes.*
If she had been bless'd, she would never have lov'd the

265 Moor. Bless'd pudding! Didst thou not see her paddle
with the palm of his hand? Didst not mark that?

RODERIGO

Yes, that I did; but that was but courtesy.

IAGO

Lechery, by this hand! An index and obscure prologue to
the history of lust and foul thoughts. They met so near

270 with their lips that their breaths embrac'd together.
Villainous thoughts, Roderigo! When these mutualities so
marshal the way, hard at hand comes the master and main
exercise, th' incorporate conclusion. Pish! But, sir, be you
rul'd by me; I have brought you from Venice. Watch you

275 tonight; for the command, I'll lay 't upon you. Cassio
knows you not. I'll not be far from you. Do you find some
occasion to anger Cassio, either by speaking too loud, or
tainting his discipline, or from what other course you
please, which the time shall more favourably minister.

---

263 *The wine . . . grapes.* Iago means Desdemona is only human.

this (since it's an obvious and logical conclusion), who possesses these qualities to a greater degree than Cassio? A very flattering rascal; having no more conscience than to put on a mask of civility and politeness, just to achieve his lecherous and secret immoral intentions? Why, no one! No one! A slippery and subtle rascal; a true opportunist; a man who knows how to sniff out an advantage, even if a real advantage never turns up; a devilish rascal! Besides, this rascal is handsome, young, and has all those qualities about him that foolish and young minds are always looking for. A completely rotten rascal! And the woman has fallen for him already. 250 255 260

RODERIGO

I can't believe that about her. She's blessed with a most admirable character.

IAGO

Blessed, my eye! The wine she drinks is still made of grapes. If she were so blessed, she wouldn't have fallen in love with the Moor. Blessed, my foot! Didn't you see her holding his hand? 265 Didn't you see that?

RODERIGO

Yes, I did; but that was just politeness.

IAGO

It was lechery, I tell you! Just the indication and secret prologue to a history of lust and filthy thoughts. Their lips were so close that their breaths embraced. Wicked thoughts, 270 Roderigo! When these mutual courtesies show the way, hard by comes the lead and main event, the carnal conclusion. Bah! But, sir, you do exactly as I say. I've brought you here from Venice. Take good care tonight; as to your orders, I'll give them 275 to you. Cassio doesn't know you. I'll be close by. Figure out some way to make Cassio angry, either by talking too loudly or slandering his conduct or whatever way you can think of when the time is most favorable.

RODERIGO

280   Well?

IAGO

Sir, he's rash and very sudden in choler, and haply may
strike at you. Provoke him, that he may, for even out of
that will I cause these of Cyprus to mutiny, whose
qualification shall come into no true taste again but by
285   the displanting of Cassio. So shall you have a shorter
journey to your desires by the means I shall then have to
prefer them, and the impediment most profitably
removed, without the which there were no expectation of
our prosperity.

RODERIGO

290   I will do this, if you can bring it to any opportunity.

IAGO

I warrant thee. Meet me by and by at the citadel. I must
fetch his necessaries ashore. Farewell.

RODERIGO

Adieu.

He exits.

IAGO

That Cassio loves her, I do well believe 't;
295   That she loves him, 'tis apt and of great credit.
The Moor, howbeit that I endure him not,
Is of a constant, loving, noble nature,
And I dare think he'll prove to Desdemona
A most dear husband. Now, I do love her too,
300   Not out of absolute lust [though peradventure
I stand accountant for as great a sin]
But partly led to diet my revenge
For that I do suspect the lusty Moor
Hath leap'd into my seat—the thought whereof
305   Doth, like a poisonous mineral, gnaw my inwards,
And nothing can or shall content my soul
Till I am even'd with him, wife for wife,
Or failing so, yet that I put the Moor
At least into a jealousy so strong
310   That judgment cannot cure. Which thing to do,

RODERIGO

Well? 280

IAGO

Sir, he is hotheaded and very short-tempered, and perhaps
he'll try to hit you with his baton. Provoke him to that. That's
all I need to start a mutiny among those of Cyprus, who won't
be happy until Cassio is thrown out. So you will have a quicker 285
route to what you desire by the means I'll then suggest. And
we'll have removed most profitably the one obstacle which
might have made it impossible for either of us to achieve our
hopes.

RODERIGO

I'll do this if it will bring me any advantage. 290

IAGO

I guarantee it. Meet me at the castle soon. I have to bring his
belongings ashore. Good-bye.

RODERIGO

Good-bye.

RODERIGO *exits.*

IAGO

That Cassio loves her, I really do believe;
that she loves him too is natural and likely. 295
The Moor, as much as I may hate him,
is of a dedicated, loving, and noble nature,
and I'm sure he'll prove to Desdemona
a very costly husband. I love her too;
not completely out of lust (although it's likely 300
that I'm guilty of a sin just as great),
but partly because she'll help me get revenge,
since I suspect the lusty Moor
has taken my place. The thought of that
gnaws at me like a poisonous mineral, 305
and nothing can or will satisfy me
till we are even, wife for wife.
Or if I fall short of that, I'll still put the Moor
in a state of jealousy so extreme
that good sense won't cure it. In order to do this, 310

If this poor trash of Venice, whom I trace
For his quick hunting, stand the putting on,
I'll have our Michael Cassio on the hip,
Abuse him to the Moor in the rank garb—
315 For I fear Cassio with my night-cap too—
Make the Moor thank me, love me, and reward me
For making him **egregiously** an ass
And practising upon his peace and quiet
Even to madness. 'Tis here, but yet confus'd;
320 Knavery's plain face is never seen till us'd.

[*Exit.*]

if this worthless Venetian, whom I'm hounding
to keep him on track, will only do as I've urged him,
I'll have Michael Cassio in my pocket,
slander him to the Moor in the proper fashion,
because I'm afraid Cassio has been in my bed too,   315
make the Moor thank me, love me, and reward me
for making a complete fool of him
and scheming against his peace and quiet—
even to the point of madness. That's the plan, though the
    details must be flushed out.
Villainous work is never recognized until the villainy's been   320
    done.

    IAGO *exits.*

ACT II, SCENE II

[*A street.*] *Enter Othello's* HERALD, *with a proclamation.* [*People following.*]

HERALD

It is Othello's pleasure, our noble and valiant general,
that, upon certain tidings now arriv'd, importing the mere
perdition of the Turkish fleet, every man put himself into
triumph; some to dance, some to make bonfires, each
5   man to what sport and revels his addition leads him; for,
beside these beneficial news, it is the celebration of his
nuptial. So much was his pleasure should be proclaimed.
All offices are open, and there is full liberty of feasting
from this present hour of five till the bell have told eleven.
10   Heaven bless the isle of Cyprus and our noble general
Othello!

[*Exeunt.*]

ACT 2, SCENE 2

A street. Othello's HERALD *enters with a proclamation; people follow him.*

HERALD

It is the wish of Othello, our noble and brave general, that, because of the news we've just heard, relating the total destruction of the Turkish fleet, everyone should rejoice. Some should dance, some should make bonfires, and everyone should engage in whatever amusement and celebration that   5
is to their taste. Because, besides this welcome news, it's also his wedding celebration. His joy is so great, he wants it proclaimed. All kitchens are open, and there's free feasting from the present hour of five until the bell rings eleven. Heaven bless the island of Cyprus and our noble general   10
Othello!

Exit.

ACT II, SCENE III

[*A hall in the castle.*] *Enter* OTHELLO, DESDEMONA, CASSIO, *and* ATTENDANTS.

OTHELLO

Good Michael, look you to the guard tonight.
Let's teach ourselves that honourable stop
Not to outsport discretion.

CASSIO

Iago hath direction what to do;
5 But, not withstanding, with my personal eye
Will I look to 't.

OTHELLO

          Iago is most honest.
Michael, good night; tomorrow with your earliest
Let me have speech with you. [*to* DESDEMONA] Come,
10   my dear love,
The purchase made, the fruits are to ensue;
That profit's yet to come 'tween me and you.
Good night.

       [*Exeunt* OTHELLO, DESDEMONA, *and*
       ATTENDANTS.]

       Enter IAGO.

CASSIO

Welcome, Iago; we must to the watch.

IAGO

15 Not this hour, Lieutenant; 'tis not yet ten o' th' clock. Our
general cast us thus early for the love of his Desdemona;
who let us not therefore blame. He hath not yet made
wanton the night with her; and she is sport for Jove.

CASSIO

She's a most exquisite lady.

IAGO

20 And, I'll warrant her, full of game.

CASSIO

Indeed, she's a most fresh and delicate creature.

ACT 2, SCENE 3

A hall in the castle. OTHELLO, DESDEMONA, CASSIO, *and* ATTENDANTS *enter.*

OTHELLO
Good Michael, you are in charge of the guard tonight.
Let's make sure things don't get out of hand
and no one celebrates indiscreetly.

CASSIO
Iago already has instructions to do so.
Nevertheless, I'll see to it   5
myself.

OTHELLO
Iago is very honest.
Good night, Michael. The first thing tomorrow morning,
come and talk to me. (*to* DESDEMONA) Come, my dear love.   10
Once the purchase has been made, the fruits will follow;
the two of us have not yet enjoyed our profits.
Good night.

> OTHELLO, DESDEMONA, *and* ATTENDANTS *exit.*

> IAGO *enters.*

CASSIO
Welcome, Iago. We'd better go on watch.

IAGO
Not at this hour, Lieutenant; it's not ten o'clock yet. Our general   15
dismissed us early because of his love for Desdemona, but let's
not blame her for that. He hasn't yet enjoyed the night with
her, and she's a lover worthy of Jove.

CASSIO
She's a very beautiful lady.

IAGO
And I'll bet she's full of fire.   20

CASSIO
Certainly, she's a very young and refined creature.

IAGO

What an eye she has! Methinks it sounds a parley to **provocation**.

CASSIO

An inviting eye; and yet methinks right modest.

IAGO

25 And when she speaks, is it not an alarum to love?

CASSIO

She is indeed perfection.

IAGO

Well, happiness to their sheets! Come, Lieutenant, I have a stoup of wine; and here without are a brace of Cyprus gallants that would fain have a measure to the health of
30 black Othello.

CASSIO

Not tonight, good Iago. I have very poor and unhappy brains for drinking. I could well wish courtesy would invent some other custom of entertainment.

IAGO

O, they are our friends. But one cup; I'll drink for you.

CASSIO

35 I have drunk but one cup tonight, and that was craftily qualified too, and, behold, what innovation it makes here. I am unfortunate in the **infirmity** and dare not task my weakness with any more.

IAGO

What, man! 'Tis a night of revels. The gallants desire it.

CASSIO

40 Where are they?

IAGO

Here at the door; I pray you, call them in.

CASSIO

I'll do't; but it dislikes me.

[*Exit.*]

IAGO

What an eye she has! I think it's downright provocative.

CASSIO

An inviting eye; but a modest one, I think.

IAGO

And when she speaks, isn't it a temptation to love? 25

CASSIO

She is certainly perfect.

IAGO

Well, happiness to their sheets! Come, Lieutenant, I have a cup
of wine, and just outside are a few fellows of Cyprus who would
like to drink to the health of black Othello. 30

CASSIO

Not tonight, good Iago. Wine goes straight to my head.
I really wish there was some other mean of courteous
entertainment.

IAGO

But they are our friends. Just one cup! I'll drink when you
make a toast.

CASSIO

I've had just one cup tonight and that was quite diluted. But 35
look how flushed I am just from that. I really can't handle wine
and must not overdo it with any more.

IAGO

What! This is a night of celebration. The fellows wish it.

CASSIO

Where are they? 40

IAGO

Right here at the door. Please call them in.

CASSIO

I'll do it, but I don't like the idea.

> CASSIO *exits.*

IAGO

If I can fasten but one cup upon him,
With that which he hath drunk tonight already,
45　He'll be as full of quarrel and offence
As my young mistress's dog. Now, my sick fool Roderigo,
Whom love hath turn'd almost the wrong side out,
To Desdemona hath tonight carous'd
Potations pottle-deep; and he's to watch.
50　Three else of Cyprus, noble swelling spirits
That hold their honours in a wary distance,
The very elements of this warlike isle,
Have I tonight fluster'd with flowing cups,
And they watch too. Now, 'mongst this flock of drunkards
55　Am I to put our Cassio in some action
That may offend the isle. But here they come.
If consequence do but approve my dream,
My boat sails freely, both with wind and stream.

Enter CASSIO, MONTANA, *and* GENLEMEN.
[SERVANTS *follow with wine.*]

CASSIO

'Fore God, they have given me a rouse already.

MONTANO

60　Good faith, a little one; not past a pint, as I am a soldier.

IAGO

Some wine, ho!

[*Sings.*]

"And let me the cannikin clink, clink;
And let me the cannikin clink.
　A soldier's a man;
　O, man's life's but a span;
Why, then, let a soldier drink."

Some wine, boys!

CASSIO

'Fore God, an excellent song.

IAGO

If I can get him to drink just one more cup
on top of what he's had to drink tonight already,
he'll be as quarrelsome and disagreeable   45
as my young lady's dog. Now my sick fool Roderigo,
who has been turned almost inside out by love,
has been toasting Desdemona tonight
and draining many cups to the bottom; and he's supposed to
     be on guard.
Three boys of Cyprus—fine and noble fellows,   50
who are very quick to respond to an insult,
and of a very suitable temperament to this warlike island—
I've made tipsy tonight with overflowing cups,
and they're on guard, too. Now, amid this flock of drunkards,
I'll provoke Cassio to some action   55
that's bound to cause offense on this island. But here they come.
If things only go the way I hope,
my boat will sail freely, with both the wind and the stream.

> CASSIO, MONTANO, and several GENTLEMEN enter.
> SERVANTS follow with some wine.

CASSIO

By God, they've given me a huge cup already.

MONTANO

Really now, it's just a little one; no more than a pint, or I'm not   60
a soldier.

IAGO

Some wine over here!

> (He sings.)

> *And let me clink the cup, clink;*
> *And let me clink the cup.*
>   *A soldier's a man;*
>   *A life is short,*   65
> *So then let a soldier drink.*

Some wine, boys!

CASSIO

By God, that's an excellent song!

IAGO

70 I learn'd it in England, where, indeed, they are most
potent in potting; your Dane, your German, and your
swag-belli'd Hollander—drink, ho!—are nothing to your
English.

CASSIO

Is your Englishman so exquisite in his drinking?

IAGO

Why, he drinks you, with facility, your Dane dead drunk;
75 he sweats not to overthrow your Almain; he gives your
Hollander a vomit ere the next pottle can be fill'd.

CASSIO

To the health of our general!

MONTANO

I am for it, Lieutenant; and I'll do you justice.

IAGO

O Sweet England!

80 [*Sings.*] "King Stephen was and-a worthy peer,
        His breeches cost him but a crown;
He held them sixpence all too dear,
        With that he call'd the tailor lown.
He was a wight of high renown,
85   And thou art but of low degree.
'Tis pride that pulls the country down;
        Then take thy auld cloak about thee."

Some wine, ho!

CASSIO

Fore God, this is a more exquisite song than the other.

IAGO

90 Will you hear 't again?

CASSIO

No, for I hold him to be unworthy of his place that does
those things. Well, God's above all; and there be souls
must be saved, and there be souls must not be saved.

IAGO

I learned it in England, where they really know how to drink.
Your Danes, your Germans, and your pot-bellied Hollanders—   70
drink up!—are nothing compared to your English.

CASSIO

Is your Englishman such an expert drinker?

IAGO

Why, he'll drink your Dane dead drunk with no trouble; it's no
sweat for him to outdo your German; he'll have your Hollander   75
vomiting before the next cup gets filled.

CASSIO

To the health of our general!

MONTANO

I'll drink to that, Lieutenant, and I'll match your toast.

IAGO

Oh, sweet England!

(*He sings.*)

King Stephen was a worthy gentleman;   80
  His pants only cost him a crown;
He thought they were a sixpence too expensive,
  So he called the tailor a lout.
He was a man of great renown,
  And you are but of low birth.   85
It's pride that's ruining this country;
  So keep wearing your old coat.
Some wine, over here!

CASSIO

By God, this is an even better song than the other one.

IAGO

Do you want to hear it again?   90

CASSIO

No, because I don't think a man who does those things is
worthy of his rank. Well, God's above us all; and there are souls
that will be saved, and there are souls that will not be saved.

IAGO

It's true, good Lieutenant.

CASSIO

95   For mine own part—no offence to the general, nor any man of quality—I hope to be saved.

IAGO

And so do I too, Lieutenant.

CASSIO

Ay, but, by your leave, not before me; the lieutenant is to be saved before the ancient. Let's have no more of this;
100   let's to our affairs.—God forgive us our sins!—Gentlemen, let's look to our business. Do not think, gentlemen, I am drunk. This is my ancient; this is my right hand, and this is my left. I am not drunk now; I can stand well enough, and I speak well enough.

GENTLEMEN

105   Excellent well.

CASSIO

Why, very well then; you must not think then that I am drunk.

    [*Exit.*]

MONTANO

To the platform, masters; come, let's set the watch.

IAGO

You see this fellow that is gone before:
110   He is a soldier fit to stand by Caesar
And give direction; and do but see his vice.
'Tis to his virtue a just equinox,
The one as long as th' other; 'tis pity of him.
I fear the trust Othello puts him in,
115   On some odd time of his infirmity,
Will shake this island.

MONTANO

                  But is he often thus?

IAGO

That's the truth, good Lieutenant.

CASSIO

For my own part—I mean no offense to the general, nor to 95
any other man of high rank—I hope to be saved.

IAGO

And so do I, Lieutenant.

CASSIO

Yes, but if you don't mind, not before me. The lieutenant has
to be saved before the ensign. Let's not talk about this anymore;
let's get down to business. God forgive us for our sins! 100
Gentlemen, let's see to our business. Gentlemen, don't think
I'm drunk. This is my ensign. This is my right hand, and this is
my left. I'm not drunk now. I can stand well enough and speak
well enough.

ALL

Extremely well. 105

CASSIO

Well, very good then. As long as you don't think I'm drunk.

    CASSIO *exits.*

MONTANO

Let's go on guard, gentlemen. Come, let's begin the watch.

IAGO

Take a look at this fellow who has gone ahead.
He is a soldier fit to stand beside Caesar 110
and give orders; and take a look at this vice of his.
It's the exact counterpart of his virtue—
the one's the equal of the other. It's a pity about him.
I'm afraid that the trust Othello puts in him,
due to his infirmity, will one of these days 115
cause trouble on this island.

MONTANO

But is he like this very often?

IAGO

'Tis evermore the prologue to his sleep.
He'll watch the horologe a double set
120 If drink rock not his cradle.

MONTANO

It were well
The general were put in mind of it.
Perhaps he sees it not; or his good nature
Prizes the virtue that appears in Cassio,
125 And looks not on his evils. Is not this true?

Enter RODERIGO.

IAGO [*aside to* RODERIGO]

How now, Roderigo!
I pray you, after the lieutenant; go.

[*Exit* RODERIGO.]

MONTANO

And 'tis great pity that the noble Moor
Should hazard such a place as his own second
130 With one of an engraffed infirmity.
It were an honest action to say so
To the Moor.

IAGO

Not I, for this fair island.
I do love Cassio well; and would do much
135 To cure him of this evil.— [*cry within:* "Help! Help!"]
But, hark! What noise?

Reenter CASSIO, *pursuing* RODERIGO.

CASSIO

'Zounds, you rogue! You rascal!

MONTANO

What's the matter, Lieutenant?

CASSIO

A knave teach me my duty? I'll beat the knave into a
140 twiggen bottle.

IAGO

All the time, before he goes to bed.
He'll watch the clock for twenty-four hours
if his drinking doesn't put him to sleep.   120

MONTANO

It would be a good idea
to let the general know about this.
Maybe he doesn't know about this, or his good nature
values Cassio's good qualities
and overlooks his evils. Isn't this true?   125

      RODERIGO *enters.*

IAGO (*aside to* RODERIGO)

What is this, Roderigo?
I'm telling you, go after the lieutenant!

      RODERIGO *exits.*

MONTANO

It's a terrible pity that the noble Moor
should risk the position of his own second in command
to a man with such an ingrained infirmity.   130
It would be an honest deed to say so to the Moor.

IAGO

I wouldn't do it for this entire lovely island!
I love Cassio very much, and will do what I can
to cure him of this problem.—   135

      A voice from offstage cries "Help! Help!"

But listen! What's that noise?

      CASSIO *enters, chasing* RODERIGO.

CASSIO

Damn, you villain! You rascal!

MONTANO

What's the matter, Lieutenant?

CASSIO

Do I need some villain to teach me my duty?
I'll beat this villain until he's ready to crawl inside a wicker-
covered bottle.   140

RODERIGO
Beat me?

CASSIO
Dost thou prate, rogue?

[*striking* RODERIGO]

MONTANO
Nay, good lieutenant;

[*staying him*]

I pray you, sir, hold your hand.

CASSIO
145   Let me go, sir, or I'll knock you o'er the mazard.

MONTANO
Come, come, you're drunk.

CASSIO
Drunk? [*They fight.*]

IAGO [*aside to* RODERIGO]
Away, I say; go out, and cry a mutiny.

[*Exit* RODERIGO.]

Nay, good lieutenant—God's will, gentlemen;—
150   Help, ho!—Lieutenant—sir—Montano—sir;—
Help, masters! Here's a goodly watch indeed!

[*Bell rings.*]

Who's that which rings the bell?—Diablo, ho!
The town will rise. Fie, fie, Lieutenant, hold!
You will be sham'd forever.

Reenter OTHELLO *and* ATTENDANTS.

OTHELLO
155   What is the matter here?

MONTANO
                'Zounds, I bleed still;
I am hurt to the death. He dies!

RODERIGO
Beat me?

CASSIO
Still rattling on, rascal?

He strikes RODERIGO.

MONTANO
No, good lieutenant!

He grabs CASSIO *by the arm.*

Please, sir, stop fighting.

CASSIO
Let go of me, sir,   145
or I'll beat you over the head.

MONTANO
Come, come, you're drunk!

CASSIO
Drunk?

MONTANO *and* CASSIO *fight.*

IAGO (*aside to* RODERIGO)
Get going, I tell you! Go and warn everybody of a mutiny!

RODERIGO *exits.*

Stop, good lieutenant.—For God's sake, gentlemen!
Help, please!—Lieutenant—sir—Montano—sir—   150
Help, gentlemen!—This is certainly a fine watch!

A bell rings.

Who's that ringing the bell? Oh, the devil!
The whole town will be awakened. For God's sake, Lieutenant,
   stop!
You'll be humiliated forever.

OTHELLO *and* ATTENDANTS *enter.*

OTHELLO
What's the matter here?   155

MONTANO
Damn, I'm bleeding!
I'm fatally wounded! He'll die for it!

OTHELLO

Hold, for your lives!

IAGO

Hold, ho! Lieutenant—sir—Montano—gentlemen—
160   Have you forgot all sense of place and duty?
Hold! The General speaks to you; hold, for shame!

OTHELLO

Why, how now, ho! From whence ariseth this?
Are we turn'd Turks, and to ourselves do that
Which Heaven hath forbid the Ottomites?
165   For Christian shame, put by this barbarous brawl.
He that stirs next to carve for his own rage
Holds his soul light; he dies upon his motion.
Silence that dreadful bell; it frights the isle
From her propriety. What is the matter, masters?
170   Honest Iago, that looks dead with grieving,
Speak, who began this? On thy love, I charge thee.

IAGO

I do not know. Friends all but now, even now,
In quarter, and in terms like bride and groom
Divesting them for bed; and then, but now—
175   As if some planet had unwitted men—
Swords out, and tilting one at other's breast,
In opposition bloody. I cannot speak
Any beginning to this **peevish** odds;
And would in action glorious I had lost
180   Those legs that brought me to a part of it!

OTHELLO

How comes it, Michael, you are thus forgot?

CASSIO

I pray you, pardon me; I cannot speak.

OTHELLO

Worthy Montano, you were wont to be civil;
The gravity and stillness of your youth
185   The world hath noted, and your name is great
In mouths of wisest censure. What's the matter
That you unlace your reputation thus,

OTHELLO

Stop, if you want to live!

IAGO

Stop, stop! Lieutenant—sir—Montano—gentlemen!
Have you lost all sense of your position and duty? 160
Stop! The General is talking to you. Stop, stop; shame on you!

OTHELLO

Why, what is this? How did this get started?
Have we turned into Turks, and are we doing to ourselves
what heaven has stopped the Ottomites from doing?
Out of Christian dignity, stop this barbarous fighting! 165
The man who next makes a move to vent his anger
values his life lightly; he'll be killed at once.
Silence that awful bell! It scares the island
out of its peace and quiet. What's the matter, gentlemen?
Honest Iago, you look like you're sick with grief. 170
Speak up. Who started this? If you love me, I command you to
speak.

IAGO

I don't know. They were friends just a moment ago,
at peace, just like a bride and groom
getting ready for bed; and then, the next moment—
as if the influence of some planet had made them crazy— 175
the swords were out and pointed at each other's chests
in a bloody fight. I can't tell you
how this silly quarrel started,
but I wish I had lost in glorious battle
these legs that brought me here to take part in it. 180

OTHELLO

Michael, why have you forgotten yourself like this?

CASSIO

Please, pardon me; I cannot speak.

OTHELLO

Worthy Montano, you've always been well-behaved.
The seriousness and earnestness of your younger days
was noted by the world, and your name is always mentioned 185
by people with the best judgment. What happened
to cause you to ruin your reputation this way

And spend your rich opinion for the name
Of a night-brawler? Give me answer to it.

MONTANO

190 Worthy Othello, I am hurt to danger.
Your officer, Iago, can inform you—
While I spare speech, which something now offends me—
Of all that I do know; nor know I aught
By me that's said or done amiss this night,
195 Unless self-charity be sometimes a vice,
And to defend ourselves it be a sin
When violence **assails** us.

OTHELLO

                       Now, by heaven,
My blood begins my safer guides to rule;
200 And passion, having my best judgment collied,
Assays to lead the way. 'Zounds if I stir
Or do but lift this arm, the best of you
Shall sink in my **rebuke**. Give me to know
How this foul rout began, who set it on;
205 And he that is approv'd in this offence,
Though he had twinn'd with me, both at a birth,
Shall lose me. What! In a town of war,
Yet wild, the people's hearts brimful of fear,
To manage private and domestic quarrel,
210 In night, and on the court and guard of safety!
'Tis monstrous. Iago, who began 't?

MONTANO

If partially affin'd, or leagu'd in office,
Thou dost deliver more or less than truth,
Thou art no soldier.

IAGO

215   Touch me not so near.
I had rather have this tongue cut from my mouth
Than it should do offence to Michael Cassio;
Yet, I persuade myself, to speak the truth
Shall nothing wrong him. Thus it is, General:
220 Montano and myself being in speech,
There comes a fellow crying out for help;

and waste the value of your good name to become known as
a night-brawler? Give me an answer.

MONTANO

Worthy Othello, I am seriously hurt.　　　　　　　　　190
Your officer, Iago, can tell you,
while I spare myself from talking—which is painful to me—
of everything I know. And I don't know anything
I've said or done that's wrong tonight,
unless it's not right to look out for one's safety,　　　　195
and if it's a sin to defend oneself
when one is violently attacked.

OTHELLO

Now, by God,
my anger is starting to overcome my prudence,
and passion, blotting out my better judgment,　　　　200
is taking charge. If I just make a move
or only lift this arm, the best of you
will be cut down by my sword. I want to know
how this disgusting fight began and who started it.
And the one who is proved at fault,　　　　　　　　205
even if he were my twin, born from the same mother,
will lose my friendship. I can't believe that in a garrison town,
still on edge and filled with frightened people,
you'd start a private, personal fight like this.
At night, and while you're on guard and at headquarters?　　210
This is outrageous. Iago, who started it?

MONTANO

If you're biased because of friendship or comradeship
and tell more or less than the truth,
you're no real soldier.

IAGO

Please, that comes too close to the truth.　　　　　　215
I'd rather have this tongue cut out of my mouth
than say anything to hurt Michael Cassio.
Still, I've convinced myself that speaking the truth
will do no harm to him. So here it is, General.
As Montano and I were talking,　　　　　　　　　220
a young fellow, crying for help, came upon us,

And Cassio following him with determin'd sword
To execute upon him. Sir, this gentleman [*pointing to*
   MONTANO]
Steps in to Cassio and entreats his pause;
225   Myself the crying fellow did pursue,
Lest by his clamour—as it so fell out—
The town might fall in fright. He, swift of foot,
Outran my purpose; and I return'd the rather
For that I heard the clink and fall of swords,
230   And Cassio high in oath; which till tonight
I ne'er might say before. When I came back—
For this was brief—I found them close together,
At blow and thrust; even as again they were
When you yourself did part them.
235   More of this matter cannot I report.
But men are men; the best sometimes forget.
Though Cassio did some little wrong to him,
As men in rage strike those that wish them best,
Yet surely Cassio, I believe, receiv'd
240   From him that fled some strange indignity
Which patience could not pass.

OTHELLO
                        I know, Iago,
Thy honesty and love doth mince this matter,
Making it light to Cassio. Cassio, I love thee;
245   But nevermore be officer of mine.

       Reenter DESDEMONA, *attended.*

Look, if my gentle love be not rais'd up!
I'll make thee an example.

DESDEMONA
What's the matter, dear?

OTHELLO
                      All's well now, sweeting;
250   come away to bed. [*to* MONTANO]
Sir, for your hurts, myself will be your surgeon.—
Lead him off. [MONTANO *is led off.*]

with Cassio following him with a drawn sword
trying to kill him. Sir, this gentleman (*pointing to* MONTANO)
stepped up to Cassio and begged him to stop.
I chased down the fellow who'd been crying out,   225
to see that the terrible racket he was making—but it did
        anyway—
wouldn't frighten the whole town. He, being fast-footed,
got away from me, and I returned quickly
because I heard the clanking and rattling of swords
and Cassio swearing loudly—which until this night,   230
I could never have said about him. When I came back—
and I was fast about it—I found them close together
thrusting and striking at each other, just as they were
when you yourself parted them.
I have nothing more to report about this matter.   235
But men are like that—even the best sometimes slip.
While Cassio did Montano a small injustice,
as enraged men will strike those who only wish them the best,
I still believe that Cassio received
an insult of some sort from the man that ran away,   240
which was beyond his patience to tolerate.

OTHELLO
I know, Iago,
that, in your honesty and love, you make light of this matter,
making it easier on Cassio. Cassio, I love you,
but you will never again serve as my officer.   245

        DESDEMONA *enters with* ATTENDANTS.

Look; my gentle love has been awakened!
I'll make an example of you.

DESDEMONA
What's the matter, dear?

OTHELLO
Everything's all right now, sweetheart;
let's go to bed. (*to* MONTANO) Sir, I'll personally see to your   250
        injuries.—
Help him away.

        MONTANO *exits, attended.*

Iago, look with care about the town,
And silence those whom this vile brawl distracted.
255 Come, Desdemona; 'tis the soldiers' life
To have their balmy slumbers wak'd with strife.

[*Exeunt all but* IAGO *and* CASSIO.]

IAGO

What, are you hurt, Lieutenant?

CASSIO

Ay, past all surgery.

IAGO

Marry, God forbid!

CASSIO

260 Reputation, reputation, reputation! O, I have lost my
reputation! I have lost the immortal part of myself, and
what remains is bestial. My reputation, Iago, my
reputation!

IAGO

As I am an honest man, I thought you had received some
265 bodily wound; there is more sense in that than in
reputation. Reputation is an idle and most false
imposition; oft got without merit, and lost without
deserving. You have lost no reputation at all, unless you
repute yourself such a loser. What, man! There are more
270 ways to recover the general again. You are but now cast in
his mood, a punishment more in policy than in malice;
even so as one would beat his offenceless dog to affright
an **imperious** lion. Sue to him again, and he's yours.

CASSIO

I will rather sue to be despis'd than to deceive so good a
275 commander with so slight, so drunken, and so **indiscreet**
an officer. Drunk? And speak parrot? And squabble?
Swagger? Swear? And discourse fustian with one's own
shadow? O thou invisible spirit of wine, if thou hast no
name to be known by, let us call thee devil!

Iago, look carefully around the town
and calm down those who have been disturbed by this
    terrible fight.—
Come, Desdemona. It's the story of a soldier's life   255
to have a quiet sleep disturbed with fighting.

    Everyone exits except IAGO *and* CASSIO.

IAGO

What, have you been hurt, Lieutenant?

CASSIO

Yes, beyond any hope of recovery.

IAGO

Oh, God forbid!

CASSIO

Reputation, reputation, reputation! Oh, I have lost my   260
reputation! I've lost the one immortal part of myself, and
everything that remains is bestial. My reputation, Iago, my
reputation!

IAGO

As sure as I'm honest, I thought you'd been physically
wounded; that's more serious than your reputation. Reputation 265
is a foolish thing, falsely imposed by others; it's often gained
without merit and lost undeservedly. You haven't lost your
reputation at all unless you really believe you have lost it.
Come on, man! There are ways to get back in the general's
favor again. You were only dismissed because of his anger— 270
more as a disciplinary example than because of real resentment,
just as one might beat an innocent dog to scare off a
threatening lion. Appeal to him again, and he'll listen.

CASSIO

I'd rather appeal to him to hate me than deceive such a good
commander with a weak, drunken, and indiscreet officer like 275
me. Drunk? And babbling? And quarreling? Swaggering?
Swearing? And talking nonsense with my own shadow? Oh,
you unseen spirit of wine, if you have no name to be known
by, let us call you the devil!

IAGO

280   What was he that you follow'd with your sword? What
had he done to you?

CASSIO

I know not.

IAGO

Is 't possible?

CASSIO

I remember a mass of things, but nothing distinctly; a
285   quarrel, but nothing wherefore. O God, that men should
put an enemy in their mouths to steal away their brains!
That we should, with joy, pleasance, revel, and applause,
transform ourselves into beasts!

IAGO

Why, but you are now well enough. How came you
290   thus recovered?

CASSIO

It hath pleas'd the devil drunkenness to give place to the
devil wrath. One unperfectness shows me another, to
make me frankly despise myself.

IAGO

Come, you are too severe a moraler. As the time, the place,
295   and the condition of this country stands, I could heartily
wish this had not so befallen; but since it is as it is, mend
it for your own good.

CASSIO

I will ask him for my place again; he shall tell me I am a
drunkard! Had I as many mouths as Hydra,* such an
300   answer would stop them all. To be now a sensible man, by
and by a fool, and presently a beast! O strange! Every
inordinate cup is unbless'd and the ingredient is a devil.

IAGO

Come, come, good wine is a good familiar* creature, if it
be well us'd; exclaim no more against it. And, good
305   lieutenant, I think you think I love you.

---

299   *Hydra* a mythical monster with many heads

303   *familiar* means both "friendly" as well as "a spirit summoned by an enchanter."
(This latter meaning plays on Cassio's remark about the devil in wine.)

IAGO

Who was the man you were chasing with your sword? What   280
had he done to you?

CASSIO

I don't know.

IAGO

Is that possible?

CASSIO

I remember a lot of things, but nothing clearly; a quarrel, but I
don't know why. Oh, God, why do men drink an enemy to steal   285
their brains! To think that we should, with joy, merriment,
celebration, and applause, turn ourselves into beasts!

IAGO

Well, you seem a lot better now. How did you recover so quickly?   290

CASSIO

That devil of drunkenness has been so kind as to make way for
the devil of anger. One flaw in myself leads me to another, and
I'm starting to really hate myself.

IAGO

Come, you're being too moralistic. As far as the time, place, and
the way things stand in this country, I certainly wish this hadn't   295
happened. But since it has, make the best of it.

CASSIO

I'll ask him for my position again. He'll tell me I'm a drunkard!
If I had as many mouths as Hydra, I'd have nothing to say to
that. To be a sensible man one minute, a fool the next, and   300
soon after a beast! How strange! Every excess cup of wine is
wicked and contains the devil.

IAGO

Come, come, good wine is a very friendly thing if it's wisely
taken. Don't say anything else against it. And, good lieutenant,
I'm sure you realize that I love you.   305

CASSIO

I have well approved it, sir. I drunk!

IAGO

You or any man living may be drunk at a time, man. I'll
tell you what you shall do. Our general's wife is now the
general;—I may say so in this respect, for that he hath
310   devoted and given up himself to the contemplation, mark
and denotement of her parts and graces;—confess yourself
freely to her; importune her help to put you in your place
again. She is of so free, so kind, so apt, so blessed a
disposition, she holds it a vice in her goodness not to do
315   more than she is requested. This broken joint between
you and her husband entreat her to splinter; and, my
fortunes against any lay worth naming, this crack of your
love shall grow stronger than it was before.

CASSIO

You advise me well.

IAGO

320   I protest, in the sincerity of love and honest kindness.

CASSIO

I think it freely; and betimes in the morning I will beseech
the virtuous Desdemona to undertake for me. I am
desperate of my fortunes if they check me here.

IAGO

You are in the right. Good night, Lieutenant; I must to
325   the watch.

CASSIO

Good night, honest Iago.

      [*Exit.*]

IAGO

And what's he then that says I play the villain?
When this advice is free I give and honest,
Probal to thinking and indeed the course
330   To win the Moor again? For 'tis most easy
Th' inclining Desdemona to subdue
In any honest suit; she's fram'd as fruitful
As the free elements. And then for her

CASSIO

I can testify to that, sir. But even when I'm drunk?

IAGO

You or any other man alive may be drunk on occasion, man.
I'll tell you what to do. The general's wife is practically in charge.
The reason I say this is he has completely given himself over
to contemplating, observing, and cataloging her wonderful   310
qualities. Tell her everything freely. Ask for her help to get your
position back. She is of such a generous, kind, sympathetic,
and blessed temper that she considers it wrong not to do
more than people ask her to do. Ask her to put a splint on   315
this break between you and her husband; and I'll bet all my
fortune against any wager you want to make, this break in
your love will grow back stronger than it was before.

CASSIO

You give me good advice.

IAGO

I assure you, it is out of the sincerest love and honest kindness.   320

CASSIO

I'm convinced of that; and first thing in the morning, I'll beg
the virtuous Desdemona to speak on my behalf. I'll be in a
very bad way if I'm stopped by this.

IAGO

You're making the right choice. Good night, Lieutenant; I must
go on guard duty.   325

CASSIO

Good night, honest Iago.

> CASSIO *exits.*

IAGO

And why would anyone say I'm playing the villain
when I give away such free and honest advice,
so sensible when you think about it, and obviously the way
to get back in the Moor's good favor? Because it's very easy   330
to win over the agreeable Desdemona
to any honest cause. She is as generous
as nature itself. And then it's easy for her

To win the Moor, were 't to **renounce** his baptism,
335 All seals and symbols of redeemed sin,
His soul is so enfetter'd to her love,
That she may make, unmake, do what she list,
Even as her appetite shall play the god
With his weak function. How am I then a villain
340 To counsel Cassio to this parallel course,
Directly to his good? Divinity of hell!
When devils will the blackest sins put on,
They do suggest at first with heavenly shows,
As I do now; for whiles this honest fool
345 Plies Desdemona to repair his fortune
And she for him pleads strongly to the Moor,
I'll pour this pestilence into his ear,
That she repeals him for her body's lust;
And by how much she strives to do him good,
350 She shall undo her credit with the Moor.
So will I turn her virtue into pitch,
And out of her own goodness make the net
That shall enmesh them all.

       Reenter RODERIGO.

How now, Roderigo!

RODERIGO

355 I do follow here in the chase, not like a hound that hunts,
but one that fills up the cry.* My money is almost spent; I
have been tonight exceedingly well cudgell'd; and I think
the issue will be, I shall have so much experience for my
pains; and so, with no money at all and a little more wit,
360 return again to Venice.

IAGO

How poor are they that have not patience!
What wound did ever heal but by degrees?
Thou know'st we work by wit, and not by witchcraft;
And wit depends on dilatory time.

355–56 *not like a hound . . . cry* In hunting, dogs were sometimes used only for the
sound of their barking and not for actual tracking. Roderigo is saying that he
had felt useless during the preceding events.

to persuade the Moor—even to renounce his baptism,
or his entire religious faith—   335
because his soul is so infatuated with her
that she can help him, ruin him, or do whatever she pleases;
her wishes completely control
his weak reason. Why, then, should I be called a villain
for advising Cassio to take this same way   340
that is directly in his best interests? Why, that's hell's own
    preaching!
When devils urge you to do the most wicked things,
they tempt you by making everything seem heavenly—
the same as I'm doing now. Because while this honest fool
is appealing to Desdemona to make things better for him,   345
and she pleads strongly to the Moor on his behalf,
I'll tell him this poisonous thing about Cassio—
that she asks for him to be reinstated only out of lust for him.
And the more good she tries to do for him,
the worse she'll look in the eyes of the Moor.   350
This is how I'll turn her virtue into wickedness,
and, out of her own goodness, make a net
to catch everyone in.

      RODERIGO *enters.*

What is it, Roderigo?

RODERIGO

I've come here after the chase, not like a real tracker, but like   355
one that does nothing but bark. My money is almost gone,
I've been thoroughly beaten tonight, and I think the result will
be that I'll have nothing to show for my trouble except my
pains. And so, with no money at all and just a little more wit,
I'll end up going back to Venice.   360

IAGO

How pathetic are people who don't have any patience!
What wound doesn't take some time to heal?
You know we accomplish things by scheming and not by
    witchcraft,
and our schemes need time to unfold.

365 Does 't not go well? Cassio hath beaten thee,
And thou, by that small hurt, hast cashier'd Cassio.
Though other things grow fair against the sun,
Yet fruits that blossom first will first be ripe.
Content thyself awhile. In troth, 'tis morning;
370 Pleasure and action make the hours seem short.
Retire thee; go where thou art billeted.
Away, I say; thou shalt know more hereafter.
Nay, get thee gone. [*Exit* RODERIGO.] Two things are to
    be done:
375 My wife must move for Cassio to her mistress;
I'll set her on.
Myself the while to draw the Moor apart
And bring him jump when he may Cassio find
Soliciting his wife. Ay, that's the way;
380 Dull not device by coldness and delay.

    [*Exit.*]

Didn't things go well? Cassio has beaten you,   365
and because of that small hurt, you've ruined Cassio.
No matter how things seem to be going,
things will come to pass in their own sweet time.
Be patient awhile. Good Lord, it's morning!
Pleasure and action make the time pass quickly.   370
Get to bed; go to where you've been put up.
Go on, I say! You'll know more later on.
Go on, get going! (RODERIGO *exits.*) Two things have to be done:
my wife must intercede on Cassio's behalf to her mistress;   375
I'll put her up to it.
In the meantime, I'll work on the Moor separately
and bring him in at the very moment when he'll find Cassio
appealing to his wife. Yes, that's how to do it!
I won't spoil this plan by hesitation or delay.   380

    IAGO *exits.*

Act II Review

Discussion Questions

1. What happens to the threat of a Turkish invasion of Cyprus?

2. How does Montano react to the news that Othello is about to take his place as governor? Discuss what his reaction reveals about him and also about Othello.

3. What do Cassio's actions in Scene i tell us about his character?

4. What judgments does Iago pass on women in his conversation with Desdemona and Emilia? Explain what his statements tell you about his character.

5. In Scene ii, why do you think Shakespeare introduced a herald to announce the night's festivities? Discuss other ways he might have supplied this information.

6. How does Iago set about ruining Cassio?

7. How do you think Iago feels about Cassio's drunken remark, "The lieutenant is to be saved before the ancient"?

8. How does Iago manipulate Cassio after the lieutenant's humiliating dismissal?

Literary Elements

1. **Foreshadowing** refers to hints in the text about what will occur later. For example, Iago's aside in Scene i ("He takes her by the palm") clearly foreshadows how he intends to make trouble for Cassio. What other examples of foreshadowing can you find in the play so far?

2. Shakespeare depended heavily on dialogue to establish **settings** because scenery was minimal. How does he use characters' words to differentiate between the worlds of Venice and Cyprus?

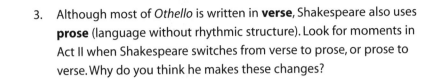

3. Although most of *Othello* is written in **verse**, Shakespeare also uses **prose** (language without rhythmic structure). Look for moments in Act II when Shakespeare switches from verse to prose, or prose to verse. Why do you think he makes these changes?

Writing Prompts

1. Write Montano's resignation letter to the Duke of Venice. What is the tone of his letter? What does he have to say about his successor, Othello?

2. Roderigo and Cassio begin their fight offstage. Write this episode as a dramatic scene. What does Roderigo say to provoke the drunken Cassio to anger? Use this line of Cassio's as a clue: "A knave teach me my duty?"

3. Pretend you are a journalist in Cyprus. Try to find out what really provoked the fight on the night of Othello's arrival. Interview Montano, Cassio, and Iago about what happened. Of course, you wouldn't know that Roderigo was the other person involved; even so, you might want to speculate on the identity of the "mystery man" who quarreled with Cassio.

4. Can you identify with Cassio's feelings after his dismissal? Write about a situation in which your own reputation suffered a blow. What did you do to try to redeem yourself?

5. From what you know about Iago so far, make a list of his character traits. Then cite lines from the text that support each trait. Finally, write a description of Iago based on the first two acts.

Othello

Act III

Bob Hoskins, top, as Iago and Anthony Hopkins as Othello, 1981 TV production

"O, beware, my lord, of jealousy!
It is the green-ey'd monster which
doth mock the meat it feeds on."

Before You Read

1. Have you ever been troubled by a suspicion that you could neither prove nor disprove? Describe this experience.

2. Based on what you know so far, how do you think Cassio feels about Desdemona?

3. At this point in the play, what do you think Iago expects to achieve by his plotting and scheming?

4. What role do you expect Iago's wife to play in the rest of the drama?

Literary Elements

1. **Comic relief** refers to humor found in otherwise serious drama. Even in his most intense tragedies, such as *Romeo and Juliet* and *Macbeth*, there are humorous characters, scenes, and wordplay that offer a different perspective on the action and keep the plays from being unbearably tragic.

2. A **metaphor** makes a comparison between two unlike things that nevertheless have something in common. In Act I, for example, Iago compares Othello to a ram and and Desdemona to a ewe; he wants the sexual implication of the comparison to alarm Desdemona's father. An **extended metaphor** draws out a comparison at length.

3. A **theme** is an ongoing topic, idea, or concern of a literary work. One of the themes of *Othello* concerns the harmful effects of jealousy.

4. **Conflict** is the struggle between opposing forces in a piece of writing. **External conflict** refers to a struggle between humans and an outside force such as nature or another individual. In *Othello*, the war between the Turks and Cypriots exemplifies external conflict. **Internal conflict** refers to a mental struggle within the individual. Othello is internally conflicted when Iago makes him doubt Desdemona's love and faithfulness.

Words to Know

The following vocabulary words appear in Act III in the original text of Shakespeare's play. However, they are words that are still used today. Read the definitions here and pay attention to the words as you read the play (they will be in boldfaced type).

affinity	kinship; similarity
castigation	criticism; scolding
chide	scold; blame
discern [discern'st]	tell the difference; distinguish
dissemble	conceal; lie
edified	taught; instructed
indicted	accused; charged
inference	suggestion; proposal
languishes	suffers; pines away
recoiling	retreating; withdrawing
ruminate	reflect; ponder
sequester	separation; removal
surmises	guesses; inferences
vehement	intense; passionate
veritable	true; authentic

Act Summary

The next morning, Cassio meets with Desdemona, who promises to help him. True to her word, Desdemona sweetly nags her husband to reinstate Cassio.

Iago immediately sets to work on Othello's suspicions. He feigns reluctance to speak ill of Cassio and warns Othello to beware of jealousy. Still, Iago hints that something might be amiss between Cassio and Desdemona. After all, Desdemona acted rashly in marrying Othello, and she betrayed her own father. Might she not now regret her rashness, preferring a lover of her own society and complexion? Might she not betray Othello?

David Suchet as Iago and Janet Dale as Emilia, 1986 production by the Royal
Shakespeare Company, Barbican Theatre, London

Desdemona loses a handkerchief—the first gift the Moor ever gave
her. It is found by Emilia, Desdemona's serving lady and Iago's wife.
Iago has asked Emilia many times to steal it, so she gives it to him.

Meanwhile, Othello's suspicions spin out of control. He demands
that Iago give him proof that Desdemona has been unfaithful. Iago says
that he once heard Cassio talking in his sleep of his love for Desdemona.
Moreover, he claims to have seen Cassio wipe his beard with the
handkerchief Othello gave Desdemona.

All but convinced, Othello demands the handkerchief from
Desdemona. She is afraid to admit that she has lost it. Desperate to
change the subject, she talks of Cassio's suit. She cannot understand why
this makes Othello even angrier.

Iago places the handkerchief in Cassio's room. Cassio finds it and is
delighted by its embroidery. He gives it to his mistress, Bianca, so she can
copy the design.

ACT III, SCENE I

[*Cyprus before the castle.*] *Enter* CASSIO, *with*
MUSICIANS.

CASSIO

Masters, play here; I will content your pains;
Something that's brief; and bid "Good morrow, General."

[*They play.*]

Enter CLOWN. *

CLOWN

Why, masters, have your instruments been in Naples, that
they speak i' th' nose thus?*

1. MUSICIAN

5 How, sir, how?

CLOWN

Are these, I pray you, wind instruments?

1. MUSICIAN

Ay, marry, are they, sir.

CLOWN

O, thereby hangs a tail.

1. MUSICIAN

Whereby hangs a tale, sir?

CLOWN

10 Marry, sir, by many a wind instrument that I know. But,
masters, here's money for you; and the General so likes
your music, that he desires you, for love's sake, to make
no more noise with it.

1. MUSICIAN

Well, sir, we will not.

---

s.d. *Clown* means "fool" or comic servant

3-4 *have your instruments . . . thus* a reference not only to the Neapolitans' nasal
voices but to an outbreak of syphilis in Naples. Syphilis can cause
decomposition in the nose.

ACT 3, SCENE 1

Cyprus, in front of the castle. CASSIO *enters with several*
MUSICIANS.

CASSIO
Gentlemen, play here, I'll reward your efforts,
Play something short, and say good day to the general.

They play.

The CLOWN *enters.*

CLOWN
Well, gentlemen, is it because your instruments have been to
Naples that they have that nasal sound?

FIRST MUSICIAN
What do you mean, sir? 5

CLOWN
I ask you, aren't these called wind instruments?

FIRST MUSICIAN
They certainly are, sir.

CLOWN
Well, there's a tail hanging from that.

FIRST MUSICIAN
Where does a tale hang, sir?

CLOWN
Why, sir, from many wind instruments I know about. But here's 10
some money for you, gentlemen. The General likes your music
so much that he asks, for the respect you bear for him, that
you not play anymore.

FIRST MUSICIAN
Well, sir, we won't.

CLOWN

15 If you have any music that may not be heard, to 't again;
but, as they say, to hear music the General does not
greatly care.

1. MUSICIAN

We have none such, sir.

CLOWN

Then put up your pipes in your bag, for I'll away. Go,
20 vanish into air, away!

[*Exeunt* MUSICIANS.]

CASSIO

Dost thou hear, mine honest friend?

CLOWN

No, I hear not your honest friend; I hear you.

CASSIO

Prithee, keep up thy quillets. There's a poor piece of gold
for thee. If the gentlewoman that attends the General's
25 wife be stirring, tell her there's one Cassio entreats her a
little favour of speech. Wilt thou do this?

CLOWN

She is stirring, sir. If she will stir hither, I shall seem to
notify unto her.*

CASSIO

Do, good my friend.

[*Exit* CLOWN.]

Enter IAGO.

30   In happy time, Iago.

IAGO

You have not been abed, then?

CASSIO

Why, no; the day had broke
Before we parted. I have made bold, Iago,
To send in to your wife. My suit to her

27-28 *If . . . her.* The clown is mimicking Cassio's overblown courtesy.

CLOWN
If you know any music that can't be heard, go right ahead.   15
But, as they say, the General doesn't much care for music.

FIRST MUSICIAN
We don't know any music like that, sir.

CLOWN
Then put your instruments back in your bags, because I must
leave. Go, vanish into thin air, go on!   20

> *The* MUSICIANS *exit.*

CASSIO
Can you hear me, my honest friend?

CLOWN
No, I don't hear your honest friend. I hear you.

CASSIO
Please, keep your puns to yourself. Here's a little gold piece for you.
If the lady that waits on the General's wife is awake, tell her
a certain Cassio begs to talk to her for a bit. Will you do that?   25

CLOWN
She's awake, sir. If she comes this way, I'll agree to notify her.

CASSIO
Do so, good friend.

> CLOWN *exits.*
>
> IAGO *enters.*

What luck meeting with you, Iago.   30

IAGO
You haven't been to bed, then?

CASSIO
Why, no. Day had come
before we left each other. Iago, I have been so bold
as to ask to see your wife. What I wish to ask from her

35 Is that she will to virtuous Desdemona
Procure me some access.

IAGO

I'll send her to you presently;
And I'll devise a mean to draw the Moor
Out of the way, that your converse and business
40 May be more free.

CASSIO

I humbly thank you for 't. [*Exit* IAGO.] I never knew
A Florentine* more kind and honest.

Enter EMILIA.

EMILIA

Good morrow, good Lieutenant. I am sorry
For your displeasure; but all will sure be well.
45 The General and his wife are talking of it,
And she speaks for you stoutly. The Moor replies
That he you hurt is of great fame in Cyprus
And great **affinity**, and that in wholesome wisdom
He might not but refuse you; but he protests he loves you,
50 And needs no other suitor but his likings
To take the safest occasion by the front
To bring you in again.

CASSIO

Yet, I beseech you,
If you think fit, or that it may be done,
55 Give me advantage of some brief discourse
With Desdemona alone.

EMILIA

Pray you, come in.
I will bestow you where you shall have time
To speak your bosom freely.

CASSIO

60 I am much bound to you.

[*Exeunt.*]

---

42 *Florentine* Cassio is from Florence; he means that not even his fellow citizens are
as kind and honest as Iago.

is that she will arrange for me 35
to talk to the virtuous Desdemona.

IAGO

I'll have her come to you right away,
and I'll figure out some means to get the Moor
out of the way so that your business and your conversation
won't be interrupted. 40

CASSIO

I humbly thank you. (IAGO *exits*.) I never knew
any Florentine who was as kind and honest.

EMILIA *enters*.

EMILIA

Good day, good Lieutenant. I'm sorry
that you've been disgraced; but everything will be better soon.
The General and his wife are talking about it, 45
and she's strongly defending you. The Moor has replied
that the man you hurt is very famous in Cyprus,
with a good family, and for the sake of discretion,
his only choice is to refuse you. But he still says he loves you,
and he needs no other suitor than his own feelings 50
to find the best possible moment
to reinstate you.

CASSIO

Still, I beg you,
if you think it appropriate or possible,
give me a chance to talk a little 55
alone to Desdemona.

EMILIA

Please come in, then.
I'll take you to where you'll have the time
to freely speak your mind to her.

CASSIO

I'm very indebted to you. 60

They exit.

ACT III, SCENE II

[A room in the castle.] Enter OTHELLO, IAGO, *and* GENTLEMEN.

OTHELLO

These letters give, Iago, to the pilot;
And by him do my duties to the Senate.
That done, I will be walking on the works;
Repair there to me.

IAGO

5   Well, my good lord, I'll do 't.

OTHELLO

This fortification, gentlemen, shall we see 't?

GENTLEMEN

We wait upon your Lordship.

[Exeunt.]

ACT 3, SCENE 2

Inside the castle. OTHELLO, IAGO, *and* GENTLEMEN *enter.*

OTHELLO
Iago, give these letters to the pilot
so that my duties in the Senate will be taken care of.
When you've finished, I'll be walking on the castle walls.
Come and see me there.

IAGO
Certainly, my good lord; I'll see to everything.   5

OTHELLO
Shall we examine the fortifications, gentleman?

GENTLEMEN
Whatever you wish, your Lordship.

They exit.

ACT III, SCENE III

[The garden of the castle.] Enter DESDEMONA,
CASSIO, *and* EMILIA.

DESDEMONA

Be thou assur'd, good Cassio, I will do
All my abilities in thy behalf.

EMILIA

Good madam, do. I warrant it grieves my husband
As if the cause were his.

DESDEMONA

5   O, that's an honest fellow. Do not doubt, Cassio,
But I will have my lord and you again
As friendly as you were.

CASSIO

                              Bounteous madam,
Whatever shall become of Michael Cassio,
10   He's never anything but your true servant.

DESDEMONA

I know 't; I thank you. You do love my lord;
You have known him long; and be you well assur'd
He shall in strangeness stand no farther off
Than in a politic distance.

CASSIO

15   Ay, but, lady,
That policy may either last so long,
Or feed upon such nice and waterish diet,
Or breed itself so out of circumstance,
That, I being absent and my place supplied,
20   My general will forget my love and service.

DESDEMONA

Do not doubt that; before Emilia here
I give thee warrant of thy place. Assure thee,
If I do vow a friendship, I'll perform it
To the last article. My lord shall never rest;
25   I'll watch him tame* and talk him out of patience;

---

25   *watch him tame* Hawks were sometimes tamed by being kept awake.

ACT 3, SCENE 3

The castle garden. DESDEMONA, CASSIO, *and* EMILIA *enter.*

DESDEMONA
Good Cassio, rest assured that I'll do
everything in my power that I can for you.

EMILIA
Please do, dear lady. I tell you, it makes my husband so unhappy,
you'd think it was his own cause.

DESDEMONA
Oh, there's an honest fellow. You can be certain, Cassio,   5
that I'll make sure that you and my lord
will be as friendly as ever.

CASSIO
Generous lady,
whatever else might happen to Michael Cassio,
he'll never be anything but your faithful servant.   10

DESDEMONA
I know that and thank you. You love my lord;
you've known him for a long time; so be assured
that he'll only be cold to you
for the sake of appearance.

CASSIO
Yes, but lady,   15
that attitude might exist for a long time,
or be fed by small and trifling considerations,
or grow out of all proportion due to some new circumstances,
so that, while I'm gone and my position is filled by another,
my general will forget my love and good service.   20

DESDEMONA
Don't worry about that. As Emilia here is my witness,
I guarantee you your position. Rest easy;
when I promise something out of friendship, I'll see it through
to the last detail. My lord won't get any rest;
I'll keep him awake and talk enough to him to wear out his   25
   patience;

His bed shall seem a school, his board a shrift;
I'll intermingle everything he does
With Cassio's suit. Therefore be merry, Cassio;
For thy solicitor shall rather die
30   Than give thy cause away.

> *Enter* OTHELLO *and* IAGO.

EMILIA
Madam, here comes my lord.

CASSIO
Madam, I'll take my leave.

DESDEMONA
Why, stay, and hear me speak.

CASSIO
Madam, not now; I am very ill at ease,
35   Unfit for mine own purposes.

DESDEMONA
Well, do your discretion.

> [*Exit* CASSIO.]

IAGO
Ha! I like not that.

OTHELLO
                    What dost thou say?

IAGO
Nothing, my lord; or if—I know not what.

OTHELLO
40   Was not that Cassio parted from my wife?

IAGO
Cassio, my lord? No, sure, I cannot think it
That he would steal away so guiltylike,
Seeing your coming.

OTHELLO
I do believe 'twas he.

DESDEMONA
45   How now, my lord?

his bed will seem like a school and his table like a confessional.
With everything he does, I'll mix in talk
of Cassio's suit. So cheer up, Cassio,
for your intercessor would rather die
than fail in your cause.   30

       OTHELLO *and* IAGO *enter.*

EMILIA
Madam, here comes my lord.

CASSIO
Madam, I'll leave now.

DESDEMONA
Why, stay here and listen to me speak.

CASSIO
Not now, madam. I'm very ill at ease,
which won't help my situation at all.   35

DESDEMONA
Well, do as you think best.

       CASSIO *exits.*

IAGO
Ha! I don't like the looks of that.

OTHELLO
What did you say?

IAGO
Nothing, my lord; or maybe—I just don't know.

OTHELLO
Wasn't that Cassio who just left my wife?   40

IAGO
Cassio, my lord? No, surely not, I can't believe
he'd sneak away so guilty-looking
when he saw you coming.

OTHELLO
I really think it was him.

DESDEMONA
How are you doing, my lord?   45

I have been talking with a suitor here,
A man that **languishes** in your displeasure.

OTHELLO
Who is 't you mean?

DESDEMONA
Why, your lieutenant, Cassio. Good my lord,
50 If I have any grace or power to move you,
His present reconciliation take;
For if he be not one that truly loves you,
That errs in ignorance and not in cunning,
I have no judgment in an honest face.
55 I prithee, call him back.

OTHELLO
                              Went he hence now?

DESDEMONA
Yes, faith, so humbled
That he hath left part of his grief with me
To suffer with him. Good love, call him back.

OTHELLO
60 Not now, sweet Desdemona; some other time.

DESDEMONA
But shall 't be shortly?

OTHELLO
                              The sooner, sweet, for you.

DESDEMONA
Shall 't be tonight at supper?

OTHELLO
                              No, not tonight.

DESDEMONA
65 Tomorrow dinner, then?

OTHELLO
I shall not dine at home;
I meet the captains at the citadel.

I have been talking to a man who has a problem here,
someone who suffers from your disapproval.

OTHELLO
Who do you mean?

DESDEMONA
Why, your lieutenant, Cassio. My good lord,
if I have any ability or power to persuade you,   50
take his apology at once.
Because if he doesn't love you very sincerely,
and if he hasn't erred out of ignorance and not deliberately,
then I can't tell an honest face when I see one.
Please, call him back.   55

OTHELLO
Was that him who left just now?

DESDEMONA
Yes, it was; and he was so humbled
that he made me feel his grief
and suffer with him. My love, call him back.

OTHELLO
Not now, sweet Desdemona; some other time.   60

DESDEMONA
But will it be shortly?

OTHELLO
As soon as possible, sweetheart, on your account.

DESDEMONA
Will it be tonight at suppertime?

OTHELLO
No, not tonight.

DESDEMONA
Before dinner tomorrow, then?   65

OTHELLO
I will not dine at home.
I'm meeting the captains at the castle.

DESDEMONA

Why, then, tomorrow night; or Tuesday morn;
On Tuesday noon, or night; on Wednesday morn.
70 I prithee, name the time, but let it not
Exceed three days. In faith, he's penitent;
And yet his trespass, in our common reason—
Save that, they say, the wars must make example
Out of her best—is not almost a fault
75 T' incur a private check. When shall he come?
Tell me, Othello. I wonder in my soul
What you would ask me that I should deny,
Or stand so mamm'ring on. What? Michael Cassio,
That came a-wooing with you, and so many a time,
80 When I have spoke of you dispraisingly,
Hath ta'en your part—to have so much to do
To bring him in! By 'r Lady, I could do much—

OTHELLO

Prithee, no more; let him come when he will,
I will deny thee nothing.

DESDEMONA

85 Why, this is not a boon.
'Tis as I should entreat you wear your gloves,
Or feed on nourishing dishes, or keep you warm,
Or sue to you to do a peculiar profit
To your own person. Nay, when I have a suit
90 Wherein I mean to touch your love indeed,
It shall be full of poise and difficult weight
And fearful to be granted.

OTHELLO

I will deny thee nothing;
Whereon, I do beseech thee, grant me this,
95 To leave me but a little to myself.

DESDEMONA

Shall I deny you? No. Farewell, my lord.

OTHELLO

Farewell, my Desdemona; I'll come to thee straight.

DESDEMONA

Well then, make it tomorrow night, or Tuesday morning,
or Tuesday noon or night, or Wednesday morning.
Please name the time, but don't let it   70
be more than three days. Really, he's very sorry;
and his crime, by everyday standards
(except that, as they say, military order demands that
the best men serve as examples), isn't even enough of a fault
to merit a private scolding. When will he come?   75
Tell me, Othello. In my heart, I wonder
what kind of thing you might ask of me that I would deny
or hesitate so much about as you do. What? Michael Cassio,
who came wooing with you, and so many times
when I've said disagreeable things about you,   80
took your part—why is it so much trouble
to make up with him? Trust me, I could do much—

OTHELLO

Please, say no more. He can come when he wants to!
I won't deny you anything.

DESDEMONA

Why, I'm not asking for some favor.   85
It's as if I were telling you to wear your gloves,
or eat nourishing food, or stay warm,
or ask you to do something helpful
for yourself. No, when I want to ask something
and appeal to you out of your love,   90
it will be a weighty and serious thing
and difficult to grant.

OTHELLO

I won't deny you anything!
And so I ask you to do this for me;
just leave me alone for a little while.   95

DESDEMONA

Would I refuse you? No. Good-bye, my lord.

OTHELLO

Good-bye, Desdemona. I'll join you at once.

DESDEMONA

Emilia, come.—Be as your fancies teach you;
Whate'er you be, I am obedient.

[*Exeunt* DESDEMONA *and* EMILIA.]

OTHELLO

100   Excellent wretch! Perdition catch my soul,
But I do love thee! and when I love thee not,
Chaos is come again.

IAGO

                      My noble lord—

OTHELLO

What dost thou say, Iago?

IAGO

105   Did Michael Cassio,
When you woo'd my lady,
Know of your love?

OTHELLO

He did, from first to last. Why dost thou ask?

IAGO

But for a satisfaction of my thought;
110   No further harm.

OTHELLO

               Why of thy thought, Iago?

IAGO

I did not think he had been acquainted with her.

OTHELLO

O, yes, and went between us very oft.

IAGO

Indeed?

OTHELLO

115   Indeed? Ay, indeed! **Discern**'st thou aught in that?
Is he not honest?

IAGO

Honest, my lord?

DESDEMONA

Emilia, come along. (*to* OTHELLO) Do whatever you like. Whatever you want, I'll obey you.

DESDEMONA *and* EMILIA *exit.*

OTHELLO

You sweet thing! Hell take me,   100
but I really love you! And when I don't love you,
chaos will have come again.

IAGO

My noble lord—

OTHELLO

What is it, Iago?

IAGO

When you wooed my lady, did Michael Cassio   105
know about your love for her?

OTHELLO

Yes, from beginning to end. Why do you ask?

IAGO

I just wanted to satisfy my curiosity about something;
nothing important.   110

OTHELLO

What were you curious about, Iago?

IAGO

I didn't realize that he had known her.

OTHELLO

Oh, yes, and he often served as our go-between.

IAGO

Really?

OTHELLO

Really? Yes, really! Do you see anything wrong with that?   115
Isn't he honest?

IAGO

Honest, my lord?

OTHELLO
Honest! Ay, honest.

IAGO
My lord, for aught I know.

OTHELLO
What dost thou think?

IAGO
Think, my lord?

OTHELLO
"Think, my lord?" By heaven, thou echo'st me,
As if there were some monster in thy thought
Too hideous to be shown.—Thou dost mean something.
I heard thee say even now, thou lik'st not that,
When Cassio left my wife. What didst not like?
And when I told thee he was of my counsel
In my whole course of wooing, thou criedst, "Indeed?"
And didst contract and purse thy brow together,
As if thou then hadst shut up in thy brain
Some horrible conceit. If thou dost love me,
Show me thy thought.

IAGO
My lord, you know I love you.

OTHELLO
I think thou dost;
And, for I know thou 'rt full of love and honesty,
And weigh'st thy words before thou giv'st them breath,
Therefore these stops of thine fright me the more;
For such things in a false disloyal knave
Are tricks of custom; but in a man that's just
They're close dilations, working from the heart
That passion cannot rule.

IAGO
For Michael Cassio,
I dare be sworn I think that he is honest.

OTHELLO
I think so too.

OTHELLO
Honest? Yes, honest.

IAGO
For all I know, my lord.

OTHELLO
What are you thinking? 120

IAGO
Thinking, my lord?

OTHELLO
"Thinking, my lord?" By God, he's echoing me
as if he had something so awful on his mind
that he was afraid to tell me. You have something on your mind.
I heard you say just a moment ago that you didn't like it 125
when you saw Cassio leaving my wife. What didn't you like?
And when I told you that he was in my confidence
during my whole courtship, you cried, "Really?"
And you wrinkled your forehead
as if you had shut up inside your brain 130
some terrible thought. If you love me,
tell me what you're thinking.

IAGO
My lord, you know I love you.

OTHELLO
I believe you do;
and, because I know you are full of love and honesty 135
and weigh your words carefully before you say them,
I'm all the more frightened by your hesitation.
This kind of behavior in a dishonest, disloyal rascal
is a customary trick; but in a good man,
it is a true sign of secret concern, coming from the heart 140
in spite of one's intentions.

IAGO
As for Michael Cassio,
I'd venture to swear that I think he is honest.

OTHELLO
I think so too.

IAGO

145   Men should be what they seem;
        Or those that be not, would they might seem none!

OTHELLO
        Certain, men should be what they seem.

IAGO
        Why, then, I think Cassio's an honest man.

OTHELLO
        Nay, yet there's more in this.
150   I prithee speak to me as to thy thinkings,
        As thou dost **ruminate**, and give thy worst of thoughts
        The worst of words.

IAGO
                  Good my lord, pardon me.
        Though I am bound to every act of duty,
155   I am not bound to that all slaves are free to.
        Utter my thoughts? Why, say they are vile and false;
        As where's that palace whereinto foul things
        Sometimes intrude not? Who has that breast so pure
        But some uncleanly apprehensions
160   Keep leets and law days* and in sessions sit
        With meditations lawful?

OTHELLO
        Thou dost conspire against thy friend, Iago,
        If thou but think'st him wrong'd and mak'st his ear
        A stranger to thy thoughts.

IAGO
165   I do beseech you—
        Though I perchance am vicious in my guess—
        As, I confess, it is my nature's plague
        To spy into abuses, and oft my jealousy
        Shapes faults that are not—that your wisdom,
170   From one that so imperfectly conceits,
        Would take no notice, nor build yourself a trouble
        Out of his scattering and unsure observance.
        It were not for your quiet nor your good,

---

160   *leets and law days* days when the local courts held sessions

IAGO

Men should be what they seem to be;   145
and men who aren't men shouldn't seem like men.

OTHELLO

Certainly, men should be what they seem to be.

IAGO

Well then, I think Cassio's an honest man.

OTHELLO

No, you're still not telling me something.
Please, tell me what you're thinking,   150
what's on your mind, and give me your worst thoughts
as bluntly as you can.

IAGO

My good lord, pardon me.
Though I am obliged to perform all sorts of duties to you,
I am not obliged to do something even slaves are free not to do. 155
Tell my thoughts? Why, suppose they are rotten and untrue?
And what palace is so secure that bad things
don't sometimes get in? Who has such a pure heart
that unclean ideas
don't keep regular session, sitting side by side   160
with better thoughts?

OTHELLO

You are doing an injustice to a friend, Iago,
if you believe he's been wronged and you won't tell him
what you're thinking.

IAGO

I beg you—   165
since I may be wrong in my suspicion,
and I admit it is a flaw in my nature
to seek out wrongs, and often my suspicious mind
finds faults that aren't real—that, in your wisdom,
you keep in mind that I often imagine things,   170
and take no notice, and don't get worked up
about my random and doubtful observations.
It's not good for your peace of mind or your best interests,

Nor for my manhood, honesty, and wisdom,
175　To let you know my thoughts.

OTHELLO

What dost thou mean?

IAGO

Good name in man and woman, dear my lord,
Is the immediate jewel of their souls.
Who steals my purse steals trash; 'tis something, nothing;
180　'Twas mine, 'tis his, and has been slave to thousands;
But he that filches from me my good name
Robs me of that which not enriches him,
And makes me poor indeed.

OTHELLO

By heaven, I'll know thy thoughts.

IAGO

185　You cannot, if my heart were in your hand;
Nor shall not, whilst 'tis in my custody.

OTHELLO

Ha?

IAGO

O, beware, my lord, of jealousy!
It is the green-ey'd monster which doth mock
190　The meat it feeds on. That cuckold lives in bliss
Who, certain of his fate, loves not his wronger;
But, O, what damned minutes tells he o'er
Who dotes, yet doubts, suspects, yet strongly loves!

OTHELLO

O misery!

IAGO

195　Poor and content is rich, and rich enough;
But riches fineless is as poor as winter
To him that ever fears he shall be poor.
Good God, the souls of all my tribe defend
From jealousy!

or for my manhood, honesty, or wisdom,
to tell you what I'm thinking.   175

OTHELLO

What do you mean?

IAGO

A man or a woman's good name, my dear lord,
is the most important thing they have.
Someone who steals my money steals trash; it was something,
    now it's nothing;
it was mine, now it's his—and has belonged to thousands of
    others.   180
But someone who takes my good name away from me
robs me of something which does him no good
and leaves me very poor indeed.

OTHELLO

By God, I want to know what you're thinking!

IAGO

You couldn't, even if you were holding my heart in your hand;   185
and you won't as long as it's in my custody.

OTHELLO

Ha!

IAGO

Oh, watch out for jealousy, my lord!
It is a green-eyed monster, and it laughs at
the meat it eats. A cuckold can be happy   190
who, sure of his situation, hates the man who wrongs him.
But, oh, how time drags on for the man
who adores, but doubts; suspects, but loves strongly!

OTHELLO

Oh, misery!

IAGO

To be poor and happy is to be rich, and plenty rich;   195
but limitless wealth is just so much poverty
to a man who is frightened he'll wind up poor.
May heaven protect the souls of everyone I know
from jealousy!

OTHELLO

200 Why, why is this?
Think'st thou I'd make a life of jealousy,
To follow still the changes of the moon
With fresh suspicions? No! To be once in doubt
Is once to be resolv'd. Exchange me for a goat
205 When I shall turn the business of my soul
To such exsufflicate and blown **surmises**,
Matching thy **inference**. 'Tis not to make me jealous
To say my wife is fair, feeds well, loves company,
Is free of speech, sings, plays, and dances well;
210 Where virtue is, these are more virtuous.
Nor from mine own weak merits will I draw
The smallest fear or doubt of her revolt;
For she had eyes, and chose me. No, Iago;
I'll see before I doubt; when I doubt, prove;
215 And on the proof, there is no more but this—
Away at once with love or jealousy!

IAGO

I am glad of this, for now I shall have reason
To show the love and duty that I bear you
With franker spirit; therefore, as I am bound,
220 Receive it from me. I speak not yet of proof.
Look to your wife; observe her well with Cassio;
Wear your eyes thus, not jealous nor secure.
I would not have your free and noble nature,
Out of self-bounty, be abus'd; look to 't.
225 I know our country disposition well;
In Venice they do let Heaven see the pranks
They dare not show their husbands. Their best conscience
Is not to leave 't undone, but keep 't unknown.

OTHELLO

Dost thou say so?

IAGO

230 She did deceive her father, marrying you;
And when she seem'd to shake and fear your looks,
She lov'd them most.

OTHELLO

Why, why do you say this?   200
Do you think I'd choose to live for jealousy,
to follow continually the changes of the moon,
eyeing them suspiciously? No! To be in doubt once
is to be satisfied as to the truth. Exchange me for a goat
when I become obsessed   205
with such inflated and far-fetched thoughts
as you suggest. You won't make me jealous
by saying that my wife is lovely, dines elegantly, likes company,
speaks freely, sings, plays, and dances well.
These good qualities make a virtuous person all the more
   virtuous.   210
And though I might not be the best-looking man alive,
I won't fear rejection on that account
because she had eyes and chose me. No, Iago;
I must see evidence before I doubt, and when I doubt, I must
   have proof;
and when there's proof, that's the end of it—   215
and that's the end of love or jealousy!

IAGO

I'm glad to hear that; now I have cause
to show the love and duty that I owe you
more openly. Therefore, since I'm obliged,
listen to me. I've no proof yet.   220
Watch your wife; observe her carefully when she's with Cassio;
just keep your eyes open, neither suspicious nor careless.
I don't want your generous and noble nature
to be abused because of your natural kindness.
Keep your eyes open.   225
In Venice, women let heaven see them do wicked things
that their husbands never see. The height of their morality
is not to do no wrong, but to not get caught.

OTHELLO

Do you really mean it?

IAGO

She deceived her father by marrying you;   230
and when she seemed most frightened by your looks,
she really loved them most.

OTHELLO

And so she did.

IAGO

Why, go to then.

235　She that, so young, could give out such a seeming,
To seel her father's eyes up close as oak—*
He thought 'twas witchcraft—but I am much to blame.
I humbly do beseech you of your pardon
For too much loving you.

OTHELLO

240　I am bound to thee for ever.

IAGO

I see this hath a little dash'd your spirits.

OTHELLO

Not a jot, not a jot.

IAGO

I' faith, I fear it has.
I hope you will consider what is spoke
245　Comes from my love. But I do see you're mov'd.
I am to pray you not to strain my speech
To grosser issues nor to larger reach
Than to suspicion.

OTHELLO

I will not.

IAGO

250　Should you do so, my lord,
My speech should fall into such vile success
As my thoughts aim not at. Cassio's my worthy friend—
My lord, I see you're mov'd.

OTHELLO

No, not much mov'd.
255　I do not think but Desdemona's honest.

236　*close as oak* Iago means Brabantio's eyes were closed up as tightly as the close
wood grain of the oak.

OTHELLO

And so she did.

IAGO

Well, there you have it!
Here's a girl who is so young but could still put on an   235
    appearance
to completely hoodwink her father;
he thought it was witchcraft—but I shouldn't be saying this.
I humbly beg your pardon
for being too concerned about you.

OTHELLO

I'm forever indebted to you.   240

IAGO

I see this has dampened your good spirits a little.

OTHELLO

Not a bit, not a bit.

IAGO

Really, I'm afraid it has.
I hope you'll remember that what I've said
was spoken simply out of love. But I see you're disturbed.   245
I really beg you not to apply what I've said
to larger issues or to go further
than my suspicions.

OTHELLO

I will not.

IAGO

If you should do that, my lord,   250
my words would have evil consequences
that I really didn't intend. Cassio's my very good friend—
My lord, I see you're disturbed.

OTHELLO

No, not terribly disturbed.
I can't think that Desdemona's anything but honest.   255

IAGO

Long live she so! And long live you to think so!

OTHELLO

And yet, how nature erring from itself—

IAGO

Ay, there's the point; as—to be bold with you—
Not to affect many proposed matches

260 Of her own clime, complexion, and degree,
Whereto we see in all things nature tends—
Foh! One may smell in such, a will most rank,
Foul disproportion, thoughts unnatural.
But pardon me; I do not in position

265 Distinctly speak of her, though I may fear
Her will, **recoiling** to her better judgment,
May fall to match you with her country forms,
And happily repent.

OTHELLO

                    Farewell, farewell!

270 If more thou dost perceive, let me know more;
Set on thy wife to observe. Leave me, Iago.

IAGO [*going*]

My lord, I take my leave.

OTHELLO

Why did I marry? This honest creature doubtless
Sees and knows more, much more, than he unfolds.

IAGO [*returning*]

275 My lord, I would I might entreat your Honor
To scan this thing no farther; leave it to time.
Although 'tis fit that Cassio have his place,
For sure he fills it up with great ability,
Yet, if you please to hold him off awhile,

280 You shall by that perceive him and his means.
Note if your lady strain his entertainment
With any strong or **vehement** importunity;
Much will be seen in that. In the meantime,
Let me be thought too busy in my fears—

285 As worthy cause I have to fear I am—
And hold her free, I do beseech your Honor.

IAGO

And long may she live so! And long may you live to think so!

OTHELLO

But still, one can sometimes forget oneself—

IAGO

Yes, that's the point! Since—to be quite blunt—
she hasn't shown an inclination toward another match
of her own temperament, nature, and social status,   260
which is simply the tendency of all things in nature—
Really! One might smell in that kind of desire rotten
and foul abnormalities, unnatural thoughts—
but pardon me—in delivering this argument, I don't
specifically speak about her; although I'm afraid   265
that her desires, overwhelming her better judgment,
might bring her to compare you to men of her own race
and perhaps lead her to reject you.

OTHELLO

Good-bye, good-bye!
If you see anything else, let me know.   270
Tell your wife to keep her eyes open too. Leave me alone, Iago.

IAGO (*walking away from him*)

My lord, I'll take my leave.

OTHELLO

Why did I get married? This honest man doubtless
has seen and knows more, much more, than he's told me.

IAGO (*returning*)

My lord, I would really like to beg your Honor   275
to think no more about this business. Give it time.
Though it's right that Cassio should have his position back,
for he certainly does his job well,
still, if you'll only make him wait awhile,
you'll get a chance to watch him and see how he goes about   280
    appealing to you.
Watch if your lady pushes for his reappointment
too strongly or too vehemently.
You'll be able to tell much by that. In the meantime,
just assume that my fears are groundless—
as I have good cause to think they are—   285
and consider her innocent, I beg you, your Honor.

OTHELLO

Fear not my government.

IAGO

I once more take my leave.

[Exit.]

OTHELLO

This fellow's of exceeding honesty,
290 And knows all qualities with a learned spirit,
Of human dealings. If I do prove her haggard,*
Though that her jesses* were my dear heartstrings,
I'd whistle her off* and let her down the wind*
To prey at fortune. Haply, for I am black
295 And have not those soft parts of conversation
That chamberers have, or for I am declin'd
Into the vale of years,—yet that's not much—
She's gone. I am abus'd; and my relief
Must be to loathe her. O curse of marriage,
300 That we can call these delicate creatures ours
And not their appetites! I had rather be a toad
And live upon the vapour of a dungeon
Than keep a corner in the thing I love
For others' uses. Yet, 'tis the plague of great ones;
305 Prerogativ'd are they less than the base.
'Tis destiny unshunnable, like death.
Even then this forked plague* is fated to us
When we do quicken. Look where she comes,

Reenter DESDEMONA *and* EMILIA.

If she be false, heaven mocks itself!
310 I'll not believe 't.

DESDEMONA

How now, my dear Othello!
Your dinner, and the generous islanders
By you invited, do attend your presence.

---

291   *haggard* Othello uses falconry terminology in this speech. A haggard is an untamed hawk. The word also means "unchaste."

292   *jesses* straps of leather which held a falcon to a leash

293   *whistle her off* send her away; a whistle was a falconer's signal for a bird to take wing

OTHELLO

Don't worry about my self-control.

IAGO

Once again, I'll take my leave.

      IAGO *exits.*

OTHELLO

This fellow's exceptionally honest
and knows all types of people, as well as having a keen eye   290
for human behavior. If I find out she's unfaithful,
even if she was tethered to me by my own dear heartstrings,
I'd pack her off and let her fend her own way
against fortune. Possibly because I'm black
and don't have that gentle way of behaving   295
which gallants have, or because I'm getting along
in years—though still not very old—
she's betrayed me. I've been wronged, and my only comfort
will be to hate her. Oh, what a curse of marriage
that we can call these delicate creatures our own   300
and not control their longings! I'd rather be a toad
and live in some damp dungeon
than let a part of something I loved
be used by others. Yet this is the curse of those in high positions;
they're less likely to be free of it than the lowborn.   305
It's an inescapable destiny, like death:
we're doomed to wear the horns of the cuckold
from the moment we're born. Desdemona is coming.

      DESDEMONA *and* EMILIA *enter.*

If she's unfaithful, oh, then heaven has given itself an insult!
I won't believe it.   310

DESDEMONA

How are you, my dear Othello?
Your dinner and the noble islanders
you've invited are waiting for you to come.

---

293   *down the wind* A hawk was usually flown against the wind. To fly down the wind was a phrase that indicated someone was facing formidable odds.

307   *forked plague* a reference to the tradition that cuckolds supposedly had horns

Act 3, Scene 3   177

OTHELLO

I am to blame.

DESDEMONA

315   Why do you speak so faintly? Are you not well?

OTHELLO

I have a pain upon my forehead here.*

DESDEMONA

Faith, that's with watching: 'twill away again.
Let me but bind it hard, within this hour
It will be well.

OTHELLO

320   Your napkin is too little; [*He puts the
handkerchief from him and it drops.*]
Let it alone.
              Come, I'll go in with you.

DESDEMONA

I am very sorry that you are not well.

[*Exeunt* OTHELLO *and* DESDEMONA.]

EMILIA [*picking up the handkerchief*]

I am glad I have found this napkin;
325   This was her first remembrance from the Moor.
My wayward husband hath a hundred times
Woo'd me to steal it; but she so loves the token,
(For he conjur'd her she should ever keep it)
That she reserves it evermore about her
330   To kiss and talk to. I'll have the work ta'en out
And give 't Iago. What he will do with it
Heaven knows, not I.
I nothing but to please his fantasy.

Reenter IAGO.

IAGO

How now! What do you here alone?

---

316   *I have a pain . . . here.* Othello is pointing to the place on his head where his
cuckold's "horns" would be.

OTHELLO

I am to blame.

DESDEMONA

Why are you speaking so softly?   315
Aren't you well?

OTHELLO

I have a pain in my forehead, here.

DESDEMONA

Well, that's from staying up too long; it will go away.
I'll bind it up, and in less than an hour,
it will be just fine.

OTHELLO

Your handkerchief isn't large enough.   320
Don't bother with it. (*He pushes it away, and it falls to the
    ground.*)
Come along, I'll go with you.

DESDEMONA

I'm very sorry you're not feeling well.

> OTHELLO *and* DESDEMONA *exit.*

EMILIA (*picking up the handkerchief*)

I'm glad I've found this handkerchief.
This was her first gift from the Moor.   325
My willful husband has asked me a hundred times
to steal it. But she loves it so much,
since Othello made her promise she would always keep it,
that she keeps it with her all the time
to kiss and talk to. I'll have the embroidery copied   330
and give it to Iago.
What he'll do with it, heaven knows; I don't.
I want nothing but to please his whims.

> IAGO *enters.*

IAGO

What is this? What are you doing here alone?

EMILIA

335 Do not you **chide**; I have a thing for you.

IAGO

  You have a thing for me? It is a common thing—

EMILIA

  Ha?

IAGO

  To have a foolish wife.

EMILIA

  O, is that all? What will you give me now
340 For that same handkerchief?

IAGO

           What handkerchief?

EMILIA

  What handkerchief!
  Why, that the Moor first gave to Desdemona;
  That which so often you did bid me steal.

IAGO

345 Hast stol'n it from her?

EMILIA

  No, faith, she let it drop by negligence,
  And, to th' advantage, I, being here, took 't up.
  Look, here 't is.

IAGO

       A good wench; give it me.

EMILIA

350 What will you do with 't, that you have been so earnest
  To have me filch it?

IAGO [*snatching it*]

  Why, what is that to you?

EMILIA

  If it be not for some purpose of import,
  Give 't me again. Poor lady, she'll run mad
355 When she shall lack it.

EMILIA
Don't scold me; I've got something for you.   335

IAGO
Something for me? It's an ordinary something—

EMILIA
What?

IAGO
To have a foolish wife.

EMILIA
Oh, is that all? What would you give me
for that handkerchief?   340

IAGO
What handkerchief?

EMILIA
What handkerchief?
Why, the one the Moor gave to Desdemona;
the one you've asked me to steal so often.

IAGO
Have you stolen it from her?   345

EMILIA
Certainly not; she dropped it by accident,
and I was lucky enough to be on hand to pick it up.
Look, here it is.

IAGO
Good girl! Give it to me.

EMILIA
What do you want to do with it after insisting all this time   350
that I steal it?

IAGO (*snatching it away from her*)
Why, what's it to you?

EMILIA
If it's not for anything important,
give it back to me. The poor lady; she'll go crazy
when she finds out she's lost it.   355

IAGO

                            Be not acknown on 't;
I have use for it. Go, leave me.

      [*Exit* EMILIA.]

    I will in Cassio's lodging lose this napkin,
    And let him find it. Trifles light as air
360   Are to the jealous confirmations strong
    As proofs of holy writ; this may do something.
    The Moor already changes with my poison.
    Dangerous conceits are, in their natures poisons,
    Which at the first are scarce found to distaste,
365   But with a little act upon the blood
    Burn like the mines of sulphur.

      Reenter OTHELLO.

                              I did say so.
    Look, where he comes! Not poppy, nor mandragora,*
    Nor all the drowsy syrups of the world
370   Shall ever medicine thee to that sweet sleep
    Which thou ow'dst yesterday.

OTHELLO

    Ha! ha! False to me?

IAGO

    Why, how now, General! No more of that!

OTHELLO

    Avaunt! Be gone! Thou hast set me on the rack.*
375   I swear 'tis better to be much abus'd
    Than but to know 't a little.

IAGO

                       How now, my lord!

OTHELLO

    What sense had I of her stol'n hours of lust?
    I saw 't not, thought it not, it harm'd not me.
380   I slept the next night well, fed well, was free and merry;

---

368   *poppy, nor mandragora* Extracts from these plants were used to induce sleep.

374   *rack* a torture device that painfully stretched a victim's body

IAGO

Don't let on that you know anything; I have use for it.
Go on, leave me alone.

    EMILIA *exits.*

I'll put this handkerchief in Cassio's lodging
and let him find it. Little things like this
are as convincing to those of a jealous nature 360
as the Holy Scriptures themselves. This might have an effect.
The Moor already shows some change, due to my poisonous
   influence.
Dangerous ideas are poisonous by nature;
at first they do not even taste bad,
but in a short time, they get into the blood 365
and burn like sulfur mines.

    OTHELLO *enters.*

I said as much.
Look at him coming! Neither poppies nor herbs
nor all the sleeping potions in the world
will ever restore you to that sweet sleep 370
which you knew only yesterday.

OTHELLO

What! What! Unfaithful to me!

IAGO

Why, what is it, General? No more of that kind of talk!

OTHELLO

Away! Be gone! You have put me on the rack.
I swear, it's better to be greatly wronged 375
than to know anything about it.

IAGO

What do you mean, my lord?

OTHELLO

What did I know about her secret hours of lust?
I didn't see it, didn't suspect it, and wasn't hurt by it.
I slept well that night and was free and happy; 380

I found not Cassio's kisses on her lips.
He that is robb'd, not wanting what is stolen,
Let him not know 't, and he's not robb'd at all.

IAGO

I am sorry to hear this.

OTHELLO

385 I had been happy, if the general camp,
Pioners*and all, had tasted her sweet body,
So I had nothing known. O, now, for ever
Farewell the tranquil mind! Farewell content!
Farewell the plumed troops and the big wars
390 That makes ambition virtue! O, farewell!
Farewell the neighing steed and the shrill trump,
The spirit-stirring drum, th' ear-piercing fife,
The royal banner, and all quality,
Pride, pomp, and circumstance of glorious war!
395 And, O you mortal engines, whose rude throats
Th' immortal Jove's dread clamours counterfeit,
Farewell! Othello's occupation's gone!

IAGO

Is 't possible, my lord?

OTHELLO

Villain, be sure thou prove my love a whore;
400 Be sure of it. Give me the ocular proof;
Or, by the worth of mine eternal soul,
Thou hadst been better have been born a dog
Than answer my wak'd wrath!

IAGO

Is 't come to this?

OTHELLO

405 Make me to see 't; or, at the least, so prove it
That the probation bear no hinge nor loop
To hang a doubt on; or woe upon thy life!

IAGO

My noble lord—

---

386 *Pioners* the lowest rank of soldiers; they dug trenches and laid mines

I didn't know that Cassio had been kissing her.
If a man's been robbed and has no need of what's been stolen,
he shouldn't be told; then he's not really robbed at all.

IAGO

I'm sorry to hear this.

OTHELLO

I'd have been happy if the whole army,   385
foot soldiers and everyone, had made love to her,
as long as I didn't know. Oh, now I must say
farewell to peace of mind forever! Farewell to contentment!
Farewell to the glorious troops and the great wars
that make ambition into a virtue! Oh, farewell!   390
Farewell to the neighing horse and the shrill trumpet,
to the spirit-stirring drum, and the ear-shattering fife,
the royal banner, and all the good men,
pride, pomp, and pageantry of glorious war!
And, oh, you deadly cannons whose horrible voices   395
imitate the thunderclaps of the god Jove,
farewell! Othello's occupation is gone!

IAGO

Can this be possible, my lord?

OTHELLO

Villain, you'd better be sure you prove my love's a whore!
Be sure of it; give me visible proof;   400
or, by the value of a man's eternal soul,
you would have been better off to have been born a dog
than to face my roused wrath!

IAGO

Has it come to this?

OTHELLO

Make me see it; or at least prove it so well   405
that there's no hinge or loop in the proof
to hang a doubt on—or woe upon your life!

IAGO

My noble lord—

OTHELLO

If thou dost slander her and torture me,
410 Never pray more; abandon all remorse;
On horror's head horrors accumulate;
Do deeds to make heaven weep, all earth amaz'd;
For nothing canst thou to damnation add
Greater than that.

IAGO

415   O grace! O heaven forgive me!
Are you a man? Have you a soul or sense?
God b' wi' you; take mine office.—O wretched fool,
That liv'st to make thine honesty a vice!—
O monstrous world! Take note, take note, O world.
420 To be direct and honest is not safe.—
I thank you for this profit; and from hence
I'll love no friend, sith love breeds such offence.

OTHELLO

Nay, stay. Thou shouldst be honest.

IAGO

I should be wise, for honesty's a fool
425 And loses that it works for.*

OTHELLO

                            By the world,
I think my wife be honest and think she is not;
I think that thou art just and think thou art not.
I'll have some proof. Her name, that was as fresh
430 As Dian's visage,* is now begrim'd and black
As mine own face. If there be cords, or knives,
Poison, or fire, or suffocating streams,
I'll not endure it. Would I were satisfied!

IAGO

I see you are eaten up with passion;
435 I do repent me that I put it to you.
You would be satisfied?

---

425 *loses that it works for* Iago means honesty does not gain the trust it deserves.

430 *Dian's visage* refers to the Greek goddess of chastity and hunting

OTHELLO

If you're slandering her and torturing me,
never pray again; stop feeling remorse; 410
heap new horrors on top of horrors;
do deeds that will make heaven weep, and shock the world
   into speechlessness;
for you can't add anything to your own damnation
greater than that.

IAGO

Oh, God! Oh, heaven forgive me! 415
Are you a man? Have you a soul or reason?
May God be with you! You do my duty. What a fool I am,
who has lived to see his honesty become a vice!
Oh, monstrous world! Take note, take note, world:
to be truthful and honest is not safe. 420
I thank you for teaching me this lesson; and from now on,
I'll love no friend, since love causes such offense.

OTHELLO

No, stay. You should be honest.

IAGO

I should be wise; honest men are fools
and lose what they try to gain. 425

OTHELLO

By all the world
I believe my wife to be honest, and I believe that she is not;
I believe that you are truthful and believe that you are not.
I must have some proof. Her name used to be as clean
as Diana's face, but is now as grimy and black 430
as my own face. As long as there are ropes, knives,
poison, fires, or rivers where I can drown myself,
I won't suffer this. I wish I were certain!

IAGO

I see, sir, that you are eaten up by your emotions.
I'm very sorry that I brought this on. 435
Do you really want to be certain?

OTHELLO

Would? Nay, and I will.

IAGO

And may; but, how? How satisfied, my lord?
Would you, the supervisor, grossly gape on—
440   Behold her topp'd?

OTHELLO

                    Death and damnation! O!

IAGO

It were a tedious difficulty, I think,
To bring them to that prospect; damn them then,
If ever mortal eyes do see them bolster
445   More than their own! What then? How then?
What shall I say? Where's satisfaction?
It is impossible you should see this,
Were they as prime as goats, as hot as monkeys,
As salt as wolves in pride, and fools as gross
450   As ignorance made drunk. But yet, I say,
If imputation and strong circumstances
Which lead directly to the door of truth
Will give you satisfaction, you might have 't.

OTHELLO

Give me a living reason she's disloyal.

IAGO

455   I do not like the office;
But, sith I am enter'd in this cause so far,
Prick'd to 't by foolish honesty and love,
I will go on. I lay with Cassio lately;
And, being troubled with a raging tooth,
460   I could not sleep. There are a kind of men
So loose of soul, that in their sleeps will mutter
Their affairs; One of this kind is Cassio.
In sleep I heard him say, "Sweet Desdemona,
Let us be wary, let us hide our love."
465   And then, sir, would he gripe and wring my hand,
Cry, "O sweet creature!" then kiss me hard,
As if he pluck'd up kisses by the roots

OTHELLO

Want to be? No, I will be.

IAGO

And you might be. But how? How will you be certain my lord?
Do you want to be an onlooker, grossly staring at it all?
Do you want to see her in the act?   440

OTHELLO

Death and damnation! Oh!

IAGO

I think it would be very difficult
to get them to do it where they can be seen. Damn them, then,
if mortal eyes ever do see them go to bed,
other than their own! So how? How then?   445
What's there to say? How will you be satisfied?
It's impossible that you would see it happen,
even if they were as ready as goats, as hot as monkeys,
as lustful as wolves in heat, and as stupidly foolish
as if they were drunk. But still, let me tell you,   450
if accusation and the strongest circumstantial evidence
which point straight to the truth of the matter
will satisfy you, you may have that.

OTHELLO

Give me absolute proof that she's unfaithful.

IAGO

I don't like being put in this position.   455
But since I'm so deep into this business already,
driven on by my foolish honesty and love,
I'll continue. I was lying next to Cassio recently,
and since I had a terrible toothache,
I couldn't sleep. There's a certain kind of man   460
of so loose a soul that he'll talk about his private business in
    his sleep.
Cassio is this kind of man.
In his sleep, I heard him say, "Sweet Desdemona,
let's be careful, let's hide our love!"
And then, sir, he'd grip and wring my hand,   465
cry, "Oh, sweet creature!" and then kiss me hard,
as if he were pulling up kisses by the roots

That grew upon my lips; then laid his leg
Over my thigh, and sighed, and kissed; and then
470   Cried, "Cursed fate that gave thee to the Moor!"

OTHELLO
O monstrous! Monstrous!

IAGO
                    Nay, this was but his dream.

OTHELLO
But this denoted a foregone conclusion.
'Tis a shrewd doubt, though it be but a dream.

IAGO
475   And this may help to thicken other proofs
That do demonstrate thinly.

OTHELLO
I'll tear her all to pieces.

IAGO
Nay, but be wise; yet we see nothing done.
She may be honest yet. Tell me but this,
480   Have you not sometimes seen a handkerchief
Spotted with strawberries in your wife's hand?

OTHELLO
I gave her such a one; 'twas my first gift.

IAGO
I know not that; but such a handkerchief—
I am sure it was your wife's—did I today
485   See Cassio wipe his beard with.

OTHELLO
                    If it be that—

IAGO
If it be that, or any that was hers,
It speaks against her with the other proofs.

OTHELLO
O, that the slave had forty thousand lives!
490   One is too poor, too weak for my revenge.
Now do I see 'tis true. Look here, Iago,
All my fond love thus do I blow to heaven.

which grew upon my lips. Then he laid his leg
over my thigh and sighed and kissed me, and then
cried "Curse the fate that gave you to the Moor!" 470

OTHELLO

Oh, monstrous! Monstrous!

IAGO

Still, this only happened in his dream.

OTHELLO

But it told of something which had already actually occurred.
It's very suspicious, even though it was only a dream.

IAGO

And we might use this to strengthen other evidence 475
of a flimsier nature.

OTHELLO

I'll tear her all to pieces!

IAGO

No, be sensible. We haven't seen anything done;
she still might be faithful. Just tell me this—
haven't you sometimes seen a handkerchief 480
decorated with strawberries in your wife's hand?

OTHELLO

I gave her one like that; it was my first gift to her.

IAGO

I didn't know that; but I saw a handkerchief like that
—and I'm sure it was your wife's—just today;
Cassio wiped his beard with it. 485

OTHELLO

If it's the same one—

IAGO

If it's the same one, or any one that belongs to her,
it speaks against her, along with the other evidence.

OTHELLO

Oh, I wish the wretch had forty thousand lives!
One is too little, too small to satisfy my revenge. 490
Now I see that it's true. Look here, Iago:
all my dear love for her I send straight to heaven.

'Tis gone.
Arise, black vengeance, from the hollow hell!
495 Yield up, O love, thy crown and hearted throne
To tyrannous hate! Swell, bosom, with thy fraught,
For 'tis of aspics' tongues!

IAGO
Yet be content.

OTHELLO
O, blood, blood, blood!

IAGO
500 Patience, I say. Your mind perhaps may change.

OTHELLO
Never, Iago. Like to the Pontic Sea,
Whose icy current and compulsive course
Ne'er feels retiring ebb, but keeps due on
To the Propontic and the Hellespont,
505 Even so my bloody thoughts, with violent pace,
Shall ne'er look back, ne'er ebb to humble love,
Till that a capable and wide revenge
Swallow them up. [*Kneels.*] Now, by yond marble heaven,
In the due reverence of a sacred vow
510 I here engage my words.

IAGO [*Kneels.*]
                    Do not rise yet.
Witness, you ever-burning lights above,
You elements that clip us round about,
Witness that here Iago doth give up
515 The execution of his wit, hands, heart,
To wrong'd Othello's service! Let him command,
And to obey shall be in me remorse,
What bloody business ever.

          [*They rise.*]

OTHELLO
                    I greet thy love,
520 Not with vain thanks, but with acceptance bounteous,
And will upon the instant put thee to 't:
Within these three days let me hear thee say
That Cassio's not alive.

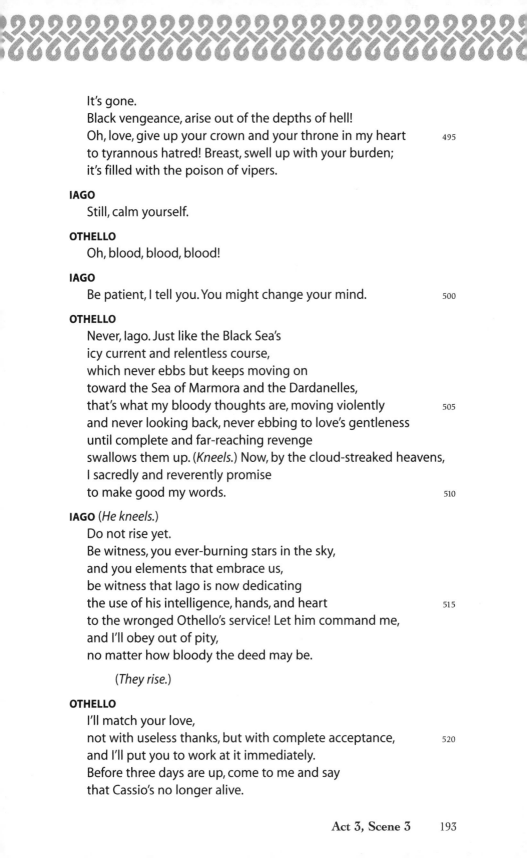

It's gone.
Black vengeance, arise out of the depths of hell!
Oh, love, give up your crown and your throne in my heart   495
to tyrannous hatred! Breast, swell up with your burden;
it's filled with the poison of vipers.

IAGO

Still, calm yourself.

OTHELLO

Oh, blood, blood, blood!

IAGO

Be patient, I tell you. You might change your mind.   500

OTHELLO

Never, Iago. Just like the Black Sea's
icy current and relentless course,
which never ebbs but keeps moving on
toward the Sea of Marmora and the Dardanelles,
that's what my bloody thoughts are, moving violently   505
and never looking back, never ebbing to love's gentleness
until complete and far-reaching revenge
swallows them up. (*Kneels.*) Now, by the cloud-streaked heavens,
I sacredly and reverently promise
to make good my words.   510

IAGO (*He kneels.*)

Do not rise yet.
Be witness, you ever-burning stars in the sky,
and you elements that embrace us,
be witness that Iago is now dedicating
the use of his intelligence, hands, and heart   515
to the wronged Othello's service! Let him command me,
and I'll obey out of pity,
no matter how bloody the deed may be.

    (*They rise.*)

OTHELLO

I'll match your love,
not with useless thanks, but with complete acceptance,   520
and I'll put you to work at it immediately.
Before three days are up, come to me and say
that Cassio's no longer alive.

IAGO

My friend is dead;

525 'tis done at your request. But let her live.

OTHELLO

Damn her, lewd minx! O, damn her! Damn her!
Come, go with me apart; I will withdraw
To furnish me with some swift means of death
For the fair devil. Now art thou my lieutenant.

IAGO

530 I am your own forever.

[*Exeunt.*]

IAGO

My friend is as good as dead;
it's done at your request. But let her live. 525

OTHELLO

Damn her, the lewd minx! Oh, damn her!
Come, step aside with me. I will leave
so I can think up some quick means to kill
that lovely devil. You are my lieutenant now.

IAGO

I'm your servant forever. 530

They exit.

ACT III, SCENE IV

[*Before the castle.*] *Enter* DESDEMONA, EMILIA, *and* CLOWN.

DESDEMONA
Do you know, sirrah, where Lieutenant Cassio lies?*

CLOWN
I dare not say he lies anywhere.

DESDEMONA
Why, man?

CLOWN
He's a soldier, and for me to say a soldier lies,
5   'tis stabbing.

DESDEMONA
Go to! Where lodges he?

CLOWN
To tell you where he lodges is to tell you where I lie.

DESDEMONA
Can anything be made of this?

CLOWN
I know not where he lodges, and for me to devise a
10 lodging and say he lies here or he lies there, were to lie in
mine own throat.

DESDEMONA
Can you inquire him out and be **edified** by report?*

CLOWN
I will catechize the world for him; that is, make questions,
and by them answer.

DESDEMONA
15 Seek him, bid him come hither. Tell him I have mov'd my
lord on his behalf, and hope all will be well.

---

1   *lies* lodges

12 *Can . . . report?* Desdemona is mimicking the clown's overly formal language.

ACT 3, SCENE 4

In front of the castle. DESDEMONA, EMILIA, *and* CLOWN *enter.*

DESDEMONA
Do you know, fellow, where Lieutenant Cassio stays?

CLOWN
I don't dare say he lies anywhere.

DESDEMONA
Why, man?

CLOWN
He's a soldier; and to say a soldier lies could get me stabbed.   5

DESDEMONA
Don't talk nonsense! Where is he staying?

CLOWN
To tell you where he's staying would be to tell you where I lie.

DESDEMONA
What's that supposed to mean?

CLOWN
I don't know where he's staying; and for me to make up an
address and say he lies here or lies there, I'd be lying for sure.   10

DESDEMONA
Can you inquire around for him and learn from a report?

CLOWN
I'll interrogate the world to find him; that is, I'll make up
questions and come back with answers.

DESDEMONA
Find him, and tell him to come here. Tell him I've persuaded my   15
lord on his behalf and have reason to hope that all will be well.

CLOWN

To do this is within the compass of man's wit; and
therefore I will attempt the doing it.

[*Exit.*]

DESDEMONA

Where should I lose that handkerchief, Emilia?

EMILIA

20   I know not, madam.

DESDEMONA

Believe me, I had rather have lost my purse
Full of crusadoes;* and, but my noble Moor
Is true of mind and made of no such baseness
As jealous creatures are, it were enough
25   To put him to ill thinking.

EMILIA

                        Is he not jealous?

DESDEMONA

Who, he? I think the sun where he was born
Drew all such humours from him.

EMILIA

                      Look, where he comes.

Enter OTHELLO.

DESDEMONA

30   I will not leave him now till Cassio
Be call'd to him.—How is 't with you, my lord?

OTHELLO

Well, my good lady. [*aside*] O, hardness to **dissemble**!—
How do you, Desdemona?

DESDEMONA

                  Well, my good lord.

OTHELLO

35   Give me your hand. This hand is moist, my lady.*

---

22   *crusadoes* Portuguese gold coins

35   *moist* a moist, warm hand was supposed to indicate lustfulness

CLOWN
It's within the range of human intelligence to do that, so I'll give it a try.

    CLOWN *exits.*

DESDEMONA
Where could I have lost that handkerchief, Emilia?

EMILIA
I don't know, madam.   20

DESDEMONA
Believe me, I'd rather have lost my purse
full of gold coins. If my noble Moor
were not sensible and were made of the same bad stuff
as jealous creatures are, this would be enough
to put evil thoughts in his head.   25

EMILIA
Isn't he jealous?

DESDEMONA
Who? Him? I think the sun where he was born
dried all such tendencies out of him.

EMILIA
Look, he's coming.

    OTHELLO *enters.*

DESDEMONA
I won't leave him until Cassio   30
is summoned. (*to* OTHELLO) How are you, my lord?

OTHELLO
Well, my good lady. (*to himself*) Oh, how hard it is to pretend!—
How are you doing, Desdemona?

DESDEMONA
Well, my good lord.

OTHELLO
Give me your hand. Your hand is moist, my lady.   35

DESDEMONA

It yet hath felt no age nor known no sorrow.

OTHELLO

This argues fruitfulness and liberal heart.
Hot, hot, and moist. This hand of yours requires
A **sequester** from liberty, fasting and prayer,
40   Much **castigation**, exercise devout;
For here's a young and sweating devil here
That commonly rebels. 'Tis a good hand,
A frank one.

DESDEMONA

          You may, indeed, say so;
45   For 'twas that hand that gave away my heart.

OTHELLO

A liberal hand!* The hearts of old gave hands;
But our new heraldry is hands, not hearts.

DESDEMONA

I cannot speak of this. Come now, your promise.

OTHELLO

What promise, chuck?

DESDEMONA

50   I have sent to bid Cassio come speak with you.

OTHELLO

I have a salt and sorry rheum offends me;
Lend me thy handkerchief.

DESDEMONA

               Here, my lord.

OTHELLO

That which I gave you.

DESDEMONA

55   I have it not about me.

---

46   *liberal* On the surface, Othello means Desdemona is generous. However, he also
is suggesting that Desdemona is too free with her favors; i.e., immoral. Othello
uses double meanings throughout the speech to hint at Desdemona's infidelity,
though she is unaware of his insinuations.

DESDEMONA
It hasn't yet felt age or known sorrow.

OTHELLO
This suggests fruitfulness and a generous heart.
Hot, hot, and moist. This hand of yours requires
a separation from the world, fasting and praying,
mortification of spirit and devout duties;   40
because I see a young, sweating devil here,
who often rebels. This is a good hand,
a frank one.

DESDEMONA
You have good reason to say so;
this was the hand that gave away my heart.   45

OTHELLO
A generous hand! In the past, hearts gave away hands.
But the new custom is to give the hands, not necessarily the
    hearts.

DESDEMONA
I don't know anything about this. Come, now, your promise!

OTHELLO
What promise do you mean, dear?

DESDEMONA
I have sent for Cassio to come and speak to you.   50

OTHELLO
I have a terrible head cold bothering me.
Lend me your handkerchief.

DESDEMONA
Here it is, my lord.

OTHELLO
I mean the one I gave you.

DESDEMONA
I don't have it with me.   55

OTHELLO

Not?

DESDEMONA

No, faith, my lord.

OTHELLO

That's a fault. That handkerchief
Did an Egyptian to my mother give;
60 She was a charmer, and could almost read
The thoughts of people. She told her, while she kept it
'Twould make her amiable and subdue my father
Entirely to her love. But if she lost it,
Or made a gift of it, my father's eye
65 Should hold her loathed and his spirits should hunt
After new fancies. She, dying, gave it me
And bid me, when my fate would have me wiv'd,
To give it her. I did so; and take heed on 't;
Make it a darling like your precious eye.
70 To lose 't or give 't away were such perdition
As nothing else could match.

DESDEMONA

Is 't possible?

OTHELLO

'Tis true; there's magic in the web of it.
A sibyl that had numb'red in the world
75 The sun to course two hundred compasses,
In her prophetic fury sew'd the work;
The worms were hallowed that did breed the silk;
And it was dy'd in mummy* which the skillful
Conserv'd of maidens' hearts.

DESDEMONA

80 Indeed! Is 't true?

OTHELLO

Most **veritable**; therefore look to 't well.

---

78 *mummy* fluids from embalmed corpses, which were supposed to have magical
powers

OTHELLO

You don't?

DESDEMONA

I really don't, my lord.

OTHELLO

That's wrong of you. That handkerchief
was given to my mother by an Egyptian.
She was a magician and could almost   60
read people's thoughts. She told her that, as long as she kept it,
it would make her desirable and cause my father
to love her completely. But if she lost it
or gave it as a gift, my father's eyes
would find her loathsome, and he'd begin   65
to seek out other women. She gave it to me when she
    was dying,
and asked me, when it came time for me to marry,
to give it to my wife. I did so; so remember what I said—
consider it as precious to you as your own eye.
If you were to lose it or give it away, that would be a loss   70
that you could never make up.

DESDEMONA

Is it possible?

OTHELLO

It's true. There's magic in the weaving of it.
A prophetess who had lived
two hundred years   75
sewed this handkerchief while she was possessed and able
    to prophesy.
The silk came from sacred worms,
and it was dyed in a liquid skillfully drained
and preserved from maidens' hearts.

DESDEMONA

Really? Is that true?   80

OTHELLO

Very true. So take good care of it.

DESDEMONA

Then would to God that I had never seen 't!

OTHELLO

Ha? Wherefore?

DESDEMONA

Why do you speak so startingly and rash?

OTHELLO

85   Is 't lost? Is 't gone? Speak, is 't out o' th' way?

DESDEMONA

Heaven bless us!

OTHELLO

Say you?

DESDEMONA

It is not lost; but what an if it were?

OTHELLO

How?

DESDEMONA

90   I say, it is not lost.

OTHELLO

Fetch 't, let me see 't.

DESDEMONA

Why, so I can, sir, but I will not now.
This is a trick to put me from my suit.
Pray you, let Cassio be receiv'd again.

OTHELLO

95   Fetch me the handkerchief. [*aside*] My mind misgives.

DESDEMONA

Come, come;
You'll never meet a more sufficient man.

OTHELLO

The handkerchief!

DESDEMONA

I pray, talk me of Cassio.

DESDEMONA
Then I wish to God I'd never seen it!

OTHELLO
What? Why is that?

DESDEMONA
Why are you speaking so angrily and abruptly?

OTHELLO
Have you lost it? Is it gone? Tell me, have you left it somewhere? 85

DESDEMONA
Heaven help us!

OTHELLO
What did you say?

DESDEMONA
It hasn't been lost. But what if it had been?

OTHELLO
What?

DESDEMONA
I tell you, it's not lost. 90

OTHELLO
Go get it; let me see it!

DESDEMONA
Well, I can do that, sir, but I won't right now.
This is just a trick to distract me from my appeal.
Please, reinstate Cassio.

OTHELLO
Get me the handkerchief! (*to himself*) I'm very mistrustful. 95

DESDEMONA
Come, come!
You'll never meet a more capable man.

OTHELLO
The handkerchief!

DESDEMONA
Please, let's talk about Cassio.

OTHELLO

100   The handkerchief!

DESDEMONA

A man that all his time
Hath founded his good fortunes on your love,
Shar'd dangers with you—

OTHELLO

The handkerchief!

DESDEMONA

105   In sooth, you are to blame.

OTHELLO

'Zounds!

OTHELLO *exits.*

EMILIA

Is not this man jealous?

DESDEMONA

I ne'er saw this before.
Sure, there's some wonder in this handkerchief;
110   I am most unhappy in the loss of it.

EMILIA

'Tis not a year or two shows us a man.
They are all but stomachs, and we all but food;
They eat us hungerly, and when they are full
They belch us.

Enter IAGO *and* CASSIO.

115   Look you—Cassio and my husband!

IAGO [*to* CASSIO]

There is no other way, 'tis she must do 't;
And, lo, the happiness! Go and importune her.

DESDEMONA

How now, good Cassio! What's the news with you?

CASSIO

Madam, my former suit. I do beseech you
120   That by your virtuous means I may again
Exist, and be a member of his love

OTHELLO

The handkerchief! 100

DESDEMONA

A man who, all his life,
has depended on your love for everything he has,
shared dangers with you—

OTHELLO

The handkerchief!

DESDEMONA

Really, you have no reason to act like this. 105

OTHELLO

Get away from me!

> OTHELLO *exits.*

EMILIA

And this man isn't jealous?

DESDEMONA

I've never seen this side of him.
There must be something magical about this handkerchief.
I'm very unlucky to have lost it. 110

EMILIA

It doesn't take a year or two to find out what a man's like.
They are only stomachs, and we are only food.
They eat us hungrily, and when they are full,
they belch us.

> IAGO *and* CASSIO *enter.*

Look, Cassio and my husband! 115

IAGO (*to* CASSIO)

There is no other way; she must be the one to do it.
And then you'll be happy! Go to her and ask her.

DESDEMONA

How are you, good Cassio? What's new with you?

CASSIO

Madam, the same appeal as before. I beg you
that, with your good help, I might 120
exist again and be one of those loved

Whom I with all the office of my heart
Entirely honour. I would not be delay'd.
If my offence be of such mortal kind
125 That nor my service past, nor present sorrows,
Nor purpos'd merit in futurity
Can ransom me into his love again,
But to know so must be my benefit;
So shall I clothe me in a forc'd content,
130 And shut myself up in some other course,
To fortune's alms.

DESDEMONA
               Alas, thrice-gentle Cassio!
My advocation is not now in tune.
My lord is not my lord; nor should I know him
135 Were he in favour as in humour alter'd.
So help me every spirit sanctified
As I have spoken for you all my best
And stood within the blank* of his displeasure
For my free speech! You must awhile be patient.
140 What I can do I will; and more I will
Than for myself I dare. Let that suffice you.

IAGO
Is my lord angry?

EMILIA
             He went hence but now,
And certainly in strange unquietness.

IAGO
145 Can he be angry? I have seen the cannon
When it hath blown his ranks into the air,
And, like the devil, from his very arm
Puff'd his own brother—and is he angry?
Something of moment then. I will go meet him.
150 There's matter in 't indeed, if he be angry.

---

138   *blank* the white bull's-eye of a target

by a man whom, with all my heart,
I deeply honor. I don't want to wait.
If my offense is of such a serious nature
that neither my past service nor my present sorrow   125
nor my promises of worthy behavior in the future
can restore me to his love again,
it would at least help me to know it.
Then I can resign myself to the situation
and accept whatever kind of life   130
fortune has in mind for me.

DESDEMONA
Oh, gentle Cassio!
My pleading won't help at the moment.
My lord is not himself; and I wouldn't recognize him
if he were as altered in looks as he is in mood.   135
I swear by every sacred spirit
that I've said everything I can for you
and found myself to be the target of his anger
because of what I frankly said! You must be patient a while.
I'll do what I can; and I'll do more   140
than I'd dare to do for myself. Please be content with that.

IAGO
Is my lord angry?

EMILIA
He left just now,
certainly very strangely agitated.

IAGO
How can he be angry? I've seen him at times when cannons   145
have blown his troops sky high
and, like some devil, blasted his own brother
standing at his arm—so can he really be angry?
There's something seriously wrong, then. I'll go meet him.
There's something very urgent, indeed, if he is angry.   150

DESDEMONA

I prithee, do so.

[*Exit* IAGO.]

Something, sure, of state,
Either from Venice, or some unhatch'd practice
Made demonstrable here in Cyprus to him,
155 Hath puddled his clear spirit; and in such cases
Men's natures wrangle with inferior things,
Though great ones are their object. 'Tis even so;
For let our finger ache, and it endues
Our other, healthful members even to a sense
160 Of pain. Nay, we must think men are not gods,
Nor of them look for such observancy
As fits the bridal. Beshrew me much, Emilia,
I was, unhandsome warrior as I am,
Arraigning his unkindness with my soul;
165 But now I find I had suborn'd the witness,
And he's **indicted** falsely.

EMILIA

Pray heaven it be
State-matters, as you think, and no conception
Nor no jealous toy concerning you.

DESDEMONA

170 Alas the day! I never gave him cause.

EMILIA

But jealous souls will not be answer'd so;
They are not ever jealous for the cause,
But jealous for they're jealous. It is a monster
Begot upon itself, born on itself.

DESDEMONA

175 Heaven keep that monster from Othello's mind!

EMILIA

Lady, amen.

DESDEMONA

I will go seek him. Cassio, walk hereabout;
If I do find him fit, I'll move your suit
And seek to effect it to my uttermost.

DESDEMONA

Please, do so. (IAGO *exits.*)
Surely some business of state,
either in Venice, or some unexecuted plot
just now revealed here in Cyprus to him,
has muddied his clear mind. In such cases,   155
it's man's nature to become obsessed with little things,
though important things are really the problem. This is the
    truth.
If one of your fingers hurts, it causes
your other healthier fingers to feel
that pain as well. No, we mustn't think that men are gods,   160
nor expect the same kind of consideration from them
that one expects from a bride. Be the first to scold me, Emilia,
since I—unsportsmanlike warrior that I am!—
thought his judgment against me was unkind of him.
Now I realize that I misunderstood him,   165
and he's been falsely accused.

EMILIA

Pray to heaven that it really is
state business, as you think, and no ideas
or jealous whims concerning you.

DESDEMONA

Heaven forbid! I never gave him cause.   170

EMILIA

But jealous minds won't take that for an answer.
They are never jealous for the apparent reason,
but they are really jealous because they are jealous. It's a
monster that creates more of itself and was born of itself.

DESDEMONA

May heaven keep that monster away from Othello's mind!   175

EMILIA

Amen to that, lady.

DESDEMONA

I'll go look for him. Cassio, stay near here.
If I find him receptive, I'll bring up your appeal
and try my best to win it for you.

CASSIO

180   I humbly thank your Ladyship.

        [Exeunt DESDEMONA *and* EMILIA.*]*

        Enter BIANCA.

BIANCA

    'Save you, friend Cassio!

CASSIO

                        What make you from home?
    How is it with you, my most fair Bianca?
    I' faith, sweet love, I was coming to your house.

BIANCA

185   And I was going to your lodging, Cassio.
    What, keep a week away? Seven days and nights,
    eightscore eight hours, and lovers' absent hours
    More tedious than the dial eightscore times?
    O weary reck'ning!

CASSIO

190   Pardon me, Bianca.
    I have this while with leaden thoughts been press'd;
    But I shall, in a more continuate time,
    Strike off this score of absence. Sweet Bianca,

        [giving her Desdemona's handkerchief]

    Take me this work out.

BIANCA

195   O Cassio, whence came this?
    This is some token from a newer friend;
    To the felt absence now I feel a cause.
    Is 't come to this? Well, well.

CASSIO

                  Go to, woman!
200   Throw your vile guesses in the devils' teeth,
    From whence you have them. You are jealous now
    That this is from some mistress, some remembrance.
    No, by my faith, Bianca.

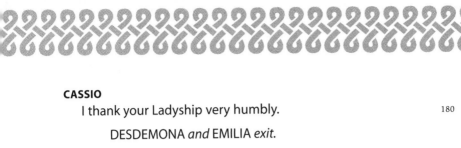

CASSIO
  I thank your Ladyship very humbly.   180

> DESDEMONA *and* EMILIA *exit.*

> BIANCA *enters.*

BIANCA
  God save you, my friend Cassio!

CASSIO
  Why are you away from home?
  How are things with you, my most lovely Bianca?
  As a matter of fact, sweet love, I was just coming to your house.

BIANCA
  And I was going to your lodging, Cassio.   185
  Why have you been away for a week? For seven days and
      nights?
  One hundred sixty-eight hours? When an hour in the absence
      of a lover
  is more tedious than a hundred sixty days?
  Oh, what tiring addition!

CASSIO
  Pardon me, Bianca.   190
  During this time, I've been weighed down by heavy thoughts;
  but, when things are better,
  I'll make up for this period of absence. Sweet Bianca,

> (*giving her Desdemona's handkerchief*)

  copy this embroidery for me.

BIANCA
  Oh, Cassio, where did you get this?   195
  This is a gift from some new friend.
  Now I know the cause of your absence.
  Has it come to this? Well, well.

CASSIO
  Go on, woman!
  Throw your wicked ideas back into the devil's teeth,   200
  where you got them in the first place. Now you're jealous
  that this is from some mistress of mine, that it's a remembrance.
  No, honestly, Bianca.

BIANCA

Why, whose is it?

CASSIO

205   I know not neither. I found it in my chamber.
I like the work well; ere it be demanded—
As like enough it will—I'd have it copied.
Take it, and do 't; and leave me for this time.

BIANCA

Leave you? Wherefore?

CASSIO

210   I do attend here on the General,
And think it no addition, nor my wish,
To have him see me woman'd.

BIANCA

Why, I pray you?

CASSIO

Not that I love you not.

BIANCA

215   But that you do not love me.
I pray you, bring me on the way a little,
And say if I shall see you soon at night.

CASSIO

'Tis but a little way that I can bring you,
For I attend here; but I'll see you soon.

BIANCA

220   'Tis very good; I must be circumstanc'd.

[*Exeunt.*]

BIANCA

Well, whose is it?

CASSIO

I don't know. I found it in my bedroom.   205
I like the embroidery very much. Before it is reclaimed,
which it probably will be, I'd like to have it copied.
Take it and do it, and leave me alone a while.

BIANCA

Leave you alone? Why?

CASSIO

I'm waiting here for the General   210
and don't think it would be to my credit, nor is it my wish,
that he should see me with a woman.

BIANCA

Why, please tell me?

CASSIO

It's not that I don't love you.

BIANCA

You seem not to love me!   215
Please walk with me a little way,
and tell me if I will see you soon at night.

CASSIO

I can only walk a little way
since I'm waiting here; but I'll see you soon.

BIANCA

That's very good. I must accept things as they are.   220

    They exit.

Act III Review

Discussion Questions

1. What is the purpose of the brief scene with the Clown and the musicians?

2. Based on what you learn in Scene iii, what kind of relationship did Cassio and Othello have before the beginning of the play?

3. In Scene iii, Iago says that "Good name in man and woman . . . / Is the immediate jewel of their souls." But in Act II, he said, "Reputation is an idle and most false imposition; oft got without merit and lost without deserving." How do you explain these contradictory statements?

4. In Othello's soliloquy in Scene iii ("This fellow's of exceeding honesty"), how does he suspect that his age, lack of sophistication, and skin color have affected his situation?

5. How does the handkerchief serve as a plot device in Act III?

6. What do Emilia's comments about men and jealousy in Scene iv tell you about her character?

7. What sort of relationship does Cassio have with Bianca?

8. What has become of Cassio's hope of appealing to Othello through Desdemona by the end of Act III?

Literary Elements

1. The addition of humor to serious plays is known as **comic relief**. The Clown, who appears in Act III, Scenes i and iv, clearly serves this function in *Othello*. And yet, some critics have pointed out that this clown is not especially funny, and that there is much less comic relief in *Othello* than in some other Shakespeare tragedies. Why do you think Shakespeare kept the mood of this play so serious?

2. In this act, Othello uses an **extended metaphor**—a drawn-out comparison of two unlike things—when he implies that Desdemona is a hawk (Scene iii, lines 289–310). Find the points of comparison and explain whether you think this metaphor is effective.

3. A **theme** is one of the main ideas in a story. One theme that gets special attention in Act III is the destructive effects of jealousy. Aside from Othello, which of the play's other characters are troubled by jealousy or envy?

4. Good drama has **conflict**: struggle between opposing forces. Find examples of both internal and external conflicts in this act.

Writing Prompts

1. In Scene ii, Othello sends a packet of letters to the Venetian Senate. Write one or more of Othello's letters, reporting on events in Cyprus.

2. List the wicked qualities that Iago attributes to all the major characters in the play—Othello, Cassio, Roderigo, and Desdemona. Do any of Iago's assumptions seem justified or realistic to you? Use a graphic organizer to sort out your thoughts. Then, using the information you have gathered, write a short essay describing Iago's view of human nature.

3. Write a step-by-step account of Othello's descent into jealousy during Scene iii. What are his feelings about Desdemona at the beginning of the scene? How have these feelings changed by the end of the scene? How has Iago managed to bring about this change?

4. Write a short story about the origins of Othello's handkerchief, based on Othello's speeches to Desdemona in Scene iv ("That handkerchief / Did an Egyptian to my mother give"). Be sure to characterize the Egyptian charmer and Othello's mother.

5. Have you or someone you know ever experienced profound jealousy? Write about the experience, relating it to events in *Othello*.

Othello

ACT IV

Orson Welles as Othello, 1953 film

"A horned man's a
monster and a beast."

✖ ✖ ✖

Before You Read

1. In Act IV, Othello will receive a message recalling him to Venice, leaving Cassio as Cyprus's governor. How do you expect this news to affect Othello's state of mind?

2. At this point in the play, what do you think it would take to convince Othello of Desdemona's innocence?

3. What is your opinion of Cassio's character? Name what you think are his virtues and faults.

4. In a typical Shakespearean tragedy, some characters die by the end of the play. Which characters in *Othello* do you expect to die? Explain.

Literary Elements

1. A **symbol** is an object that stands for or represents a more abstract concept, such as an eagle for freedom or a rose for love. The handkerchief Othello gave Desdemona is an important symbol in *Othello*.

2. **Personification** means the attribution of human characteristics to nonhuman things. In Act I, Scene iii, Othello tells Desdemona that they must obey time. Of course, time is not human and so cannot demand obedience.

3. An **allusion** is a reference to something outside the text, such as a historical, literary, biblical, or mythical figure or event. For example, in Act IV, Scene ii, Desdemona protests to Othello, "If to preserve this vessel for my lord / From any other foul unlawful touch / Be not to be a strumpet, I am none." This alludes to the Bible—1 Thessalonians 4: 4–5: "For this is the will of God . . . that ye should abstain from fornication."

Words to Know

The following vocabulary words appear in Act IV in the original text of Shakespeare's play. However, they are words that are still used today. Read the definitions here and pay attention to the words as you read the play (they will be in boldfaced type).

expostulate	demand; argue
importunes	begs; pleads
impudent	cheeky; disrespectful
insinuating	implying; suggesting
gibes	teasing; jeers
lethargy	stupor; exhaustion
palates	tastes; appetites
requite	repay; retaliate
subtle	understated; delicate
venial	forgivable; excusable

Act Summary

Iago provokes Othello's suspicions until the Moor collapses in an epileptic trance. When Othello regains consciousness, Iago promises him final proof of Desdemona's infidelity. Othello must hide nearby and overhear Iago talking with Cassio.

Othello conceals himself as Cassio arrives. Just out of Othello's earshot, Iago questions Cassio about his relationship with Bianca. Cassio replies with indecent laughter, which Othello believes to be directed at Desdemona.

At that moment, Bianca enters and returns the handkerchief to Cassio. The sight of the handkerchief convinces Othello once and for all of Desdemona's treachery. When Bianca and Cassio leave, Othello vows to kill Desdemona, and Iago to kill Cassio.

At that moment, Lodovico, a Venetian nobleman, arrives with Desdemona. Lodovico bears a letter from the Duke, recalling Othello to Venice and leaving Cassio to govern Cyprus in his place.

While Othello reads the letter, Desdemona tells Lodovico of Cassio's suit and her fondness for him. Enraged, Othello strikes her. Later, Othello accuses Desdemona of being a whore. Both she and Emilia protest her innocence, but to no avail.

Roderigo confronts Iago with a bitter grievance. Iago has long promised to make Roderigo Desdemona's lover, and Roderigo has given Iago many jewels as gifts for Desdemona. Roderigo is now penniless, but no nearer his goal.

Of course, Iago has been pocketing Roderigo's wealth all along, but he doesn't admit it. Instead, he persuades Roderigo to take decisive action by killing Cassio.

Joyce Redman as Emilia, Maggie Smith as Desdemona, and Frank Finaly as Iago, National Theatre of Great Britain, 1965

ACT IV, SCENE I

[*Cyprus before the castle.*] *Enter* OTHELLO *and* IAGO.

IAGO
Will you think so?

OTHELLO
Think so, Iago!

IAGO
What, to kiss in private?

OTHELLO
An unauthoriz'd kiss.

IAGO
5   Or to be naked with her friend in bed
An hour or more, not meaning any harm?

OTHELLO
Naked in bed, Iago, and not mean harm!
It is hypocrisy against the devil.
They that mean virtuously, and yet do so,
10   The devil their virtue tempts, and they tempt heaven.

IAGO
If they do nothing, 'tis a **venial** slip;
But if I give my wife a handkerchief—

OTHELLO
What then?

IAGO
Why, then, 'tis hers, my lord; and, being hers,
15   She may, I think, bestow 't on any man.

OTHELLO
She is protectress of her honour too;
May she give that?

IAGO
Her honour is an essence that's not seen;
They have it very oft that have it not.
20   But for the handkerchief—

ACT 4, SCENE 1

In front of the castle. OTHELLO *and* IAGO *enter.*

IAGO
Do you think so?

OTHELLO
Do I think so, Iago?

IAGO
Well, just a kiss in private?

OTHELLO
An improper kiss.

IAGO
Or maybe to be naked with her friend in bed   5
for an hour or so, but not really meaning any harm?

OTHELLO
Naked in bed, Iago, and not really meaning any harm?
They'd be putting on a show of wickedness without meaning it.
People who have virtuous intentions but act that way
will be tempted by the devil, and they will tempt heaven.   10

IAGO
Yet suppose they don't do anything; that's a forgivable sin.
But if I've given my wife a handkerchief—

OTHELLO
What then?

IAGO
Well, then, it's hers, my lord; and as long as it's hers,
she has the right, I think, to give it to any man.   15

OTHELLO
Her honor belongs to her as well.
Does she have the right to give that away?

IAGO
Her honor is a quality you cannot see.
Some seem to have it when they really don't.
But as for the handkerchief—   20

OTHELLO

By heaven, I would most gladly have forgot it.
Thou saidst—O, it comes o'er my memory
As doth the raven* o'er the infectious house,
Boding to all—he had my handkerchief.

IAGO

25   Ay, what of that?

OTHELLO

That's not so good now.

IAGO

What if I had said I had seen him do you wrong?
Or heard him say—as knaves be such abroad,
Who having, by their own importunate suit,
30   Or voluntary dotage of some mistress,
Convinced or suppli'd them, cannot choose
But they must blab—

OTHELLO

Hath he said anything?

IAGO

He hath, my lord, but be you well assur'd,
35   No more than he'll unswear.

OTHELLO

                                    What hath he said?

IAGO

Faith that he did—I know not what he did.

OTHELLO

What? What?

IAGO

Lie—

OTHELLO

40   With her?

IAGO

                        With her, on her; what you will.

---

23   *raven* an omen of death

OTHELLO

By heaven, I'd gladly have forgotten all about it!
You told me—oh, it comes over my memory
like a raven over a house of death,
boding ill to all!—that he had my handkerchief.

IAGO

Yes, what of it? 25

OTHELLO

That's not so good now.

IAGO

What if I were to tell you that I had seen him do you wrong?
Or heard him say—since there are such rascals around,
who once they have succeeded, by means of their persistence
or by the weakness of will of some lady, 30
in seducing and satisfying them, can't help it
but they have to blab—

OTHELLO

Has he said anything?

IAGO

He has, my lord; but you can be very sure
that he'll unsay everything. 35

OTHELLO

What has he said?

IAGO

To tell the truth, that he did—I don't know what he did.

OTHELLO

What? What?

IAGO

Lie—

OTHELLO

With her? 40

IAGO

With her, on her; what you will.

OTHELLO

Lie with her! Lie on her! We say "lie on her" when they
belie her. Lie with her! 'Zounds, that's fulsome!
Handkerchief—confessions—handkerchief!—To confess
45 and be hang'd for his labour—first to be hang'd, and then
to confess.—I tremble at it. Nature would not invest
herself in such shadowing passion without some
instruction. It is not words that shakes me thus. Pish!
Noses, ears, and lips.—Is 't possible?—Confess—
50 handkerchief—O devil! [*Falls in a trance.*]

IAGO

Work on,
My medicine, work! Thus credulous fools are caught;
And many worthy and chaste dames even thus,
All guiltless, meet reproach.—What, ho! My lord!
55 My lord, I say! Othello!

       Enter CASSIO.

                     How now, Cassio!

CASSIO

What's the matter?

IAGO

My lord is fall'n into an epilepsy.
This is his second fit; he had one yesterday.

CASSIO

60 Rub him about the temples.

IAGO

                  No, forbear;
The **lethargy** must have his quiet course;
If not, he foams at mouth and by and by
Breaks out to savage madness. Look, he stirs.
65 Do you withdraw yourself a little while;
He will recover straight. When he is gone,
I would on great occasion speak with you.

      [*Exit* CASSIO.]

How is it, General? Have you not hurt your head?

OTHELLO

Lie with her? Lie on her? We say this while she continues to
seem innocent. Lie with her! By God, that's repulsive.—
Handkerchief—confessions—handkerchief!—He should
confess and be hanged for this deed—hanged first, and   45
confess later! It makes me tremble. I wouldn't be so angered
by this if there weren't some truth in it. It isn't just the words
themselves that make me shake like this. What! Noses, ears,
and lips? Is it possible?—Confess?—Handkerchief?—Oh, devil!   50

(*He falls into a trance.*)

IAGO

Keep working,
my medicine, keep working! This is how gullible fools are
    caught
and how many worthy and chaste women,
all guiltless, wind up accused.—What is it? My lord!
My lord, listen! Othello!   55

CASSIO *enters.*

What is it, Cassio?

CASSIO

What's the matter?

IAGO

My lord has fallen into an epileptic seizure.
This is his second one; he had one yesterday.

CASSIO

Rub his temples.   60

IAGO

No, don't do that.
This coma must run its course quietly.
If it doesn't, he'll foam at the mouth, and soon
he'll explode into savage madness. Look, he's stirring.
Step out of the way for a little while.   65
He'll recover soon. When he's gone,
I need to talk to you about something very important.

CASSIO *exits.*

How are you, General? Have you hurt your head?

OTHELLO

Dost thou mock me?*

IAGO

70   I mock you not, by heaven.
Would you would bear your fortune like a man!

OTHELLO

A horned man's a monster and a beast.

IAGO

There's many a beast then in a populous city,
And many a civil monster.

OTHELLO

75   Did he confess it?

IAGO

                          Good sir, be a man,
Think every bearded fellow that's but yok'd
May draw with you. There's millions now alive
That nightly lie in those unproper beds
80   Which they dare swear peculiar; your case is better.
O, 'tis the spite of hell, the fiend's arch-mock,
To lip a wanton in a secure couch,
And to suppose her chaste! No, let me know;
And knowing what I am, I know what she shall be.

OTHELLO

85   O, thou art wise; 'tis certain.

IAGO

Stand you a while apart;
Confine yourself but in a patient list.
Whilst you were here o'erwhelmed with your grief—
A passion most unsuiting such a man—
90   Cassio came hither. I shifted him away,
And laid good 'scuses upon your ecstasy;
Bade him anon return and here speak with me,
The which he promis'd. Do but encave yourself,

---

69   *Dost thou mock me?* Othello believes that Iago mocks him by referring to this
proverbial cuckold's horns.

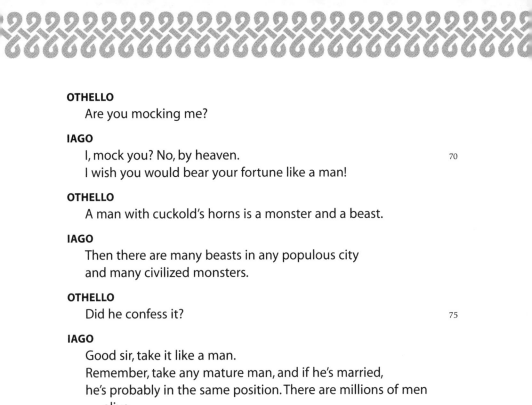

OTHELLO

Are you mocking me?

IAGO

I, mock you? No, by heaven.   70

I wish you would bear your fortune like a man!

OTHELLO

A man with cuckold's horns is a monster and a beast.

IAGO

Then there are many beasts in any populous city

and many civilized monsters.

OTHELLO

Did he confess it?   75

IAGO

Good sir, take it like a man.

Remember, take any mature man, and if he's married,

he's probably in the same position. There are millions of men
    alive

who go to beds every night that are not solely their own,

which they'll insist are theirs alone. Your case is better.   80

Oh, it's a curse of hell, the supreme mockery of fiends,

to kiss a wanton woman in a carefree bed

and imagine her to be chaste! No, I'd rather know the truth;

and as long as I know what I am, I'll know what she is, too.

OTHELLO

Oh, you are wise! That's certain.   85

IAGO

Step aside for a while;

contain yourself within the bounds of patience.

While you were lying here, overwhelmed with your grief—

in a fit most unworthy of a man like yourself—

Cassio came along. I got him away on some pretext   90

and came up with a good excuse for the trance you were in.

I told him to come back soon and to speak with me here;

he promised that he would. Go hide yourself

And mark the fleers, the **gibes**, and notable scorns
95 That dwell in every region of his face;
For I will make him tell the tale anew,
Where, how, how oft, how long ago, and when
He hath and is again to cope your wife.
I say, but make his gesture. Marry, patience,
100 Or I shall say you're all in all in spleen,
And nothing of a man.

OTHELLO

Dost thou hear, Iago?
I will be found most cunning in my patience;
But—dost thou hear?—most bloody.

IAGO

105   That's not amiss;
But yet keep time in all. Will you withdraw?

[OTHELLO *retires.*]

Now will I question Cassio of Bianca,
A huswife that by selling her desires
Buys herself bread and clothes. It is a creature
110 That dotes on Cassio, as 'tis the strumpet's plague
To beguile many and be beguil'd by one.
He, when he hears of her, cannot restrain
From the excess of laughter. Here he comes.

Reenter CASSIO.

As he shall smile, Othello shall go mad;
115 And his unbookish jealousy must construe
Poor Cassio's smiles, gestures, and light behaviours
Quite in the wrong.—How do you, Lieutenant?

CASSIO

The worser that you give me the addition
Whose want even kills me.

IAGO

120 Ply Desdemona well, and you are sure on 't.
[*speaking lower*] Now, if this suit lay in Bianca's power.
How quickly should you speed!

and observe the sneers, the contempt, and the obvious scorn
which you can see all over his face.   95
I'll make him tell the story all over again—
where, how, how often, how long ago, and when
he has, and will again, encounter your wife.
I tell you, just watch how he acts. Please, be patient!
Or I'll have to conclude that you're overwhelmed by rage   100
and not a man at all.

OTHELLO

Do you hear me, Iago?
I will prove to be very cleverly patient
but—do you hear me?—very vengeful.

IAGO

That's quite appropriate;   105
but still, think before you act. Won't you hide yourself?

(OTHELLO *hides himself.*)

Now I'll ask Cassio about Bianca,
a hussy who, by selling herself to him,
buys herself bread and clothes. She's a creature
who loves Cassio. It's the typical curse of whores   110
to gain the love of many men and only love one.
When a man hears about her love, he can't help
but laugh uncontrollably. Here he comes.

CASSIO *enters.*

When he smiles, Othello will go mad;
and his naive jealousy will interpret   115
poor Cassio's smiles, gestures, and frivolous behavior
quite the wrong way. How are you doing, Lieutenant?

CASSIO

All the worse since you call me by that title,
the lack of which is killing me.

IAGO

Work on Desdemona well, and you're sure to get it back.   120
(*speaking lower*) Now if this appeal were something Bianca
    had charge of,
everything would be taken care of quickly!

Act 4, Scene 1   231

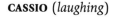

CASSIO (*laughing*)

Alas, poor caitiff!

OTHELLO

Look how he laughs already!

IAGO

125   I never knew woman love man so.

CASSIO

Alas, poor rogue! I think, i' faith, she loves me.

OTHELLO

Now he denies it faintly and laughs it out.

IAGO

Do you hear, Cassio?

OTHELLO

Now he **importunes** him

130   To tell it o'er. Go to; well said, well said.

IAGO

She gives it out that you shall marry her.
Do you intend it?

CASSIO

Ha, ha, ha!

OTHELLO

Do ye triumph, Roman? Do you triumph?

CASSIO

135   I marry her!! What? A customer? Prithee, bear some
charity to my wit; do not think it so unwholesome. Ha,
ha, ha!

OTHELLO

So, so, so, so; they laugh that wins.

IAGO

Faith, the cry goes that you marry her.

CASSIO

140   Prithee, say true.

CASSIO (*laughing*)
Oh, the poor wretch!

OTHELLO
Look! He's laughing already!

IAGO
I never knew a woman to be so in love with a man.   125

CASSIO
Oh, the poor rascal! I really do believe she loves me.

OTHELLO
Now he's feebly denying it and laughing about it.

IAGO
Haven't you heard, Cassio?

OTHELLO
Now he's begging him
to tell it over again. Go on! Well said, well said!   130

IAGO
She's spreading it around that you're going to marry her.
Do you really intend to?

CASSIO
Ha, ha, ha!

OTHELLO
Are you gloating, conqueror? Are you gloating?

CASSIO
I, marry her? What, a prostitute? Please give me credit for some   135
intelligence; don't think I'm that stupid. Ha, ha, ha!

OTHELLO
So, so, so, so. Let the winner laugh!

IAGO
Really, rumor has it that you will marry her.

CASSIO
Come, tell the truth.   140

IAGO

I am a very villain else.

OTHELLO

Have you scor'd me? Well.

CASSIO

This is the monkey's own giving out. She is persuaded I
will marry her out of her own love and flattery, not out of
145   my promise.

OTHELLO

Iago beckons me; now he begins the story.

CASSIO

She was here even now; she haunts me in every place. I
was the other day talking on the sea-bank with certain
Venetians; and thither comes the bauble. By this hand
150   she falls thus about my neck—

OTHELLO

Crying, "O dear Cassio!" as it were; his gesture imports it.

CASSIO

So hangs and lolls and weeps upon me, so shakes and
pulls me. Ha, ha, ha!

OTHELLO

Now he tells how she pluck'd him to my chamber.—Oh,
155   I see that nose of yours, but not that dog I shall throw it to.

CASSIO

Well, I must leave her company.

IAGO

Before me! Look, where she comes.

    Enter BIANCA.

CASSIO

'Tis such another fitchew!* Marry, a perfum'd one.—What
do you mean by this haunting of me?

BIANCA

160   Let the devil and his dam haunt you! What did you mean
by that same handkerchief you gave me even now? I was a

---

158   *fitchew* or a polecat, a strong-smelling animal

IAGO

I'm a true villain otherwise.

OTHELLO

Have you branded me? Well.

CASSIO

This is the monkey's own idea. Out of her own love and vanity, she thinks that I'll marry her, not because of any promise I've made.   145

OTHELLO

Iago's signaling me. Now Cassio's starting the story.

CASSIO

She was here just now; she follows me everywhere. The other day I was talking on the sea bank with some Venetians, and there came this little plaything and threw her arms around my neck—   150

OTHELLO

Crying, "Oh, dear Cassio!" as it were. His gestures say as much.

CASSIO

She hangs and droops and weeps all over me; she calls and pulls at me. Ha, ha, ha!

OTHELLO

Now he's telling how she took him to my bedroom. Oh, I see that nose of yours but not yet the dog I'll throw it to.   155

CASSIO

Well, I must get rid of her company.

IAGO

Well look! Here she comes.

> BIANCA *enters.*

CASSIO

What a polecat!—though she tries to hide it. What are you doing, chasing after me?

BIANCA

Let the devil and his mother chase you! What was the idea,   160
giving me that handkerchief just now? I was a fine fool to

fine fool to take it! I must take out the work? A likely
piece of work, that you should find it in your chamber,
and know not who left it there! This is some minx's token,
165 and I must take out the work? There, give it your hobbyhorse.
Wheresoever you had it, I'll take out no work on 't.

CASSIO
How now, my sweet Bianca? How now? How now?

OTHELLO
By heaven, that should be my handkerchief!

BIANCA
If you'll come to supper tonight, you may; if you will not,
170 come when you are next prepar'd for.

[*Exit.*]

IAGO
After her, after her.

CASSIO
Faith, I must; she'll rail in the streets else.

IAGO
Will you sup there?

CASSIO
Faith, I intend so.

IAGO
175 Well, I may chance to see you, for I would very fain speak
with you.

CASSIO
Prithee, come. Will you?

IAGO
Go to; say no more.

[*Exit* CASSIO.]

OTHELLO [*advancing*]
How shall I murder him, Iago?

take it. I'm supposed to copy the embroidery? A likely story that
you found it in your bedroom and don't know who left it
there! Some hussy gave it to you, and I'm supposed to copy
the embroidery? There! Give it to your whore. Wherever it   165
came from, I'm not copying the embroidery.

CASSIO
What is this, my sweet Bianca? What is this? What is this?

OTHELLO
By heaven, that looks like my handkerchief!

BIANCA
If you want to come to supper tonight, you may. If you don't, then
come back again when you're invited, which may be never.   170

> BIANCA *exits.*

IAGO
After her, after her!

CASSIO
Really, I'd better; she'll be yelling in the streets otherwise.

IAGO
Will you have supper there?

CASSIO
Yes, I intend to.

IAGO
Well, I might see you; for I am really eager to talk to you.   175

CASSIO
Please come. Will you?

IAGO
Certainly! Say no more.

> CASSIO *exits.*

OTHELLO (*coming forward*)
How shall I murder him, Iago?

IAGO

180 Did you perceive how he laugh'd at his vice?

OTHELLO

O Iago!

IAGO

And did you see the handkerchief?

OTHELLO

Was that mine?

IAGO

Yours, by this hand. And to see how he prizes the foolish
185 woman your wife! She gave it him, and he hath giv'n it
his whore.

OTHELLO

I would have him nine years a-killing. A fine woman! A
fair woman! A sweet woman!

IAGO

Nay, you must forget that.

OTHELLO

190 Ay, let her rot and perish and be damn'd tonight; for she
shall not live. No, my heart is turn'd to stone; I strike it,
and it hurts my hand. O, the world hath not a sweeter
creature! She might lie by an emperor's side and
command him tasks.

IAGO

195 Nay, that's not your way.

OTHELLO

Hang her! I do but say what she is. So delicate with her
needle! An admirable musician! O! She will sing the
savageness out of a bear. Of so high and plenteous wit
and invention!

IAGO

200 She's the worse for all this.

OTHELLO

O, a thousand, a thousand times! And then, of so gentle a
condition!

IAGO

Did you see how he laughed at his sin? 180

OTHELLO

Oh, Iago!

IAGO

And did you see the handkerchief?

OTHELLO

Was that mine?

IAGO

Yours, I swear! And look how much he values that foolish
woman, your wife! She gave it to him, and he's given it to his 185
whore.

OTHELLO

I wish I could spend nine years killing him!
A fine woman! A lovely woman! A sweet woman!

IAGO

No, you must forget all that.

OTHELLO

Yes, let her rot and perish and be damned tonight, for she's 190
not going to live. No, my heart has been turned to stone: when
I strike it, it hurts my hand. Oh, there's not a sweeter creature
in the world! She could lie beside an emperor and give him
commands.

IAGO

No, that's not the right attitude. 195

OTHELLO

Hang her! I'm only saying what she's like. So skillful with her
needle! An admirable musician! Oh, she could sing the
savageness right out of a bear! Such lofty and abundant
intelligence and imagination!

IAGO

She's all the worse because of this. 200

OTHELLO

Oh, a thousand, thousand times! And then she has such a
gentle temperament!

IAGO

Ay, too gentle.

OTHELLO

Nay, that's certain. But yet the pity of it, Iago! O Iago, the
205   pity of it, Iago!

IAGO

If you are so fond over her iniquity, give her patent to
offend; for if it touch not you, it comes near nobody.

OTHELLO

I will chop her into messes! Cuckold me?

IAGO

O, 'tis foul in her.

OTHELLO

210   With mine officer!

IAGO

That's fouler.

OTHELLO

Get me some poison, Iago, this night. I'll not **expostulate**
with her, lest her body and beauty unprovide my mind
again. This night, Iago.

IAGO

215   Do it not with poison; strangle her in her bed, even the
bed she hath contaminated.

OTHELLO

Good, good; the justice of it pleases. Very good.

IAGO

And for Cassio, let me be his undertaker. You shall hear
more by midnight.

OTHELLO

220   Excellent good. [*A trumpet.*]
                            What trumpet is that same?

IAGO

I warrant something from Venice.

> *Enter* LODOVICO, DESDEMONA, *and*
> ATTENDANTS.

IAGO

Yes, too gentle.

OTHELLO

Yes, that's for certain. But what a pity, Iago! Oh, Iago, what a
pity, Iago!   205

IAGO

If you're going to be so foolish about her crime, why don't
you give her a license to sin? If it doesn't bother you, it won't
bother anyone.

OTHELLO

I'll chop her up in little bits! Cuckold me!

IAGO

Oh, it's evil of her.

OTHELLO

With my officer!   210

IAGO

That's even worse.

OTHELLO

Get some poison for me tonight, Iago. I won't discuss this with
her for fear that her body and beauty might weaken my
resolve again. Tonight, Iago!

IAGO

Don't do it with poison. Strangle her in her bed, the very bed   215
she has contaminated.

OTHELLO

Good, good! The justice of that pleases me. Very good!

IAGO

As for Cassio, let me take care of him. You'll know more by
midnight.

OTHELLO

Very good! (*A trumpet blows offstage.*)   220
What was that trumpet?

IAGO

Surely someone from Venice.

LODOVICO, DESDEMONA, *and* ATTENDANTS *enter.*

'Tis Lodovico. This comes from the Duke.
See, your wife's with him.

LODOVICO
225   God save you, worthy general!

OTHELLO
With all my heart, sir.

LODOVICO [*Gives him a letter.*]
The Duke and the Senators of Venice greet you.

OTHELLO
I kiss the instrument of their pleasures. [*Opens the letter
and reads.*]

DESDEMONA
And what's the news, good cousin Lodovico?

IAGO
230   I am very glad to see you, signior;
Welcome to Cyprus.

LODOVICO
I thank you. How does Lieutenant Cassio?

IAGO
Lives, sir.

DESDEMONA
Cousin, there's fall'n between him and my lord
235   An unkind breach; but you shall make all well.

OTHELLO
Are you sure of that?

DESDEMONA
My lord?

OTHELLO [*Reads.*]
"This fail you not to do, as you will."—

LODOVICO
He did not call; he's busy in the paper.
240   Is there division 'twixt my lord and Cassio?

It's Lodovico; he's come from the Duke.
Look, your wife's with him.

LODOVICO
God save you, worthy general!   225

OTHELLO
I welcome you with all my heart, sir.

LODOVICO (*giving* OTHELLO *a letter*)
The Duke and senators of Venice send greetings.

OTHELLO
I kiss this letter. (*He opens the letter and reads it.*)

DESDEMONA
So what's the news, good cousin Lodovico?

IAGO
I am very glad to see you, signior.   230
Welcome to Cyprus.

LODOVICO
Thank you. How's Lieutenant Cassio doing?

IAGO
He lives, sir.

DESDEMONA
Cousin, there has occurred between him and my lord
an unfortunate quarrel. But you will make all that well.   235

OTHELLO
Are you sure of that?

DESDEMONA
My lord?

OTHELLO (*reading*)
"Don't fail to do this, as soon as you can—"

LODOVICO
He wasn't speaking to you; he's busy with his letter.
Has there been a falling out between my lord and Cassio?   240

DESDEMONA

A most unhappy one. I would do much
T' atone them, for the love I bear to Cassio.

OTHELLO

Fire and brimstone!

DESDEMONA

My lord?

OTHELLO

245   Are you wise?

DESDEMONA

What, is he angry?

LODOVICO

May be the letter mov'd him;
For, as I think, they do command him home,
Deputing Cassio in his government.

DESDEMONA

250   By my troth, I am glad on 't.

OTHELLO

Indeed!

DESDEMONA

My lord?

OTHELLO

I am glad to see you mad.

DESDEMONA

Why, sweet Othello—

OTHELLO [*striking her*]

255   Devil!

DESDEMONA

I have not deserv'd this.

LODOVICO

My lord, this would not be believ'd in Venice,
Though I should swear I saw 't. 'Tis very much.
Make her amends: she weeps.

DESDEMONA
A very unfortunate one. I'd do a great deal
to reconcile them because of the love I feel for Cassio.

OTHELLO
Fire and brimstone!

DESDEMONA
My lord?

OTHELLO
Are you sane?   245

DESDEMONA
What, is he angry?

LODOVICO
Maybe the letter has upset him.
I think they have commanded him to go home
and turn his position over to Cassio.

DESDEMONA
Well really, I'm glad to hear it.   250

OTHELLO
Indeed?

DESDEMONA
My lord?

OTHELLO
I'm glad to see you've gone mad.

DESDEMONA
Why, sweet Othello!

OTHELLO (*striking her*)
Devil!   255

DESDEMONA
I've done nothing to deserve this.

LODOVICO
My lord, no one would believe this in Venice,
even if I swore I saw it. This is too much.
Apologize to her; she's weeping.

OTHELLO

260   O devil, devil!
If that the earth could teem with woman's tears,
Each drop she falls would prove a crocodile.*
Out of my sight!

DESDEMONA

                         I will not stay to offend you. [*going*]

LODOVICO

265   Truly, an obedient lady:
I do beseech your Lordship, call her back.

OTHELLO

Mistress!

DESDEMONA

My lord?

OTHELLO

What would you with her, sir?

LODOVICO

270   Who, I, my lord?

OTHELLO

Ay, you did wish that I would make her turn.
Sir, she can turn, and turn, and yet go on,
And turn again; and she can weep, sir, weep;
And she's obedient, as you say, obedient.

275   Very obedient. —Proceed you in your tears.—
Concerning this, sir—O well-painted passion!—
I am commanded home.—Get you away;
I'll send for you anon.—Sir, I obey the mandate
And will return to Venice.—Hence, avaunt!—

      [*Exit* DESDEMONA.]

280   Cassio shall have my place. And, sir, tonight
I do entreat that we may sup together.
You are welcome, sir, to Cyprus. Goats and monkeys!

      [*Exit.*]

---

262   *crocodile* According to legend, crocodiles wept false tears to entrap prey.

OTHELLO

Oh, devil, devil! 260

If the earth could be sown by a woman's tears,

every drop that falls from her eyes would become a crocodile.

Out of my sight!

DESDEMONA

I won't stay to offend you. (*starting to go*)

LODOVICO

Really, she's an obedient lady. 265

I beg your Lordship to call her back.

OTHELLO

Lady!

DESDEMONA

My lord?

OTHELLO

What do you want with her, sir?

LODOVICO

Who? I, my lord? 270

OTHELLO

Yes! You wanted me to make her turn back.

Sir, she can twist and turn and yet keep moving ahead

and continue to deceive you. And she can weep, sir, weep.

And she's obedient; just as you said, obedient,

very obedient. (*to* DESDEMONA) Go ahead and cry. 275

(*to* LODOVICO) Concerning this letter, sir. (*to* DESDEMONA) Oh,

well-acted grief!

(*to* LODOVICO) I've been commanded home. (*to* DESDEMONA)

Go away;

I'll send for you soon. (*to* LODOVICO) Sir, I'll obey this command

and go back to Venice. (*to* DESDEMONA) Go, get away from me!

DESDEMONA *exits.*

Cassio will take my place. And, sir, tonight 280

I hope we can have supper together.

Sir, you are welcome to Cyprus.—Goats and monkeys!

OTHELLO *exits.*

LODOVICO

    Is this the noble Moor whom our full senate

    Call all in all sufficient? Is this the nature

285   Whom passion could not shake? Whose solid virtue

    The shot of accident nor dart of chance

    Could neither graze nor pierce?

IAGO

                           He is much chang'd.

LODOVICO

    Are his wits safe? Is he not light of brain?

IAGO

290   He's that he is; I may not breathe my censure

    What he might be. If what he might he is not,

    I would to heaven he were!

LODOVICO

                      What, strike his wife!

IAGO

    'Faith, that was not so well; yet would I knew

295   That stroke would prove the worst!

LODOVICO

                          Is it his use?

    Or did the letters work upon his blood

    And new-create this fault?

IAGO

                  Alas, alas!

300   It is not honesty in me to speak

    What I have seen and known. You shall observe him,

    And his own courses will denote him so

    That I may save my speech. Do but go after

    And mark how he continues.

LODOVICO

305   I am sorry that I am deceiv'd in him.

    [Exeunt.]

LODOVICO

Is this the same noble Moor whom our senate unanimously
called completely capable? Is this the man
who could not be shaken by anger? Whose solid virtue   285
an accidental shot or a chance arrow
could neither graze nor pierce?

IAGO

He is much changed.

LODOVICO

Is his mind all right? Has he gone mad?

IAGO

He's what he seems to be. I mustn't pass judgment.   290
The man he could be—if he is not such a man—
I wish to heaven he really were!

LODOVICO

And he struck his wife?

IAGO

Really, that wasn't so good; yet I wish I knew
that blow would prove to be his worst action.   295

LODOVICO

Is he usually like this?
Or did the letter make him angry
and just create this fault?

IAGO

Oh, no, no!
It would not be honorable of me to speak   300
of the things I've seen and known. Observe him for yourself,
and his own actions will tell you enough about him
so that I can remain silent. Just follow him
and watch what he does.

LODOVICO

I'm sorry that I was wrong about him.   305

They exit.

ACT IV, SCENE II

[*A room in the castle.*] *Enter* OTHELLO *and* EMILIA.

OTHELLO
You have seen nothing then?

EMILIA
Nor ever heard, nor ever did suspect.

OTHELLO
Yes, you have seen Cassio and she together.

EMILIA
But then I saw no harm, and then I heard
5   Each syllable that breath made up between them.

OTHELLO
What, did they never whisper?

EMILIA
                      Never, my lord.

OTHELLO
Nor send you out o' th' way?

EMILIA
Never.

OTHELLO
10   To fetch her fan, her gloves, her mask,* nor nothing?

EMILIA
Never, my lord.

OTHELLO
That's strange.

EMILIA
I durst, my lord, to wager she is honest,
Lay down my soul at stake. If you think other,
15   Remove your thought; it doth abuse your bosom.
If any wretch have put this in your head,
Let heaven **requite** it with the serpent's curse!*

---

10 *mask* In public, some Elizabethan women wore masks.

17 *serpent's curse* the curse God laid on the serpent who tempted Eve in the Garden of Eden

ACT 4, SCENE 2

Inside the castle. OTHELLO *and* EMILIA *enter.*

OTHELLO
You haven't seen anything, then?

EMILIA
Nor ever heard or even suspected anything.

OTHELLO
Yes, but you have seen Cassio and her together.

EMILIA
But I saw no harm in it, and I heard
every syllable that they said to each other.   5

OTHELLO
What, didn't they ever whisper?

EMILIA
Never, my lord.

OTHELLO
Nor tell you to go away?

EMILIA
Never.

OTHELLO
To get her fan, her gloves, her mask, or some other trifle?   10

EMILIA
Never, my lord.

OTHELLO
That's strange.

EMILIA
My lord, I would dare wager that she is faithful—
I'd bet my very soul on that. If you think otherwise,
then get that thought out of your head; it troubles you to no   15
    purpose.
If some villain has put this idea in your head,
let heaven repay him with the curse laid on the serpent!

For, if she be not honest, chaste, and true,
There's no man happy; the purest of their wives
20   Is foul as slander.

OTHELLO
                                    Bid her come hither. Go.

[*Exit* EMILIA.]

She says enough; yet she's a simple bawd
That cannot say as much. This is a **subtle** whore,
A closet lock and key of villainous secrets;
25   And yet she'll kneel and pray; I have seen her do 't.

                    Enter DESDEMONA *with* EMILIA.

DESDEMONA
My lord, what is your will?

OTHELLO
Pray you, chuck, come hither.

DESDEMONA
                                    What is your pleasure?

OTHELLO
Let me see your eyes;
30   Look in my face.

DESDEMONA
What horrible fancy's this?

OTHELLO [*to* EMILIA]
Some of your function, mistress;
Leave procreants alone, and shut the door;
Cough, or cry "hem" if anybody come.
35   Your mystery, your mystery!* Nay, dispatch.

                    [*Exit* EMILIA.]

32–35 *Some of your function . . . mystery!* Othello is suggesting that Desdemona is a
prostitute and Emilia her procurer.

If she isn't faithful, chaste, and true,
there's not a lucky man in the world; the most innocent of
    wives
is as wicked as any rumor says.   20

OTHELLO
Tell her to come here. Go.

      EMILIA *exits.*

What she says sounds good; yet it would be a stupid brothel
    keeper
who couldn't make up such a story. This is a sly whore,
a locked room and key with all kinds of villainous secrets;
but still, she kneels and prays; I've seen her do it.   25

      DESDEMONA *and* EMILIA *enter.*

DESDEMONA
My lord, what do you wish?

OTHELLO
Please, my dear, come here.

DESDEMONA
What do you desire?

OTHELLO
Let me see your eyes.
Look at my face.   30

DESDEMONA
What horrible ideas do you have?

OTHELLO (*to* EMILIA)
See to your duty, madam.
Leave the lovers alone, and shut the door;
cough or cry "ahem" if anybody comes.
Your trade, your trade! Come on, get to it!   35

      EMILIA *exits.*

DESDEMONA [*kneeling*]
Upon my knees, what doth your speech import?
I understand a fury in your words,
But not the words.

OTHELLO
Why, what art thou?

DESDEMONA
40 Your wife, my lord; your true
and loyal wife.

OTHELLO
Come, swear it, damn thyself,
Lest, being like one of heaven, the devils themselves
Should fear to seize thee; therefore be double damn'd,
45 Swear thou art honest.

DESDEMONA
                              Heaven doth truly know it.

OTHELLO
Heaven truly knows that thou art false as hell.

DESDEMONA [*standing*]
To whom, my lord? With whom? How am I false?

OTHELLO
Ah, Desdemona! Away, away! Away!

DESDEMONA
50 Alas the heavy day! Why do you weep?
Am I the motive of these tears, my lord?
If haply you my father do suspect
An instrument of this your calling back,
Lay not your blame on me. If you have lost him,
55 I have lost him too.

OTHELLO
                              Had it pleas'd heaven
To try me with affliction; had they rain'd
All kind of sores and shames on my bare head,
Steep'd me in poverty to the very lips,
60 Given to captivity me and my utmost hopes,
I should have found in some place of my soul

DESDEMONA (*kneeling*)
I ask you on my knees, what did you mean by that?
I understood the fury in your words,
but not the words themselves.

OTHELLO
Tell me, what are you?

DESDEMONA
Your wife, my lord; your true   40
and loyal wife.

OTHELLO
Come, swear it, and damn yourself
for fear that, since you look like an angel, the devils themselves
will be afraid to seize you. So damn yourself a second time—
swear you are faithful.   45

DESDEMONA
Heaven truly knows I am.

OTHELLO
Heaven truly knows that you are as unfaithful as hell.

DESDEMONA (*standing*)
To whom, my lord? With whom? How am I unfaithful?

OTHELLO
Ah, Desdemona! Get away from me! Away! Away!

DESDEMONA
Oh, what a sad day! Why are you weeping?   50
Am I the cause of these tears, my lord?
If you perhaps suspect that my father
might have had something to do with your recall,
don't blame me for it. If you have lost his affection,
then I have lost it too.   55

OTHELLO
Had it been heaven's wish
to persecute me with illness, if it had rained
all kinds of sores and shames on my bare head,
buried me in poverty up to the lips,
or given me and my highest hopes over to captivity,   60
I would have found in some part of my soul

A drop of patience; but alas, to make me
A fixed figure for the time of scorn
To point his slow and unmoving finger at!
65   Yet could I bear that too, well, very well.
But there, where I have garner'd up my heart,
Where either I must live or bear no life;
The fountain from the which my current runs
Or else dries up—to be discarded thence!
70   Or keep it as a cistern for foul toads
To knot and gender in! Turn thy complexion there,
Patience, thou young and rose-lipp'd cherubin,
Ay, there look grim as hell!

DESDEMONA
I hope my noble lord esteems me honest.

OTHELLO
75   O, ay, as summer flies are in the shambles,
That quicken even with blowing. O thou weed,
Who art so lovely fair and smell'st so sweet
That the sense aches at thee, would thou hadst ne'er been
    born!

DESDEMONA
80   Alas, what ignorant sin have I committed?

OTHELLO
Was this fair paper, this most goodly book,
Made to write "whore" upon? What committed?
Committed? O thou public commoner!
I should make very forges of my cheeks,
85   That would to cinders burn up modesty,
Did I but speak thy deeds. What committed?
Heaven stops the nose at it, and the moon winks;
The bawdy wind, that kisses all it meets
Is hush'd within the hollow mine of earth*
90   And will not hear it. What committed?
Impudent strumpet!

DESDEMONA
By heaven, you do me wrong.

---

89   *hollow mine of earth* The winds were assumed to originate in the hollow interior
of the earth.

a drop of patience. But to turn me into
a kind of target for scornful time
to point his slowly moving finger at!
Yet I could bear that too; and well, very well.   65
But that place where I have gathered up my heart,
that place that gives me reason to live or not live at all,
that fountain from which my life flows
or else dries up—to be driven away from there,
or to have it used as a reservoir for horrible toads   70
to churn and mate in, that would even turn
Patience, that young and rosy-lipped angel, pale!
This makes me grim as hell!

DESDEMONA

My noble lord, I hope you think me faithful.

OTHELLO

Oh, yes! Just like flies near a slaughterhouse,   75
which conceive even while they lay their eggs. Oh, you weed,
who are so beautifully lovely and smell so sweet
that you make the senses ache, I wish you'd never been born!

DESDEMONA

Oh, what kind of sin have I unknowingly committed?   80

OTHELLO

Was this fine paper, this handsome book,
made to write "whore" upon? What have you committed?
Committed? Oh, you common whore!
It would make my cheeks into furnaces
to burn up modesty into cinders   85
if I even spoke of your deeds. What have you committed?
Heaven holds its nose at it, and the moon closes its eyes;
the promiscuous wind, which kisses everything it meets,
hides itself inside the earth
and refuses to hear of it. What have you committed?   90
You impudent harlot!

DESDEMONA

By God, you do me wrong.

OTHELLO

Are not you a strumpet?

DESDEMONA

No, as I am a Christian.

95   If to preserve this vessel for my lord

From any other foul unlawful touch

Be not to be a strumpet, I am none.

OTHELLO

What, not a whore?

DESDEMONA

No, as I shall be sav'd.

OTHELLO

100   Is 't possible?

DESDEMONA

O, heaven forgive us!

OTHELLO

                  I cry you mercy, then.

I took you for that cunning whore of Venice

That married with Othello. [*raising his voice*] You, mistress,

    Reenter EMILIA.

105   That have the office opposite to Saint Peter

And keeps the gate of hell! You, you, ay, you!

We have done our course; there's money for your pains.

I pray you, turn the key and keep our counsel.

    [*Exit.*]

EMILIA

Alas, what does this gentleman conceive?

110   How do you, madam? How do you, my good lady?

DESDEMONA

Faith, half asleep.

EMILIA

Good madam, what's the matter with my lord?

DESDEMONA

With who?

OTHELLO

Are you not a harlot?

DESDEMONA

No, I swear to you as I am a Christian!
If keeping this body for my lord   95
from any other wicked, improper touch
means not to be a harlot, then I am not one.

OTHELLO

What, you're not a whore?

DESDEMONA

No, I swear by my salvation!

OTHELLO

Is it possible?   100

DESDEMONA

Oh, heaven help us!

OTHELLO

I ask your pardon, then.
I thought you were that conniving whore of Venice
who married Othello. (*shouting*)
You, woman,

    EMILIA *enters.*

who has the opposite job of Saint Peter's   105
and keeps the gate of hell! You, you, yes, you!
We're finished with our business. Here's money for your trouble.
Please, lock up your lips and keep this meeting secret.

    OTHELLO *exits.*

EMILIA

My God, what is this gentleman thinking?
Are you all right, madam? Are you all right, my good lady?   110

DESDEMONA

Really, I'm in a daze.

EMILIA

Good lady, what's the matter with my lord?

DESDEMONA

With whom?

EMILIA

Why, with my lord, madam.

DESDEMONA

115   Who is thy lord?

EMILIA

He that is yours, sweet lady.

DESDEMONA

I have none. Do not talk to me, Emilia;
I cannot weep, nor answers have I none
But what should go by water. Prithee, tonight
120   Lay on my bed my wedding sheets. Remember;
And call thy husband hither.

EMILIA

Here's a change indeed!

    [Exit.]

DESDEMONA

'Tis meet I should be us'd so, very meet.
How have I been behav'd that he might stick
125   The small'st opinion on my least misuse?

    Reenter EMILIA *with* IAGO.

IAGO

What is your pleasure, madam? How is 't with you?

DESDEMONA

I cannot tell. Those that do teach young babes
Do it with gentle means and easy tasks.
He might have chid me so; for, in good faith,
130   I am a child to chiding.

IAGO

What's the matter, lady?

EMILIA

Alas, Iago, my lord hath so bewhor'd her,
Thrown such despite and heavy terms upon her,
As true hearts cannot bear.

DESDEMONA

135   Am I that name, Iago?

EMILIA

Why, with my lord, madam.

DESDEMONA

Who is your lord? 115

EMILIA

The man who is yours too, sweet lady.

DESDEMONA

I have none. Don't talk to me, Emilia.
I can't weep; and I can't say anything
that shouldn't be said with tears. Please, tonight
make up the bed with my wedding sheets; remember to do it. 120
And call your husband here.

EMILIA

Things are certainly changed!

> EMILIA *exits.*

DESDEMONA

It's proper that I should be treated this way, very proper.
What have I done that he could find
the slightest reason to think me unfaithful? 125

> EMILIA *and* IAGO *enter.*

IAGO

What can I do for you, madam? How are you?

DESDEMONA

I don't know. Those who teach young babies
do it by gentle means and easy lessons.
He should have scolded me that way since, really,
I'm a child when it comes to scolding. 130

IAGO

What's the matter, lady?

EMILIA

Oh, Iago, my lord has so cruelly called her a whore
and thrown such spiteful and horrible names
that innocent hearts can't bear it.

DESDEMONA

Do I deserve that name, Iago? 135

IAGO

What name, fair lady?

DESDEMONA

Such as she said my lord did say I was.

EMILIA

He call'd her "whore." A beggar in his drink
Could not have laid such terms upon his callet.

IAGO

140 Why did he so?

DESDEMONA

I do not know; I am sure I am none such.

IAGO

Do not weep, do not weep. Alas the day!

EMILIA

Hath she forsook so many noble matches,
Her father and her country and her friends,
145 To be call'd "whore"? Would it not make one weep?

DESDEMONA

It is my wretched fortune.

IAGO

Beshrew him for 't!
How comes this trick upon him?

DESDEMONA

Nay, heaven doth know.

EMILIA

150 I will be hang'd if some eternal villain,
Some busy and **insinuating** rogue,
Some cogging, cozening slave, to get some office,
Have not devis'd this slander. I'll be hang'd else.

IAGO

Fie, there is no such man; it is impossible.

DESDEMONA

155 If any such there be, heaven pardon him!

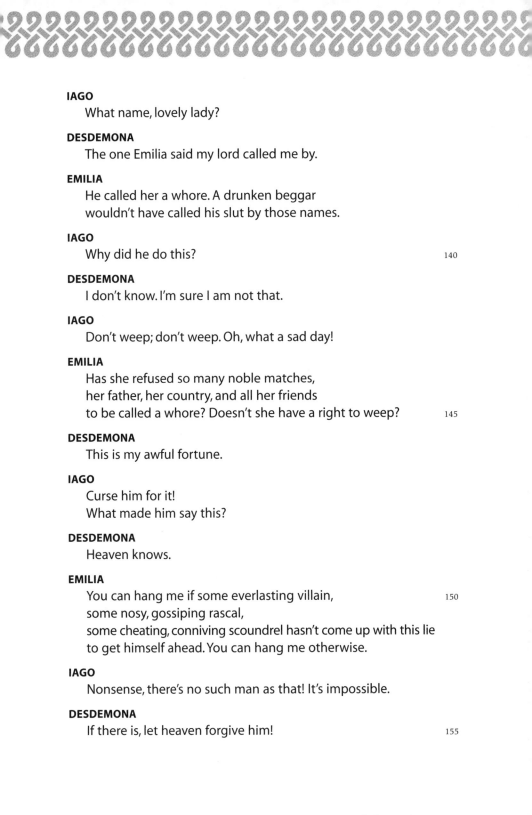

IAGO
What name, lovely lady?

DESDEMONA
The one Emilia said my lord called me by.

EMILIA
He called her a whore. A drunken beggar
wouldn't have called his slut by those names.

IAGO
Why did he do this?   140

DESDEMONA
I don't know. I'm sure I am not that.

IAGO
Don't weep; don't weep. Oh, what a sad day!

EMILIA
Has she refused so many noble matches,
her father, her country, and all her friends
to be called a whore? Doesn't she have a right to weep?   145

DESDEMONA
This is my awful fortune.

IAGO
Curse him for it!
What made him say this?

DESDEMONA
Heaven knows.

EMILIA
You can hang me if some everlasting villain,   150
some nosy, gossiping rascal,
some cheating, conniving scoundrel hasn't come up with this lie
to get himself ahead. You can hang me otherwise.

IAGO
Nonsense, there's no such man as that! It's impossible.

DESDEMONA
If there is, let heaven forgive him!   155

EMILIA

A halter pardon him, and hell gnaw his bones!
Why should he call her "whore"? Who keeps her company?
What place? What time? What form? What likelihood?
The Moor's abus'd by some most villainous knave,
160   Some base notorious knave, some scurvy fellow.
O heaven, that such companions thou'dst unfold,
And put in every honest hand a whip
To lash the rascals naked through the world
Even from the east to th' west!

IAGO

165   Speak within door.

EMILIA

O, fie upon them! Some such squire he was
That turn'd your wit the seamy side without
And made you to suspect me with the Moor.

IAGO

You are a fool. Go to!

DESDEMONA

170   Alas, Iago,
What shall I do to win my lord again?
Good friend, go to him; for, by this light of heaven,
I know not how I lost him. Here I kneel.
If e'er my will did trespass 'gainst his love,
175   Either in discourse of thought or actual deed,
Or that mine eyes, mine ears, or any sense
Delighted them in any other form;
Or that I do not yet, and ever did,
And ever will—though he do shake me off
180   To beggarly divorcement—love him dearly,
Comfort forswear me! [*She stands.*] Unkindness may do
        much,
And his unkindness may defeat my life,
But never taint my love. I cannot say "whore"—
185   It does abhor me now I speak the word;
To do the act that might the addition earn
Not the world's mass of vanity could make me.

EMILIA

May a noose forgive him! And may hell gnaw on his bones!
Why would he call her a whore? Who's been keeping her
    company?
Where did it happen? When? In what way? And how likely is it?
The Moor has been misled by some villainous rascal,
some low, infamous rascal, some low-life character.   160
Oh, heaven, I wish you'd expose such villains
and put a whip in the hand of every honest person
to whip these naked rascals around the world
all the way from the east to the west!

IAGO

Watch your tongue.   165

EMILIA

Oh, to hell with them! It was just this kind of man
that turned your thoughts to foul ideas
and made you think I was the Moor's lover.

IAGO

You are a fool. Watch yourself.

DESDEMONA

Oh, good Iago,   170
what should I do to win back the trust of my lord again?
Good friend, go talk with him; I tell you, by the light of heaven,
I don't know how I lost his affection. I'm on my knees.
If I ever deliberately did anything to betray his love,
either in thought or in action,   175
or if my eyes, my ears, or any of my other senses
were ever attracted to any other man,
or if I don't now, and always have,
and always will—even if he force me into
a penniless divorce—very dearly love him,   180
let me never know peace again! (*She stands.*) Unkindness
    may do much harm,
and his unkindness may destroy my life,
but it will not affect my love. I can't say the word "whore."
It disgusts me even now that I've said that word.   185
To actually do the act that would earn me that title—
not all the hollow treasure in the world could make me do it.

IAGO

I pray you, be content; 'tis but his humour.
The business of the state does him offence,
And he does chide with you.

DESDEMONA

If 'twere no other—

IAGO

It is but so, I warrant.

[Trumpets within.]

Hark, how these instruments summon to supper!
The messengers of Venice stays the meat.
Go in and weep not; all things shall be well.

[Exeunt DESDEMONA *and* EMILIA.]

Enter RODERIGO.

How now, Roderigo!

RODERIGO

I do not find that thou deal'st justly with me.

IAGO

What in the contrary?

RODERIGO

Every day thou daff'st me with some device, Iago; and
rather, as it seems to me now, keep'st from me all
conveniency than suppliest me with the least advantage of
hope. I will indeed no longer endure it, nor am I yet
persuaded to put up in peace what already I have foolishly
suffer'd.

IAGO

Will you hear me, Roderigo?

RODERIGO

Faith, I have heard too much, and your words and
performances are no kin together.

IAGO

You charge me most unjustly.

190

195

200

205

IAGO

Please, don't get upset. It's just a mood of his.
Business of state has made him angry,
and he's taking it out on you.   190

DESDEMONA

If it's just that—

IAGO

It's just that, I guarantee you.

> *Trumpets blow offstage.*

Listen. The trumpets are calling you to supper.
The Venetian messengers are staying to eat.
Go in, and stop crying. Everything will be all right.   195

> DESDEMONA *and* EMILIA *exit.*

> RODERIGO *enters.*

What is it, Roderigo?

RODERIGO

I've found out that you haven't been dealing with me honestly.

IAGO

In what way?

RODERIGO

Every day you've put me off with some excuse, Iago, and it
seems to me now that you've been trying to cheat me out of   200
every opportunity, rather than give me the smallest reason for
hope. I won't put up with this anymore, and I'm not going to
peacefully accept what I've already foolishly suffered.

IAGO

Will you just listen to me, Roderigo?   205

RODERIGO

I've been listening to you too much. What you say and what
you do are not connected.

IAGO

You're accusing me unjustly.

RODERIGO

With naught but truth. I have wasted myself out of my
210   means. The jewels you have had from me to deliver to
Desdemona would half have corrupted a votaress. You
have told me she hath receiv'd them and return'd me
expectations and comforts of sudden respect and
acquaintance, but I find none.

IAGO

215   Well, go to; very well.

RODERIGO

"Very well"! "Go to"! I cannot go to, man; nor 'tis not very
well. By this hand I say 'tis very scurvy, and begin to find
myself fopp'd in it.

IAGO

Very well.

RODERIGO

220   I tell you 'tis not very well. I will make myself known to
Desdemona. If she will return me my jewels, I will give
over my suit and repent my unlawful solicitation; if not,
assure yourself I will seek satisfaction of you.

IAGO

You have said now.

RODERIGO

225   Ay, and said nothing but what I protest intendment of
doing.

IAGO

Why, now I see there's mettle in thee, and even from this
instant do build on thee a better opinion than ever before.
Give me thy hand, Roderigo. Thou hast taken against me a
230   most just exception; but yet, I protest, I have dealt most
directly in thy affair.

RODERIGO

It hath not appear'd.

RODERIGO

Only with the truth. I've wasted everything I have. The jewels
you've received from me to give to Desdemona would have   210
half-corrupted a nun. You've told me that she's received them,
and led me to hope for the comfort of speedy consideration
and acquaintance. But it hasn't happened.

IAGO

Well, take it easy; things are all right.   215

RODERIGO

"All right!" "Take it easy!" I can't take it easy, man; and things aren't
all right. No, I think it's a rotten business, and I'm starting to feel
like I've been duped.

IAGO

All right, then.

RODERIGO

I'm telling you, it's not all right. I'm going to confront   220
Desdemona. If she'll give me back my jewels, I'll give up
wooing her and apologize for my improper proposal. If not,
you can be sure that I'll make you pay.

IAGO

You've had your say now.

RODERIGO

Yes, and I haven't said anything I don't intend to carry out.   225

IAGO

Well, now I can see that you've got some grit, and from this
moment on, I have a better opinion of you than ever before.
Give me your hand, Roderigo. You have good cause to say all
this. Still, I assure you, I've been very straightforward with you.   230

RODERIGO

It doesn't look like it.

IAGO

I grant indeed it hath not appear'd, and your suspicion is
not without wit and judgment. But, Roderigo, if thou hast
235   that in thee indeed, which I have greater reason to believe
now than ever, I mean purpose, courage, and valour, this
night show it. If thou the next night following enjoy not
Desdemona, take me from this world with treachery and
devise engines for my life.

RODERIGO

240   Well, what is it? Is it within reason and compass?

IAGO

Sir, there is especial commission come from Venice to
depute Cassio in Othello's place.

RODERIGO

Is that true? Why, then Othello and Desdemona return
again to Venice.

IAGO

245   O, no; he goes into Mauritania and taketh away with him
the fair Desdemona, unless his abode be ling'red here by
some accident; wherein none can be so determinate as the
removing of Cassio.

RODERIGO

How do you mean, removing him?

IAGO

250   Why, by making him uncapable of Othello's place;
knocking out his brains.

RODERIGO

And that you would have me to do?

IAGO

Ay, if you dare do yourself a profit and a right. He sups
tonight with a harlotry, and thither will I go to him; he
255   knows not yet of his honourable fortune. If you will watch
his going thence, which I will fashion to fall out between
twelve and one, you may take him at your pleasure. I will
be near to second your attempt, and he shall fall between

IAGO

I'll admit that it doesn't, and your suspicions are not foolish or improbable. But, Roderigo, if you've got some of that stuff in you which I'm more convinced than ever that you really have—I mean determination, courage, and valor—show it tonight. If Desdemona isn't yours tomorrow night, you can kidnap me and plot against my life.

235

RODERIGO

Well, what do you want me to do? Is it reasonable and possible? 240

IAGO

Sir, there's been an official order from Venice for Cassio to take Othello's place.

RODERIGO

Is that true? Why, then Othello and Desdemona will be returning to Venice.

IAGO

Oh, no. He'll go to Mauritania and take the lovely Desdemona with him—unless he has to stay here because of some accident. Nothing can be more certain to bring that about than getting rid of Cassio.

245

RODERIGO

What do you mean, getting rid of him?

IAGO

Why, by making him unable to take Othello's place—by beating out his brains.

250

RODERIGO

And that's what you want me to do?

IAGO

Yes, if you dare to do the best and most profitable thing for yourself. He's eating tonight with a harlot, and I'm going to meet him there. He hasn't heard the news of his good luck yet. If you'll wait for him to leave, which I'll arrange to have happen between twelve and one, you can finish him off at your leisure. I'll be nearby to back you up, and between the

255

260 us. Come, stand not amaz'd at it, but go along with me; I will show you such a necessity in his death that you shall think yourself bound to put it on him. It is now high supper time, and the night grows to waste. About it.

RODERIGO

I will hear further reason for this.

IAGO

And you shall be satisfi'd.

[*Exeunt.*]

two of us, he'll die. Come on, don't stand there dumbfounded, but come with me. I'll give you such good reasons for killing   260
him that you'll feel obligated to slay him. It's suppertime now, and the night is going to waste. Let's get to it!

RODERIGO
I want to hear more reasons for this.

IAGO
You'll hear them.

    They exit.

ACT IV, SCENE III

[*Another room in the castle.*] *Enter* OTHELLO,
LODOVICO, DESDEMONA, EMILIA, *and*
ATTENDANTS.

LODOVICO
I do beseech you, sir, trouble yourself no further.

OTHELLO
O, pardon me, 'twill do me good to walk.

LODOVICO
Madam, good night; I humbly thank your Ladyship.

DESDEMONA
Your Honour is most welcome.

OTHELLO
5   Will you walk, sir?—O, Desdemona—

DESDEMONA
                      My lord?

OTHELLO
Get you to bed on th' instant; I will be return'd
   forthwith.
Dismiss your attendant there. Look 't be done.

DESDEMONA
10   I will my lord.

      [*Exeunt* OTHELLO, LODOVICO, *and* ATTENDANTS.]

EMILIA
How goes it now? He looks gentler than he did.

DESDEMONA
He says he will return incontinent;
And hath commanded me to go to bed,
And bade me to dismiss you.

EMILIA
15   Dismiss me!

ACT 4, SCENE 3

Another room in the castle. OTHELLO, LODOVICO,
DESDEMONA, EMILIA, *and* ATTENDANTS *enter.*

LODOVICO
Please, sir, don't trouble yourself any further.

OTHELLO
No, allow me; the walk will do me good.

LODOVICO
Good night, madam. Thank you for the lovely evening.

DESDEMONA
You are very welcome, your Honor.

OTHELLO
Will you walk with me, sir? Oh, Desdemona—   5

DESDEMONA
Yes, my lord?

OTHELLO
Go to bed at once. I'll be back soon. Send your servant away.
Be sure to do it.

DESDEMONA
I will, my lord.   10

OTHELLO, LODOVICO, *and* ATTENDANTS *exit.*

EMILIA
How is it going now? He seems to be in a better mood than
before.

DESDEMONA
He says he'll be back immediately.
He's commanded me to go to bed
and to send you away.

EMILIA
Send me away?   15

DESDEMONA

It was his bidding; therefore, good Emilia,
Give me my nightly wearing, and adieu.
We must not now displease him.

EMILIA

I would you had never seen him!

DESDEMONA

20   So would not I. My love doth so approve him
That even his stubbornness, his checks, his frowns—
Prithee, unpin me—have grace and favour in them.

EMILIA

I have laid those sheets you bade me on the bed.

DESDEMONA

All's one. Good faith, how foolish are our minds!
25   If I do die before thee, prithee, shroud me
In one of those same sheets.

EMILIA

                       Come, come, you talk!

DESDEMONA

My mother had a maid call'd Barbary;
She was in love, and he she lov'd prov'd mad
30   And did forsake her. She had a song of "Willow";
An old thing 'twas, but it express'd her fortune,
And she died singing it. That song tonight
Will not go from my mind; I have much to do
But to go hang my head all at one side
35   And sing it like poor Barbary. Prithee, dispatch.

EMILIA

Shall I go fetch your nightgown?

DESDEMONA

No, unpin me here.
This Lodovico is a proper man.

EMILIA

A very handsome man.

DESDEMONA
That's what he told me to do. So, good Emilia,
give me my night clothes, and good-bye.
We must be careful not to displease him now.

EMILIA
I wish you had never seen him!

DESDEMONA
But I don't. I love him so much   20
that even his roughness, his criticisms, and his frowns—
please unpin me—have something graceful and good about
    them.

EMILIA (*helping her change for bed*)
I've put those sheets on the bed which you told me to.

DESDEMONA
It doesn't matter. My goodness, how foolish we are!
If I die before you do, please wrap me   25
in one of these sheets.

EMILIA
Come, come! What kind of talk is that?

DESDEMONA
My mother had a maid named Barbary.
She was in love; and the man she was in love with turned out
    to be mad
and left her. She sang a song called "Willow."   30
It was an old song, but it told her sad story,
and she died singing it. I can't get that song
out of my mind tonight. I can barely stop myself
from hanging my head to one side
and singing it like poor Barbary. Please hurry.   35

EMILIA
Should I go get your nightgown?

DESDEMONA
No, unpin me here.
That Lodovico is a fine man.

EMILIA
A very handsome man.

DESDEMONA

40   He speaks well.

EMILIA

I know a lady in Venice would have walk'd barefoot to
Palestine for a touch of his nether lip.

DESDEMONA [*singing*]

"The poor soul sat sighing by a sycamore tree,
      Sing all a green willow;
45   Her hand on her bosom, her head on her knee,
      Sing willow, willow, willow.
The fresh streams ran by her, and murmur'd her moans;
      Sing willow, willow, willow;
Her salt tears fell from her, and soft'ned the stones"—
50   Lay by these—
[*singing*] "Sing willow, willow, willow"—
Prithee, hie thee; he'll come anon—

[*singing*]

"Sing all a green willow must be my garland.
      Let nobody blame him, his scorn I approve"—
55   Nay, that's not next.—Hark! who is 't that knocks?

EMILIA

It's the wind.

DESDEMONA [*singing*]

"I call'd my love false love, but what said he then?
      Sing willow, willow, willow.
If I court more women, you'll couch with more men."—
60   So, get thee gone; good night. Mine eyes do itch;
Doth that bode weeping?

EMILIA

                                        'Tis neither here nor there.

DESDEMONA

I have heard it said so. O, these men, these men!
Dost thou in conscience think—tell me, Emilia—

DESDEMONA

He speaks well.   40

EMILIA

I know a Venetian lady who would walk barefoot to Palestine
for just one kiss.

DESDEMONA (*singing*)

A poor soul sighing sat by a sycamore tree;
   Let's all sing of a green willow.
Her hand was on her bosom, and her head was on her knee;   45
   Sing of a willow, willow, willow.
The fresh stream ran by her and echoed her moans;
   Sing of a willow, willow, willow.
Her salt tears fell from her eyes and softened the stones;
(*handing* EMILIA *her clothes*) Put these away.   50
(*singing*)—*Sing willow, willow, willow*—
Please go; he'll be coming soon.

     (*singing*)

Let's all sing of a green willow, which will be my funeral wreath.
   Let nobody blame him; I understand his scorn for me—
No, that's not what comes next. Listen! Who is that knocking?   55

EMILIA

It's just the wind.

DESDEMONA (*singing*)

I called my lover unfaithful; but what did he say to that?
   Sing of a willow, willow, willow.
If I pursue other women, you'll sleep with other men.
(*to* EMILIA) Well, get going; good night. My eyes are itching.   60
Does that mean I'll soon cry?

EMILIA

That has nothing to do with it one way or the other.

DESDEMONA

I've heard it did. Oh, these men, these men!
Do you honestly think—tell me the truth, Emilia—

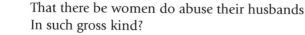

65   That there be women do abuse their husbands
In such gross kind?

EMILIA

                         There be some such, no question.

DESDEMONA

Wouldst thou do such a deed for all the world?

EMILIA

Why, would not you?

DESDEMONA

70   No, by this heavenly light!

EMILIA

Nor I neither by this heavenly light;
I might do 't as well i' th' dark.

DESDEMONA

Wouldst thou do such a deed for all the world?

EMILIA

The world's a huge thing; it is a great price for a small vice.

DESDEMONA

75   In troth, I think thou wouldst not.

EMILIA

In troth, I think I should, and undo 't when I had done it.
Marry, I would not do such a thing for a joint ring,* nor
for measures of lawn, nor for gowns, petticoats, nor caps,
nor any petty exhibition; but, for all the whole world—
80   'ud's pity, who would not make her husband a cuckold to
make him a monarch? I should venture purgatory for 't.

DESDEMONA

Beshrew me, if I would do such a wrong for the whole
world.

EMILIA

Why, the wrong is but a wrong i' th' world; and having the
85   world for your labour, 'tis a wrong in your own world, and
you might quickly make it right.

---

77   *joint ring* a ring with two interlocking halves traditionally given as a love token

that there are women who mistreat their husbands   65
in such an awful way?

EMILIA

There are some; there's no question about it.

DESDEMONA

Would you do such a thing for all the world?

EMILIA

Why, wouldn't you?

DESDEMONA

No, I swear by the light of the stars I wouldn't!   70

EMILIA

Well, I wouldn't do it by the light of the stars.
It would be easier to do in the dark.

DESDEMONA

Would you really do such a thing for all the world?

EMILIA

The world's a huge thing. It would be a great payment
for a little sin.

DESDEMONA

Really, I don't think you would.   75

EMILIA

Really, I think I would; and I'd make up for it once it was done.
Of course, I wouldn't do such a thing for a little ring, or for a
great deal of linen, or for dresses, petticoats, or caps, or any
trivial gift. But for the whole world? For God's sake! Who
wouldn't be unfaithful to her husband to make him a king? I'd   80
risk going to purgatory for that.

DESDEMONA

Curse me if I would do a wrong like that
for the whole world.

EMILIA

Why, that wrong is just one of many in the world. And if you
got the whole world for your trouble, then it's wrong in your   85
own world, and you can quickly make everything right again.

DESDEMONA

I do not think there is any such woman.

EMILIA

Yes, a dozen; and as many to th' vantage as would store
the world they play'd for.

90　But I do think it is their husbands' faults
If wives do fall. Say that they slack their duties
And pour our treasures into foreign laps,
Or else break out in peevish jealousies,
Throwing restraint upon us; or say they strike us,

95　Or scant our former having in despite;
Why, we have galls, and though we have some grace,
Yet have we some revenge. Let husbands know
Their wives have sense like them; they see and smell
And have their **palates** both for sweet and sour

100　As husbands have. What is it that they do
When they change us for others? Is it sport?
I think it is. And doth affection breed it?
I think it doth. Is 't frailty that thus errs?
It is so too. And have not we affections,

105　Desires for sport, and frailty, as men have?
Then let them use us well; else let them know,
The ills we do, their ills instruct us so.

DESDEMONA

Good night, good night. God me such uses send,
Not to pick bad from bad, but by bad mend.

　　　[*Exeunt.*]

DESDEMONA

I don't really think there is such a woman.

EMILIA

Yes, there are at least a dozen—and enough others to fill up
the world they schemed to get.
But I really think it's the fault of the husbands   90
if wives do wrong. Suppose they sluff off their duties,
or give our valuables to other women,
or else have a fit of foolish jealousy
and restrain our comings and goings. Or suppose they hit us,
or deprive us of things we usually have out of spite—   95
Well, we can become resentful too; and while we are ladylike,
we can be vengeful as well. So let all husbands know
their wives have feelings like them. They see, smell,
and have a taste for both sweet and sour things
just like their husbands. What's behind their actions   100
when they reject us for other women? Is it an amusement?
I think so. And does it result from desire?
I think it does. Is it frailty that leads them to sin?
It certainly is. And don't we have longings,
a desire for amusement, and frailties just like men?   105
Then they'd better treat us well; otherwise, let them know
the bad things we do are things we learned from them.

DESDEMONA

Good night; good night. I hope that heaven teaches me
how not to return evil with evil but to make myself better by it!

They exit.

Act IV Review

Discussion Questions

1. How does Iago continue to provoke Othello's jealousy?

2. What does the confrontation between Bianca and Cassio reveal about Cassio's character?

3. Why has Lodovico come to Cyprus, and how does he become a part of Iago's scheming?

4. How does Emilia react to Othello's initial suggestion of Desdemona's unfaithfulness?

5. How does Desdemona react to Othello's accusations in Scene ii?

6. When Desdemona asks for Iago's help, what does he say to her about Othello's jealousy? Explain why you think he responds this way.

7. How has Iago been cheating Roderigo out of his money?

8. What is your reaction to Emilia's speech about infidelity in Scene iii ("But I do think it is their husbands' faults / If wives do fall")?

Literary Elements

1. A **symbol** is an object that stands for something beyond its obvious meaning. Aside from being a plot device, the handkerchief in this play is a symbol. What things might it symbolize?

2. **Personification** means the attribution of human characteristics to nonhuman things. Consider this series of images in Scene ii: "Heaven stops the nose at it, and the moon winks; / The bawdy wind, that kisses all it meets, / Is hushed within the hollow mine of earth / And will not hear it." Heaven is seen as having a nose, the moon as having eyes, and the wind as having lips and ears. What do you think is gained by such personification?

3. An **allusion** is a reference to a historical or literary figure or event that may enhance the meaning of a story. Discuss any allusions you can find in *Othello*, especially biblical references.

Writing Prompts

1. Pretend you are a gossip columnist covering events in Cyprus. What facts could you relate? Would you have to rely on rumor? How might you misstate the facts? Write in a witty, gossipy style.

2. Write the letter Lodovico has brought to Cyprus from the Duke, calling Othello back to Venice and leaving Cassio to govern Cyprus. Since Shakespeare gives no reason for this decision, you must come up with one. Write with the formality of an official command.

3. Lodovico is undoubtedly sending reports to the Duke in Venice. Write a letter from Lodovico to the Duke, describing how Othello struck Desdemona and insulted Lodovico. What should be the tone of this letter? What action might Lodovico recommend to the Duke?

4. In Scene ii, we learn that Emilia is aware of Iago's suspicions that she has been unfaithful to him. "Some such squire he was," she tells him, "That turn'd your wit the seamy side without / And made you to suspect me with the Moor." In dramatic form, write about this earlier confrontation between Iago and Emilia. If you like, try writing it in Shakespearean blank verse.

5. Some critics find it easy to believe that Othello is so readily deceived by Iago's cunning tactics; other critics find Othello's gullibility impossible to believe. What is your own opinion? Explain your thoughts in a short essay.

Othello

Act V

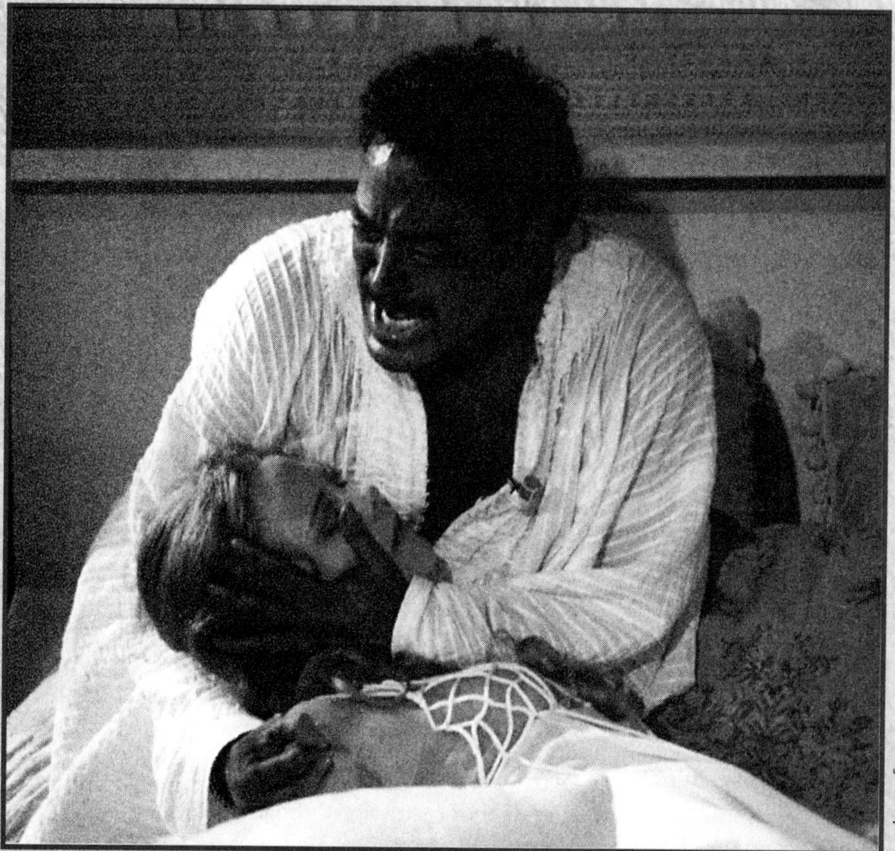

© George E. Joseph

Raul Julia and Kathryn Meisle as Othello and Desdemona, 1991 production at the Delacorte Theatre, Central Park

"That death's unnatural
that kills for loving."

Before You Read

1. What plot developments and characters' actions have surprised you so far in *Othello*?

2. In what ways have your feelings changed toward any of the characters in the play—especially Othello, Iago, Desdemona, Cassio, and Emilia?

3. Think about how Othello deals with personal uncertainties in his life. If you were Othello, how would you have gone about things differently?

4. How do you expect the pace and/or mood of the play to change during the last act?

Literary Elements

1. Shakespeare skillfully uses language to create **mood**, or atmosphere, in his plays. From the beginning of this play, Iago's poisonous comments about Cassio establish an atmosphere of paranoia and mistrust.

2. **Dramatic irony** occurs when the audience has important information that characters in the story lack. In Acts III and IV, Desdemona's handkerchief is used to trick Othello into believing she is unfaithful to him. The audience is aware that he has been deceived.

3. **Hyperbole** is an exaggeration or overstatement not meant to be taken literally. When Cassio fights with Roderigo in Act II, Scene iii, he declares that he will beat him until he's ready to crawl inside a bottle.

Words to Know

The following vocabulary words appear in Act V in the original text of Shakespeare's play. However, they are words that are still used today. Read the definitions here and pay attention to the words as you read the play (they will be in boldfaced type).

direful	frightening; dreadful
extenuate	explain away; justify
impediments	obstacles; barriers
malignant	nasty; cruel
notorious	dishonorable; disreputable
odious	horrible; hateful
perjury	lies under oath
pernicious	destructive; evil
portents	signs; omens
restitution	repayment; compensation

Act Summary

That night on a dark street, Iago and Roderigo wait in ambush for Cassio. When Cassio appears, Roderigo attacks him but fails to hurt him. Instead, Cassio injures Roderigo. Iago then attacks Cassio, badly wounds him, and flees.

Lodovico and his kinsman Gratiano arrive, quickly followed by Iago. Cassio has no idea who attacked him. Unseen by the others, Iago kills Roderigo to silence him.

Othello goes to Desdemona's bedroom and finds her asleep. He awakens her with a kiss, then tells her she is about to die. Ignoring her pleas for mercy and protestations of innocence, he smothers her with a pillow.

Emilia then knocks on the door, and Othello lets her in. Desdemona briefly revives, saying that she's been murdered. But with her last breath, she lies to protect her husband from guilt.

Othello admits to Emilia that he killed Desdemona. He also tells

Emilia that Iago convinced him of Desdemona's guilt. Emilia suddenly begins to grasp her husband's treachery.

Her shouts bring Montano, Gratiano, and Iago. She tells Othello how she found the handkerchief and gave it to Iago because he'd asked her to steal it. To silence his wife, Iago stabs her to death—but too late. Othello now knows of Iago's treachery and Desdemona's innocence.

Othello wounds Iago, but not fatally. Cassio arrives with further evidence of Iago's treachery. Othello takes his own punishment into his hands and stabs himself to death. Cassio will continue to rule Cyprus as its governor. Iago will be tortured to death.

Imogene Stubbs as Desdemona and Zoë Wannamaker as Emilia, 1990 production at The Other Place, Stratford-upon-Avon

ACT V, SCENE I

[*Cyprus. A street.*] *Enter* IAGO *and* RODERIGO.

IAGO
    Here, stand behind this bulk;* straight will he come.
    Wear thy good rapier bare, and put it home.
    Quick, quick! Fear nothing; I'll be at thy elbow.
    It makes us, or it mars us—think on that,
5   And fix most firm thy resolution.

RODERIGO
    Be near at hand; I may miscarry in 't.

IAGO
    Here, at thy hand; be bold, and take thy stand.

      [*Retires.*]

RODERIGO
    I have no great devotion to the deed,
    And yet he hath given me satisfying reasons.
10   'Tis but a man gone. Forth, my sword! He dies.

IAGO
    I have rubb'd this young quat almost to the sense,
    And he grows angry. Now, whether he kill Cassio,
    Or Cassio him, or each do kill the other,
    Every way makes my gain. Live Roderigo,
15   He calls me to a **restitution** large
    Of gold and jewels that I bobb'd from him
    As gifts to Desdemona;
    It must not be. If Cassio do remain,
    He hath a daily beauty in his life
20   That makes me ugly. And besides, the Moor
    May unfold me to him; there stand I in much peril.
    No, he must die. Be 't so; I hear him coming.

    Enter CASSIO.

RODERIGO
    I know his gait, 'tis he.—Villain, thou diest!

    [*Makes a pass at* CASSIO.]

---

1 *bulk* part of a building that juts out

ACT 5, SCENE 1

Cyprus. A street. IAGO *and* RODERIGO *enter.*

IAGO

Here, hide behind this thing; he'll be here any minute.
Keep your sword out, and be ready to use it.
Quick, quick! Don't be afraid; I'll be right at your elbow.
This will either bring us success or ruin us—remember that,
and resolve yourself to it.   5

RODERIGO

Stay close by. I might make a mistake.

IAGO

I'll be right here. Be bold, and be ready to fight.

>   IAGO *hides himself.*

RODERIGO

My heart really isn't in doing this;
but still, he's given me good reasons for it.
It will be just another man dead. My sword is drawn! He'll die!   10

IAGO

I've rubbed this young pimple almost raw,
and he's getting angry. It doesn't matter if he kills Cassio
or if Cassio kills him or if they kill each other—
it'll be good for me in any case. If Roderigo lives,
he'll expect me to give back   15
all the gold and jewels I swindled him out of
as gifts to Desdemona.
That must not happen. If Cassio survives,
he has such an everyday beauty in his life
that he makes me look ugly. And besides, the Moor   20
might reveal my lies to him; that's a very great risk for me.
No, he has to die. But I hear him coming.

>   CASSIO *enters.*

RODERIGO

I know his walk. It's him. Villain, get ready to die!

>   RODERIGO *attacks* CASSIO *with a sword.*

CASSIO

That thrust had been mine enemy indeed,
25   But that my coat is better than thou know'st.
I will make proof of thine.

      [*Draws and wounds* RODERIGO.]

RODERIGO

                    O, I am slain.

      [IAGO *from behind wounds* CASSIO *in the leg and
exits.*]

CASSIO

I am maim'd for ever. Help, ho! Murder! Murder! [*Falls.*]

      Enter OTHELLO.

OTHELLO

The voice of Cassio! Iago keeps his word.

RODERIGO

30   O, villain that I am!

OTHELLO [*aside*]

It is even so.

CASSIO

O, help, ho! Light! A surgeon!

OTHELLO [*aside*]

'Tis he!—O brave Iago, honest and just,
That hast such noble sense of thy friend's wrong!
35   Thou teachest me.—Minion, your dear lies dead,
And your unblest fate hies; strumpet, I come.
Forth of my heart those charms, thine eyes, are blotted;
Thy bed, lust-stain'd, shall with lust's blood be spotted.

      [*Exit.*]

      Enter LODOVICO *and* GRATIANO.

CASSIO

What, ho! No watch? No passage? Murder! Murder!

GRATIANO

40   'Tis some mischance; the voice is very **direful**.

CASSIO

That thrust would have really done me in
if my armor weren't better than you expected.   25
I'll see how good yours is.

> CASSIO *draws his sword and wounds* RODERIGO.

RODERIGO

Oh, I've been killed!

> IAGO *comes forward, wounds* CASSIO *from behind, and exits.*

CASSIO

I've been badly wounded. Help! Murder! Murder! (*He falls.*)

> OTHELLO *enters.*

OTHELLO

That's Cassio's voice. Iago has kept his promise.

RODERIGO

Oh, what a villain I am!   30

OTHELLO (*aside*)

It's really been done.

CASSIO

Oh, help! Give me some light! Bring me a surgeon!

OTHELLO (*aside*)

It's really him. Oh, noble Iago, you honest and just man,
you really feel for a friend who has suffered a wrong!
You're my teacher. Hussy, your lover lies dead   35
and your own death is near. Harlot, I'm coming.
Those charming eyes of yours are blotted out of my heart.
Your lust-stained bed will soon be stained with your lustful
   blood.

> OTHELLO *exits.*

> LODOVICO *and* GRATIANO *enter.*

CASSIO

What's this? No one on watch? No passersby? Murder! Murder!

GRATIANO

Something terrible has happened. That's a very frightening cry.   40

CASSIO
O, help!

LODOVICO
Hark!

RODERIGO
O wretched villain!

LODOVICO
Two or three groan. 'Tis heavy night,
45   These may be counterfeits; let's think 't unsafe
To come in to the cry without more help.

RODERIGO
Nobody come? Then shall I bleed to death.

Reenter IAGO, *with a light.*

LODOVICO
Hark!

GRATIANO
Here's one comes in his shirt, with light and weapons.

IAGO
50   Who's there? Whose noise is this that cries on murder?

LODOVICO
We do not know.

IAGO
                                Did not you hear a cry?

CASSIO
Here, here! For heaven's sake, help me!

IAGO
What's the matter?

GRATIANO [*to* LODOVICO]
55   This is Othello's ancient, as I take it.

LODOVICO
The same indeed; a very valiant fellow.

IAGO [*to* CASSIO]
What are you here that cry so grievously?

CASSIO
Oh, help!

LODOVICO
Listen!

RODERIGO
Miserable villain!

LODOVICO
There are two or three men groaning. It's a very dark night.
They might be faking in order to trap us. We'd better not try to   45
approach the ones who are crying without others to help us.

RODERIGO
Won't anybody come? Then I'll bleed to death.

   IAGO *enters with a light.*

LODOVICO
Listen!

GRATIANO
A man is coming in his nightshirt, with a lamp and weapons.

IAGO
Who's there? Whose voice is it that's crying out murder?   50

LODOVICO
We don't know.

IAGO
Didn't you hear a cry?

CASSIO
Over here, over here! For heaven's sake, help me!

IAGO
What's the matter?

GRATIANO (*to* LODOVICO)
This is Othello's ensign, I assume.   55

LODOVICO
Yes it is; he's a very noble fellow.

IAGO (*to* CASSIO)
Who is that who's crying so miserably?

CASSIO

Iago? O, I am spoil'd, undone by villains!
Give me some help.

IAGO

60   O me, Lieutenant! What villains have done this?

CASSIO

I think that one of them is hereabout
And cannot make away.

IAGO

                       O treacherous villains!
[*to* LODOVICO *and* GRATIANO] What are you there?
65   Come in, and give some help.

RODERIGO

O, help me here!

CASSIO

That's one of them.

IAGO [*to* RODERIGO]

                    O murd'rous slave! O villain!

[*He stabs* RODERIGO.]

RODERIGO

O damn'd Iago! O inhuman dog!

IAGO

70   Kill men i' th' dark!—Where be these bloody thieves?
How silent is this town! Ho! Murder! Murder!—
What may you be? Are you of good or evil?

LODOVICO

As you shall prove us, praise us.

IAGO

                       Signior Lodovico?

LODOVICO

75   He, sir.

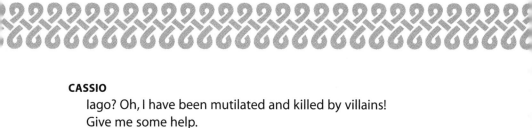

CASSIO

Iago? Oh, I have been mutilated and killed by villains!
Give me some help.

IAGO

Oh, no, Lieutenant! What villains have done this? 60

CASSIO

I think one of them is nearby
and can't get away.

IAGO

Oh, the treacherous villains!
(*to* LODOVICO *and* GRATIANO) Who's over there?
Come and give me some help. 65

RODERIGO

Oh, help me here!

CASSIO

That's one of them.

IAGO (*to* RODERIGO)

You murderous scum! You villain!

> *He stabs* RODERIGO.

RODERIGO

Damn you, Iago! You inhuman dog! (*He dies.*)

IAGO

The idea of killing men in the dark! Where are these blood- 70
thirsty thieves?
The town is so silent! Hey! Murder! Murder!
Who are you? Are you good or evil?

LODOVICO

You can judge us by what we do.

IAGO

Signior Lodovico?

LODOVICO

That's me, sir. 75

IAGO

I cry you mercy. Here's Cassio hurt by villains.

GRATIANO

Cassio!

IAGO

How is 't brother!

CASSIO

My leg is cut in two.

IAGO

80 Marry, heaven forbid!
Light, gentlemen! I'll bind it with my shirt.

Enter BIANCA.

BIANCA

What is the matter, ho? Who is 't that cried?

IAGO

Who is 't that cried?

BIANCA

O my dear Cassio! My sweet Cassio!
85 O Cassio, Cassio, Cassio!

IAGO

O notable strumpet! Cassio, may you suspect
Who they should be that have thus mangled you?

CASSIO

No.

GRATIANO

I am sorry to find you thus; I have been to seek you.

IAGO

90 Lend me a garter. So.—O, for a chair,
To bear him easily hence!

BIANCA

Alas, he faints! O Cassio, Cassio, Cassio!

IAGO

I beg your pardon. Here's Cassio, who's been hurt by villains.

GRATIANO

Cassio?

IAGO

How are you, brother?

CASSIO

My leg has been cut in two.

IAGO

Really, heaven forbid!   80
Give me some light, gentlemen. I'll bandage it with my shirt.

      BIANCA *enters.*

BIANCA

What's the matter here? Who did I hear crying out?

IAGO

Who did you hear crying out?

BIANCA

Oh, it's my dear Cassio! My sweet Cassio!
Oh, Cassio, Cassio, Cassio!   85

IAGO

You notorious harlot!—Cassio, do you have any idea
who it was that injured you like this?

CASSIO

No.

GRATIANO

I'm sorry to find you like this. I've been looking for you.

IAGO

Somebody lend me a garter. Good. Oh, if only we had a sedan   90
   chair,
so we could carry him away more easily!

BIANCA

Oh, he's fainted! Oh, Cassio, Cassio, Cassio!

IAGO

    Gentleman all, I do suspect this trash
    To be a party in this injury.—
95   Patience awhile, good Cassio.— Come, come;
    Lend me a light. [*peering at* RODERIGO] Know we this
        face or no?
    Alas, my friend and my dear countryman
    Roderigo! No! Yes, Sure! O heaven, Roderigo!

GRATIANO

100   What, of Venice?

IAGO

    Even he, sir; did you know him?

GRATIANO

    Know him? Ay.

IAGO

    Signior Gratiano? I cry your gentle pardon;
    These bloody accidents must excuse my manners
105   That so neglected you.

GRATIANO

                        I am glad to see you.

IAGO

    How do you, Cassio?—O, a chair, a chair!

GRATIANO

    Roderigo?

IAGO

    He, he, 'tis he! [*A chair is brought in.*] O, that's well said;
110   the chair.—
    Some good man bear him carefully from hence;
    I'll fetch the General's surgeon.—[*to* BIANCA] For you,
        mistress,
    Save you your labour.—He that lies slain here, Cassio,
115   Was my dear friend. What malice was between you?

CASSIO

    None in the world; nor do I know the man.

IAGO

Gentlemen, I suspect this slut
to have had a hand in this attack.—
Be patient awhile, good Cassio.—Come, come!   95
Give me some light. (*He goes over to* RODERIGO.) Do we know
     this man, or not?
Oh, is it my friend and my dear countryman
Roderigo? It can't be. Yes, it surely is. Oh, heavens! Roderigo.

GRATIANO

You mean from Venice?   100

IAGO

That's the man, sir. Did you know him?

GRATIANO

Know him? Yes.

IAGO

Signior Gratiano? I must ask you to pardon me.
These bloody actions have made me forget my manners
and neglect you.   105

GRATIANO

I'm glad to see you.

IAGO

How are you, Cassio? (*to the others*) Oh, get a chair, a chair!

GRATIANO

Roderigo!

IAGO

Yes, it's him, it's him! (*A chair is brought in.*) Yes, well done! The
     chair.   110
Some good men carry him carefully away from here.
I'll get the general's surgeon. (*to* BIANCA) And as for you, woman,
don't bother to help. The man lying dead here, Cassio, was my
dear friend. What kind of quarrel did you have with him?   115

CASSIO

None at all; I don't even know the man.

IAGO [*to* BIANCA]

What, look you pale? O, bear him out o' th' air.

[CASSIO *and* RODERIGO *are borne off.*]

[*to* GRATIANO *and* LODOVICO]

Stay you, good gentlemen. Look you pale, mistress?—
Do you perceive the gastness of her eye?—
120 Nay, if you stare, we shall hear more anon.—
Behold her well; I pray you, look upon her.
Do you see, gentlemen? Nay, guiltiness will speak,
Though tongues were out of use.

Enter EMILIA.

EMILIA

Alas, what's the matter? What's the matter, husband?

IAGO

125 Cassio hath here been set on in the dark
By Roderigo and fellows that are scap'd.
He's almost slain, and Roderigo dead.

EMILIA

Alas, good gentleman! Alas, good Cassio!

IAGO

This is the fruits of whoring. Prithee, Emilia,
130 Go know of Cassio where he supp'd tonight.
[*to* BIANCA] What, do you shake at that?

BIANCA

He supp'd at my house; but I therefore shake not.

IAGO

O, did he so? I charge you, go with me.

EMILIA

Oh, fie upon thee, strumpet!

BIANCA

135 I am no strumpet, but of life as honest
As you that thus abuse me.

EMILIA

As I? Fie upon thee!

IAGO (*to* BIANCA)

Why, you're looking very pale. (*to the others*) Carry him away.

CASSIO *and* RODERIGO *are carried off.*

(*to* GRATIANO *and* LODOVICO)

Wait, gentlemen. (*to* BIANCA) Are you looking pale, woman?
(*to the others*) Don't you see the terror in her eyes?
(*to* BIANCA) Well, if you keep staring like that, we'll soon know
  more.   120
(*to the others*) Take a good look at her; I ask you to look at her.
Do you see, gentleman? Guiltiness will speak for itself,
even if people stop talking altogether.

EMILIA *enters.*

EMILIA

Oh, what's the matter? What's the matter, husband?

IAGO

Cassio was attacked here in the dark   125
by Roderigo and some others who escaped.
He was almost killed, and Roderigo is dead.

EMILIA

Oh, such a good gentleman! Oh, good Cassio!

IAGO

This is what comes of whoring. Please, Emilia,
go ask where Cassio had supper tonight.   130
(*to* BIANCA) What, does my question cause you to shake?

BIANCA

He had supper at my house; but I'm not shaking because of that.

IAGO

Oh, he did? I order you to come with me.

EMILIA

Curses, curses on you, harlot!

BIANCA

I am no harlot; I live as honestly   135
as you people who accuse me.

EMILIA

As I? Nonsense! Curses on you!

IAGO

Kind gentlemen, let's go see poor Cassio dress'd.—
Come, mistress, you must tell 's another tale.
140   Emilia, run you to the citadel,
And tell my lord and lady what hath happ'd.
Will you go on afore? [*aside*] This is the night
That either makes me or fordoes me quite.

[*Exeunt.*]

IAGO

Kind gentlemen, let's go see that poor Cassio is tended to.
(*to* BIANCA) Come along, woman. You'd better come up with
    another story.—
Emilia, run to the castle   140
and tell my lord and lady what has happened.—
Won't you go on ahead? (*to himself*) This is a night
which will either make me or destroy me.

    They exit.

ACT V, SCENE II

[*A bedchamber in the castle:* DESDEMONA *in bed asleep.*] *Enter* OTHELLO *with a light.*

OTHELLO

It is the cause, it is the cause, my soul—
Let me not name it to you, you chaste stars!
It is the cause. Yet I'll not shed her blood,
Nor scar that whiter skin of hers than snow,
5   And smooth as monumental alabaster.
Yet she must die, else she'll betray more men.
Put out the light, and then put out the light.*
If I quench thee, thou flaming minister,
I can again thy former light restore,
10   Should I repent me; but once put out thy light,
Thou cunning'st pattern of excelling nature,
I know not where is that Promethean heat*
That can thy light relume. When I have pluck'd the rose
I cannot give it vital growth again,
15   It needs must wither. I'll smell it on the tree. [*Kisses her.*]
Oh, balmy breath, that dost almost persuade
Justice to break her sword! One more, one more.
Be thus when thou art dead, and I will kill thee
And love thee after. One more, and this the last;
20   So sweet was ne'er so fatal. I must weep,
But they are cruel tears. This sorrow's heavenly;
It strikes where it doth love. She wakes.

DESDEMONA

Who's there? Othello?

OTHELLO

                    Ay, Desdemona.

DESDEMONA

25   Will you come to bed, my lord?

---

7   *Put out the light . . . light.* Othello compares the light of the candle he holds to the "light" of Desdemona's life.

12   *Promethean heat* Prometheus was a Greek deity who stole fire from heaven and gave it to humanity.

ACT 5, SCENE 2

A bedchamber in the castle. DESDEMONA is in bed asleep.
OTHELLO enters with a candle.

OTHELLO
I know the cause of all this; I know the cause, my soul.
I won't say its name before you, you chaste stars!
I know the cause. Still, I won't shed her blood
or scar that skin of hers, which is whiter than snow
and as smooth as the alabaster of a monument.   5
Still, she has to die or else she'll betray more men.
I'll put out this light and then put out her light.
If I extinguish your light, flaming servant,
I can always relight you again
if I regret my action. But once I put out your light,   10
you skillfully designed creation of nature,
I don't know where to find that divine fire
that can relight you again. When I've picked a rose,
I can't make it grow again;
it's doomed to wither. I'll smell it on the tree. (*He kisses her.*)   15
Her sweet breath would almost persuade
Justice to break her sword! One more kiss, one more!
Be like this when you're dead, and I'll kill you
and love you afterward. One more kiss, and this is the last!
Such sweetness has never before been so fatal. I must weep,   20
but I cry cruel tears. My sorrow is like that of God
when punishing his beloved sinners. She's awakening.

DESDEMONA
Who's there? Othello?

OTHELLO
Yes, Desdemona.

DESDEMONA
Won't you come to bed, my lord?   25

OTHELLO
Have you pray'd tonight, Desdemon?

DESDEMONA
Ay, my lord.

OTHELLO
If you bethink yourself of any crime
Unreconcil'd as yet to heaven and grace,
30   Solicit for it straight.

DESDEMONA
                Alack, my lord,
what may you mean by that?

OTHELLO
Well, do it, and be brief; I will walk by.
I would not kill thy unprepared spirit;
35   No; heaven forfend! I would not kill thy soul.

DESDEMONA
Talk you of killing?

OTHELLO
Ay, I do.

DESDEMONA
Then heaven have mercy on me!

OTHELLO
Amen, with all my heart!

DESDEMONA
40   If you say so, I hope you will not kill me.

OTHELLO
Hum!

DESDEMONA
And yet I fear you; for you're fatal then
When your eyes roll so. Why I should fear I know not,
Since guiltiness I know not: but yet I feel I fear.

OTHELLO
45   Think on thy sins.

OTHELLO

Have you prayed tonight, Desdemona?

DESDEMONA

Yes, my lord.

OTHELLO

If you can think of any crime
which you haven't yet confessed to heaven,
ask forgiveness for it now.   30

DESDEMONA

Oh, my lord,
 what do you mean by that?

OTHELLO

Well, get on with it, and be quick; I will wait nearby
I don't want to kill your unrepentant spirit.
No, heaven forbid! I don't want to kill your soul.   35

DESDEMONA

Do you talk of killing?

OTHELLO

Yes, I do.

DESDEMONA

Then heaven have mercy on me!

OTHELLO

I say amen, with all my heart!

DESDEMONA

If you mean that, I hope you will not kill me.   40

OTHELLO

Hum!

DESDEMONA

Still, I'm afraid of you; you are dangerous
when your eyes roll like that. I don't know why I fear you,
since I don't know what crimes I'm guilty of. Still, I'm afraid.

OTHELLO

Think about your sins.   45

DESDEMONA

                       They are loves I bear to you.

OTHELLO

Ay, and for that thou diest.

DESDEMONA

That death's unnatural that kills for loving.
Alas, why gnaw you so your nether lip?

50   Some bloody passion shakes your very frame.
These are **portents**; but yet I hope, I hope,
They do not point on me.

OTHELLO

                         Peace, and be still!

DESDEMONA

I will so. What's the matter?

OTHELLO

55   That handkerchief
Which I so lov'd and gave thee, thou gav'st to
     Cassio.

DESDEMONA

No, by my life and soul!
Send for the man, and ask him.

OTHELLO

60   Sweet soul, take heed,
Take heed of **perjury**; thou art on thy deathbed.

DESDEMONA

Ay, but not yet to die.

OTHELLO

                     Yes, presently.
Therefore confess thee freely of thy sin;

65   For to deny each article with oath
Cannot remove nor choke the strong conception
That I do groan withal. Thou art to die.

DESDEMONA

Then Lord have mercy on me!

OTHELLO

                     I say, "Amen."

DESDEMONA
They are all the different loves I've had for you.

OTHELLO
Yes, and that's why you'll die.

DESDEMONA
It's unnatural to kill out of love.
Oh, why are you gnawing on your lower lip like that?
Some violent anger is causing you to shake.   50
These are bad signs. But still I hope, I hope,
they won't mean any harm to me.

OTHELLO
Hold your tongue and be still!

DESDEMONA
I will do so. What's the matter?

OTHELLO
The handkerchief   55
I loved so much and gave to you, you gave to
    Cassio.

DESDEMONA
No, I swear by my life and soul!
Send for the man and ask him.

OTHELLO
Sweet soul, be careful,   60
be careful of perjury; you're on your deathbed.

DESDEMONA
Yes, but it's not time for me to die.

OTHELLO
Yes, immediately.
Therefore, confess your sins openly,
since solemnly denying each charge   65
won't lift or kill the set purpose
that causes me to groan like this. You must die.

DESDEMONA
Then may the Lord have mercy on me!

OTHELLO
I say "amen."

DESDEMONA

70   And have you mercy too! I never did
Offend you in my life; never lov'd Cassio
But with such general warranty of heaven
As I might love. I never gave him token.

OTHELLO

By heaven, I saw my handkerchief in 's hand!
75   O perjur'd woman! Thou dost stone my heart
And mak'st me call what I intend to do
A murder, which I thought a sacrifice.*
I saw the handkerchief!

DESDEMONA

                    He found it then;
80   I never gave it him. Send for him hither;
Let him confess a truth.

OTHELLO

                    He hath confess'd.

DESDEMONA

What, my lord?

OTHELLO

That he hath us'd thee.

DESDEMONA

85   How? Unlawfully?

OTHELLO

Ay.

DESDEMONA

He will not say so.

OTHELLO

               No, his mouth is stopp'd.
Honest Iago hath ta'en order for 't.

DESDEMONA

90   O, my fear interprets. What, is he dead?

---

77   *A murder . . . sacrifice.* Desdemona's protests have so incensed Othello that his
killing of Desdemona will more resemble a murder of passion than an execution
dispassionately carried out.

DESDEMONA

And may you have mercy too! I never   70
offended you in my life. I never loved Cassio
except in such a way that heaven
would find permissible. I never gave him a token of love.

OTHELLO

By heaven, I saw my handkerchief in his hand!
You lying woman! You have turned my heart into stone   75
and make me call what I intend to do
a murder, when I intended it as a sacrifice.
I saw the handkerchief.

DESDEMONA

He must have found it then.
I never gave it to him. Summon him here.   80
Let him confess the truth.

OTHELLO

He has confessed already.

DESDEMONA

To what, my lord?

OTHELLO

That he has had you.

DESDEMONA

How? Improperly?   85

OTHELLO

Yes.

DESDEMONA

He won't say that.

OTHELLO

No, his mouth has been stopped.
Honest Iago was given orders to see to that.

DESDEMONA

Oh, my fear makes me wonder. Is he dead?   90

OTHELLO
    Had all his hairs been lives, my great revenge
    Had stomach for them all.

DESDEMONA
    Alas! He is betray'd, and I undone.

OTHELLO
    Out, strumpet! Weep'st thou for him to my face?

DESDEMONA
95   O, banish me, my lord, but kill me not!

OTHELLO
    Down, strumpet!

DESDEMONA
    Kill me tomorrow; let me live tonight!

OTHELLO
    Nay, if you strive—

DESDEMONA
    But half an hour!

OTHELLO
100   Being done, there is no pause.

DESDEMONA
    But while I say one prayer!

OTHELLO
                        It is too late.

        [*He smothers her.*]

EMILIA [*at the door*]
    My lord, my lord! What, ho! My lord, my lord!

OTHELLO
    What noise is this?—Not dead? Not yet quite dead?
105   I that am cruel am yet merciful;
    I would not have thee linger in thy pain.
    So, so.

EMILIA [*within*]
    What, ho! My lord, my lord!

OTHELLO
If all of his hairs had been lives, my vengefulness
would have killed them all.

DESDEMONA
Oh, he has been betrayed, and I am finished!

OTHELLO
Enough, harlot! Are you weeping for him to my very face?

DESDEMONA
Oh, banish me, my lord, but don't kill me!   95

OTHELLO
Down with you, harlot!

DESDEMONA
Kill me tomorrow; let me live tonight!

OTHELLO
No, if you even try—

DESDEMONA
Just half an hour!

OTHELLO
Since this is the end, there can be no delay.   100

DESDEMONA
Just let me say one prayer!

OTHELLO
It's too late for that.

>   OTHELLO *smothers* DESDEMONA.

EMILIA (*at the door*)
My lord, my lord! Can you hear me? My lord, my lord!

OTHELLO
What is this noise? Isn't she dead? Not yet quite dead?
I may be cruel but I'm also merciful;   105
I won't allow you to suffer anymore.
There, there.

EMILIA (*from offstage*)
Can you hear me? My lord, my lord!

OTHELLO

Who's there?

EMILIA [*within*]

110   O, good my lord, I would speak a word with you!

OTHELLO

Yes. 'Tis Emilia.—By and by.—She's dead.
'Tis like she comes to speak of Cassio's death.
The noise was here. Ha! No more moving?
Still as the grave. Shall she come in? Were 't good?—

115   I think she stirs again. No. What's best to do?
If she come in, she'll sure speak to my wife.
My wife! My wife! What wife? I have no wife.
O, insupportable! O heavy hour!
Methinks it should be now a huge eclipse

120   Of sun and moon, and that th' affrighted globe
Should yawn at alteration.*

EMILIA [*within*]

I do beseech you
That I may speak with you, O, good my lord!

OTHELLO

I had forgot thee. O, come in, Emilia.—

125   Soft, by and by, let me the curtains draw.—
Where art thou? [*Unlocks the door.*]

Enter EMILIA.

What's the matter with thee now?

EMILIA

O, my good lord, yonder's foul murders done!

OTHELLO

What, now?

EMILIA

130   But now, my lord.

120–122   *Methinks . . . alteration.* The Elizabethans thought nature sometimes echoed
major tragedies or other important events that humans experienced.

OTHELLO
Who's there?

EMILIA (*from offstage*)
Oh, my good lord, I would like to have a word with you! 110

OTHELLO
(*calling to her*) Yes. (*to himself*) It's Emilia. (*calling*) In a
  moment. (*to himself*) She's dead.
It's likely that she's come to tell me of Cassio's death;
she called very loudly. What! Have you stopped moving?
You're as still as the grave. Should I let her in? Is that wise?
I think she's moving again. No. What's the best thing to do? 115
If she comes in, she'll surely speak to my wife.
My wife! My wife! What wife? I do not have a wife.
Oh, this is unbearable! Oh, what a terrible hour!
I think that now a complete eclipse should come
of the sun and moon, and the frightened world 120
should gape with an earthquake.

EMILIA (*from offstage*)
I beg you
to let me talk with you, my good lord!

OTHELLO
I'd forgotten you. Oh, come in, Emilia.
Just a moment, I'll be right there. (*to himself*) I'll pull the 125
  curtains.
(*to* EMILIA) Where are you? (*He opens the door.*)

  EMILIA *enters.*

What's the matter with you now?

EMILIA
Oh, my good lord, a foul murder has been committed!

OTHELLO
What? Now?

EMILIA
Just now, my lord. 130

OTHELLO

It is the very error of the moon;
She comes more nearer earth than she was wont,
And makes men mad.

EMILIA

                        Cassio, my lord, hath kill'd
135   A young Venetian call'd Roderigo.

OTHELLO

Roderigo kill'd!
And Cassio kill'd!

EMILIA

No, Cassio is not kill'd.

OTHELLO

Not Cassio kill'd! Then murder's out of tune,
140   And sweet revenge grows harsh.

DESDEMONA

O, falsely, falsely murder'd!

EMILIA

O Lord, what cry is that?

OTHELLO

                    That! What?

EMILIA

Out, and alas! That was my lady's voice.
145   Help! Help, ho! Help! O lady, speak again!
Sweet Desdemona! O sweet mistress, speak!

DESDEMONA

A guiltless death I die.

EMILIA

O, who hath done this deed?

DESDEMONA

Nobody; I myself. Farewell!
150   Commend me to my kind lord. O, farewell! [*Dies.*]

OTHELLO

    This is due to the irregular course of the moon.
    It has come closer to earth than usual
    and makes men mad.

EMILIA

    My lord, Cassio has killed a young Venetian   135
    named Roderigo.

OTHELLO

    Has Roderigo been killed? And Cassio's been killed?

EMILIA

    No, Cassio's not been killed.

OTHELLO

    Cassio's not been killed? Then the wrong murder has been
        committed,
    and my sweet revenge has turned bitter.   140

DESDEMONA

    Wrongly, wrongly murdered!

EMILIA

    Oh, lord! What is that cry?

OTHELLO

    That? What?

EMILIA

    Oh, no! That was my lady's voice.
    (*pulling back the bed curtains*) Help! Help, somebody! Help!   145
        Oh, lady, speak again!
    Sweet Desdemona! Oh, sweet lady, speak!

DESDEMONA

    I shall die guiltless.

EMILIA

    Oh, who has done this deed?

DESDEMONA

    Nobody. I, myself. Good-bye.
    Speak well of me to my kind lord. Oh, good-bye! (*She dies.*)   150

OTHELLO
Why, how should she be murd'red?

EMILIA
                                        Alas, who knows?

OTHELLO
You heard her say herself, it was not I.

EMILIA
She said so; I must needs report the truth.

OTHELLO
155   She's like a liar gone to burning hell.
'Twas I that kill'd her.

EMILIA
O, the more angel she,
and you the blacker devil!

OTHELLO
She turn'd to folly, and she was a whore.

EMILIA
160   Thou dost belie her, and thou art a devil.

OTHELLO
She was false as water.*

EMILIA
Thou art rash as fire to say
That she was false. O, she was heavenly true!

OTHELLO
Cassio did top her; ask thy husband else.
165   O, I were damn'd beneath all depth in hell
But that I did proceed upon just grounds
To this extremity. Thy husband knew it all.

EMILIA
My husband?

OTHELLO
Thy husband.

---

161   *false as water* Water was said to be false because it holds no shape of its own but
shifts to fill whatever container it is in.

OTHELLO

Why, how could she have been murdered!

EMILIA

Oh, who knows?

OTHELLO

You heard her say herself, it wasn't me who did it.

EMILIA

She did say so; I'd testify to that.

OTHELLO

She's like a liar who's gone to burning hell!   155
It was I who killed her.

EMILIA

Oh, then she's all the more an angel.
and you're an even blacker devil!

OTHELLO

She became an adulteress; she was a whore.

EMILIA

You are slandering her, and you are a devil.   160

OTHELLO

She was as inconstant as water.

EMILIA

You are as rash as fire to say
that she was inconstant. Oh, she was as true as heaven!

OTHELLO

Cassio made love to her. Ask your husband if that isn't true.
Oh, I would be damned to the lowest depths of hell   165
if I hadn't proceeded upon just grounds
to such an extreme action. Your husband knew all about it.

EMILIA

My husband?

OTHELLO

Your husband.

EMILIA

170 That she was false to wedlock?

OTHELLO

Ay, with Cassio. Had she been true,
If heaven would make me such another world
Of one entire and perfect chrysolite,
I'd not have sold her for it.

EMILIA

175 My husband?

OTHELLO

Ay, 'twas he that told me on her first.
An honest man he is, and hates the slime
That sticks on filthy deeds.

EMILIA

My husband?

OTHELLO

180 What needs this iterance, woman? I say, thy husband.

EMILIA

O mistress, villainy hath made mocks with love!—
My husband say she was false?

OTHELLO

He, woman.
I say thy husband. Dost understand the word?
185 My friend, thy husband, honest, honest Iago.

EMILIA

If he say so, may his **pernicious** soul
Rot half a grain a day! He lies to th' heart.
She was too fond of her most filthy bargain.

OTHELLO

Hah?

EMILIA

190 Do thy worst!
This deed of thine is no more worthy heaven
Than thou wast worthy her.

OTHELLO

Peace, you were best!

EMILIA

That she was unfaithful to her marriage vows? 170

OTHELLO

Yes, with Cassio. No, if she had been true,
heaven could have made me another world
entirely out of perfect topaz,
and I wouldn't have sold her for it.

EMILIA

My husband? 175

OTHELLO

Yes, he told me first.
He's an honest man, and he hates the slime
that sticks to filthy deeds.

EMILIA

My husband?

OTHELLO

Why do you repeat yourself, woman? I said your husband. 180

EMILIA

Oh, my lady, a villain has toyed with your love!
My husband said she was unfaithful?

OTHELLO

It was he, woman.
I said your husband. Do you understand the word?
My friend, your husband; honest, honest Iago. 185

EMILIA

If he said so, I hope his lying soul
rots little by little! He's lying in his heart.
She was all too devoted to her filthy marriage.

OTHELLO

Ha!

EMILIA

Do your worst. 190
This deed you've done is no more worthy of heaven
than you were worthy of her.

OTHELLO

You'd better be quiet.

EMILIA

Thou hast not half that power to do me harm
195 As I have to be hurt. O gull! O dolt,
As ignorant as dirt! Thou has done a deed—
I care not for thy sword; I'll make thee known
Though I lost twenty lives. Help! Help, ho! Help!
The Moor hath kill'd my mistress! Murder! Murder!

Enter MONTANO, GRATIANO, and IAGO.

MONTANO
200 What is the matter? How now, General!

EMILIA

O, are you come, Iago? You have done well,
That men must lay their murders on your neck.

GRATIANO

What is the matter?

EMILIA [*to* IAGO]

Disprove this villain, if thou be'st a man.
205 He says thou told'st him that his wife was false.
I know thou didst not, thou'rt not such a villain.
Speak, for my heart is full.

IAGO

I told him what I thought, and told no more
Than what he found himself was apt and true.

EMILIA
210 But did you ever tell him she was false?

IAGO

I did.

EMILIA

You told a lie, an **odious**, damned lie;
Upon my soul, a lie, a wicked lie.
She false with Cassio? Did you say with Cassio?

IAGO
215 With Cassio, mistress. Go to! Charm your tongue.

EMILIA

I will not charm my tongue; I am bound to speak.
My mistress here lies murdered in her bed.

EMILIA

You can only hurt my body;
you can't harm my soul. You fool! You dolt!   195
You're as ignorant as dirt! You've done a deed—
I'm not afraid of your sword. I'll make your murder known,
even if you kill me twenty times. Help! Help, somebody! Help!
The Moor has killed my lady! Murder! Murder!

> MONTANO, GRATIANO, IAGO, *and others enter.*

MONTANO

What's the matter? What is it, General?   200

EMILIA

Oh, you've come too, Iago? You've done very well
to have other men blame their murders on you.

GRATIANO

What's the matter?

EMILIA (*to* IAGO)

Prove this villain wrong if you are a man.
He says you told him that his wife was unfaithful.   205
I know you didn't; you are not such a villain.
Tell me; my heart is in anguish.

IAGO

I told him what I thought and told no more
than what he himself found to be perfectly true.

EMILIA

But did you ever tell him she was unfaithful?   210

IAGO

I did.

EMILIA

You told a lie, a foul, damned lie!
By my very soul, a lie! A wicked lie!
She, unfaithful with Cassio? Did you say with Cassio?

IAGO

With Cassio, woman. Calm down and hold your tongue.   215

EMILIA

I will not hold my tongue; I have to speak.
My mistress is lying here, murdered in her bed—

ALL
O heavens forfend!

EMILIA [*to* IAGO]
And your reports have set the murder on!

OTHELLO
220   Nay, stare not, masters; it is true, indeed.

GRATIANO
'Tis a strange truth.

MONTANO
O monstrous act!

EMILIA
                    Villainy, villainy, villainy!
I think upon 't I think I smell 't! O villainy!
225   I thought so then. I'll kill myself for grief!
O villainy, villainy!

IAGO
What, are you mad? I charge you, get you home.

EMILIA
Good gentlemen, let me have leave to speak;
'Tis proper I obey him, but not now.
230   Perchance, Iago, I will ne'er go home.

OTHELLO
O! O! O!   [*He falls on the bed.*]

EMILIA
Nay, lay thee down and roar;
For thou hast kill'd the sweetest innocent
That e'er did lift up eye.

OTHELLO [*rising*]
235   O, she was foul!—
I scarce did know you, uncle. There lies your niece,
Whose breath indeed these hands have newly stopp'd.
I know this act shows horrible and grim.

ALL
    Oh, heaven forbid!

EMILIA (*to* IAGO)
    And things you said brought about this murder.

OTHELLO
    Stop staring, gentlemen. It is really the truth.   220

GRATIANO
    It is a terrible truth.

MONTANO
    A monstrous act!

EMILIA
    Villainy, villainy, villainy!
    I sense it—I think I smell it!—Oh, villainy!
    I realize it now—I'll kill myself out of grief!—   225
    Oh, villainy, villainy!

IAGO
    What's the matter? Are you mad? I order you to go home.

EMILIA
    Good gentlemen, just let me speak.
    It's proper that I obey him, but not now.
    Perhaps, Iago, I'll never go home.   230

OTHELLO
    Oh! Oh! Oh!

      He falls on the bed.

EMILIA
    Go right ahead and lie there roaring!
    You've killed the sweetest, most innocent creature
    who ever looked upward.

OTHELLO (*He rises.*)
    Oh, she was wicked!   235
    (*to* GRATIANO) I hardly recognized you, uncle. There lies your niece,
    whose breath has, indeed, just been stopped by these hands.
    I know this act appears to be horrible and grim.

GRATIANO

240 Poor Desdemona! I am glad thy father's dead.
Thy match was mortal to him, and pure grief
Shore his old thread in twain. Did he live now,
This sight would make him do a desperate turn,
Yea, curse his better angel from his side,
And fall to reprobance.

OTHELLO

245 'Tis pitiful. But yet Iago knows
That she with Cassio hath the act of shame
A thousand times committed. Cassio confess'd it;
And she did gratify his amorous works
With that recognizance and pledge of love
250 Which I first gave her. I saw it in his hand;
It was a handkerchief, an antique token
My father gave my mother.

EMILIA

O God! O heavenly God!

IAGO

'Zounds, hold your peace.

EMILIA

255 'Twill out, 'twill out! I peace?
No, I will speak as liberal as the north.
Let heaven and men and devils, let them all,
All, all, cry shame against me, yet I'll speak.

IAGO

Be wise, and get you home. [IAGO *draws his sword.*]

EMILIA

260 I will not.

GRATIANO

Fie!
Your sword upon a woman?

GRATIANO

Poor Desdemona! I'm glad your father is already dead.
Your marriage killed him and sheer grief   240
cut his thread of life in two. If he were still alive,
this sight would cause him to do something desperate—
he might even have renounced his better nature
and given himself up to damnation.

OTHELLO

It's a pitiful thing; but still, Iago knows   245
that she committed adultery with Cassio
a thousand times. Cassio confessed it;
and she rewarded his acts of love
with a present and token of love
which I first gave to her. I saw it in his hand.   250
It was a handkerchief, an old gift
which my father gave to my mother.

EMILIA

Oh, God! Oh, heavenly powers!

IAGO

By God, keep quiet!

EMILIA

It will all come out; it will all come out! I, hold my tongue?   255
No, I'll speak as freely as the north wind.
Let angels, men, and devils, let all of them—
all, all—denounce me for it, but I'll still speak.

IAGO

Be wise and go home. (IAGO *draws his sword and threatens*
      EMILIA.)

EMILIA

I will not.   260

GRATIANO

For shame!
Would you use your sword against a woman?

EMILIA

O thou dull Moor! That handkerchief thou speak'st of
I found by fortune and did give my husband—
265 For often, with a solemn earnestness,
More than indeed belong'd to such a trifle,
He begg'd of me to steal 't.

IAGO

Villainous whore!

EMILIA

She give it Cassio? No, alas! I found it,
270 And I did give 't my husband.

IAGO

Filth, thou liest!

EMILIA

By heaven, I do not, I do not, gentlemen!
[*to* OTHELLO] O murd'rous coxcomb! What should such
    a fool
275 Do with so good a wife?

OTHELLO

Are there no stones in heaven
But what serves for the thunder?—Precious villain!

[*He runs at* IAGO *but is disarmed;* IAGO *kills* EMILIA.]

GRATIANO

The woman falls! Sure, he hath kill'd his wife.

EMILIA

Ay, ay! O, lay me by my mistress's side.

[*Exit* IAGO.]

GRATIANO

280 He's gone, but his wife's kill'd.

MONTANO

'Tis a **notorious** villain. Take you this weapon
Which I have here recover'd from the Moor.
Come, guard the door without; let him not pass,
But kill him rather. I'll after that same villain,
285 For 'tis a damned slave.

EMILIA

Oh, you stupid Moor, the handkerchief you speak of
I found by luck and gave it to my husband
because he often, and with deadly earnestness—   265
more than seemed appropriate for such a small thing—
asked me to steal it.

IAGO

You villainous whore!

EMILIA

Did she give it to Cassio? No, sadly, I found it,
and I gave it to my husband.   270

IAGO

You filthy thing, you lie!

EMILIA

By heaven, I do not, I do not, gentlemen.
(*to* OTHELLO) Oh, you murderous idiot! What was a fool like you
doing with such a good wife?   275

OTHELLO

Aren't there any bolts in the sky
except those used for thunder? You clever villain!

> OTHELLO *attacks* IAGO, *but is disarmed.* IAGO *stabs* EMILIA.

GRATIANO

The woman has fallen. He has certainly killed his wife.

EMILIA

Yes, yes. Oh, lay me by my lady's side.

> IAGO *exits.*

GRATIANO

He's gone, but his wife's been killed.   280

MONTANO

He's a complete villain. Take this weapon,
which I just took away from the Moor.
Come, guard the outside door. Don't let him pass;
if he tries, kill him. I'll go after the villain myself;
he's a damned scoundrel.   285

[*Exeunt* MONTANO *and* GRATIANO.]

OTHELLO
    I am not valiant neither,
    But every puny whipster gets my sword.
    But why should honour outlive honesty?
    Let it go all.

EMILIA
290   What did thy song bode, lady?
    Hark, canst thou hear me? I will play the swan,
    And die in music.* [*singing*] "Willow, willow, willow!"—
    Moor, she was chaste; she lov'd thee, cruel Moor;
    So come my soul to bliss, as I speak true;
295   So speaking as I think, alas, I die. [*Dies.*]

OTHELLO
    I have another weapon in this chamber;
    It is a sword of Spain, the ice brook's temper—
    O, here it is. Uncle, I must come forth.

GRATIANO [*within*]
    If thou attempt it, it will cost thee dear,
300   Thou hast no weapon, and perforce must suffer.

OTHELLO
    Look in upon me then and speak with me,
    Or, naked as I am, I will assault thee.

        Reenter GRATIANO.

GRATIANO
    What is the matter?

OTHELLO
                Behold, I have a weapon;
305   A better never did itself sustain
    Upon a soldier's thigh. I have seen the day
    That, with this little arm and this good sword,
    I have made my way through more **impediment**s
    Than twenty times your stop. But, O vain boast!
310   Who can control his fate? 'Tis not so now.

291–292 *swan . . . music* Swans were believed to sing as they died.

MONTANO *and* GRATIANO *exit with others, leaving* OTHELLO *and* EMILIA *alone.*

OTHELLO
My courage is gone along with everything else;
any contemptible fellow can get my sword now.
But why should my good reputation outlive what I really am?
Let me lose it all.

EMILIA
What was that song you sang to me, lady?   290
Listen, can't you hear me? I'll pretend to be a swan
and die with music. (*She sings.*) *Willow, willow, willow.*
Moor, she was faithful; she loved you, cruel Moor.
As I hope for eternal happiness, I'm telling the truth.
So, speaking my mind, I die; I die. (*She dies.*)   295

OTHELLO
I have another weapon in this room;
it's a Spanish sword, tempered in ice-cold water.
Oh, here it is. (*calling outside*) Uncle, I must come out.

GRATIANO (*from offstage*)
If you try it, you'll pay for it dearly.
You don't have a weapon, so you'll undoubtedly suffer.   300

OTHELLO
Come in here, then, and talk to me,
or I'll attack you, even though I'm unarmed.

          GRATIANO *enters.*

GRATIANO
What's the matter?

OTHELLO
Look, I do have a weapon.
A better sword was never carried   305
at a soldier's side. I have seen a day
when, with this little arm and this good sword,
I've fought my way past more obstacles
than twenty of your kind. But what a useless boast!
Who can control his fate? It's not like that now.   310

Be not afraid though you do see me weapon'd;
Here is my journey's end, here is my butt
And very sea-mark of my utmost sail.
Do you go back dismay'd? 'Tis a lost fear;
315 Man but a rush against Othello's breast
And he retires. Where should Othello go?
Now, how dost thou look now? O ill-starr'd wench!
Pale as thy smock! When we shall meet at compt,
This look of thine will hurl my soul from heaven,
320 And fiends will snatch at it. Cold, cold, my girl!
Even like thy chastity.—O cursed, cursed slave!—
Whip me, you devils,
From the possession of this heavenly sight!
Blow me about in winds! Roast me in sulphur!
325 Wash me in steep-down gulfs of liquid fire!
O Desdemona! Dead, Desdemona! Dead! Oh! Oh!

Enter LODOVICO, MONTANO, CASSIO, *carried in a chair, and* OFFICERS, *with* IAGO *prisoner.*

LODOVICO
Where is this rash and most unfortunate man?

OTHELLO
That's he that was Othello; here I am.

LODOVICO
Where is that viper? Bring the villain forth. [IAGO *brought forward.*]

OTHELLO
330 I look down towards his feet; but that's a fable.—*
If that thou be'st a devil, I cannot kill thee. [*Wounds* IAGO.]

LODOVICO
Wrench his sword from him.

[*OTHELLO is disarmed.*]

IAGO
I bleed, sir, but not kill'd.

---

330   *I . . . feet* Othello is looking to see if Iago has cloven feet like Satan.

Don't be afraid, though you see me with a weapon.
This is my journey's end; this is my arrow's target,
the landmark of my ship's final destination.
Are you backing away from me out of fear? No need.
If you attack Othello with only a reed, 315
he'll retreat. Where should Othello go?
(*to* DESDEMONA) How do you look now? Oh, unfortunate
   woman!
As pale as your gown! When we meet at the Judgment Day,
this innocent look of yours will cause my soul to be damned,
and devils will snatch at it. Are you cold, cold, my girl? 320
Just like your good virtue. Oh, what a cursed fool I am!
Devils, whip
the sight of this heavenly vision from my mind!
Blow me about with the wind! Roast me in sulfur!
Wash me down into deep seas of liquid fire! 325
Oh, Desdemona, Desdemona! Dead!
Oh! Oh! Oh!

> LODOVICO, MONTANO, CASSIO, *carried in a chair, and*
> OFFICERS *enter with* IAGO *as a prisoner.*

LODOVICO
Where is this rash and very unfortunate man?

OTHELLO
You're speaking of the man who used to be Othello. Here I am.

LODOVICO
Where is that snake, Iago? Bring the villain forward. (IAGO *is*
   brought forward.)

OTHELLO
I'm looking at his feet—but that's only a myth. 330
If you really are a devil, I can't kill you. (*He stabs* IAGO.)

LODOVICO
Get that sword away from him.

> OTHELLO *is disarmed.*

IAGO
I'm bleeding, sir, but I've not been killed.

OTHELLO

I am not sorry neither. I'd have thee live,
335   For in my sense 'tis happiness to die.

LODOVICO

O thou Othello, that wert once so good,
Fall'n in the practice of a damned slave,
What shall be said to thee?

OTHELLO

Why, anything.
340   An honourable murderer, if you will,
For naught I did in hate, but all in honour.

LODOVICO

This wretch hath part confess'd his villainy.
Did you and he consent in Cassio's death?

OTHELLO

Ay.

CASSIO

345   Dear general, I never gave you cause.

OTHELLO

I do believe it, and I ask your pardon.
Will you, I pray, demand that demi-devil
Why he hath thus ensnar'd my soul and body?

IAGO

Demand me nothing; what you know, you know.
350   From this time forth I never will speak word.

LODOVICO

What, not to pray?

GRATIANO

Torments will ope your lips.

OTHELLO

Well, thou dost best.

OTHELLO

I'm not sorry to hear that. I'd rather you lived on.
From my point of view, it would be happiness to die. 335

LODOVICO

Oh, Othello, you used to be so good,
but you've fallen prey to the plot of a damned villain.
What can I say to you?

OTHELLO

Why, anything.
Call me an honorable murderer, if you wish, 340
for I did nothing out of hate but everything out of honor.

LODOVICO

This wretch has partially confessed to his villainy.
Did you and he plot to kill Cassio?

OTHELLO

Yes.

CASSIO

Dear general, I never gave you any cause. 345

OTHELLO

I believe you, and I ask your pardon.
Please, will you ask that half-devil
why he trapped me, soul and body, into this?

IAGO

Don't ask me any questions, you know everything you'll ever
know.
I'll never say a word from now on. 350

LODOVICO

What, you won't even pray?

GRATIANO

Torture will make you talk.

OTHELLO

You are right not to speak.

LODOVICO

    Sir, you shall understand what hath befall'n,
355   Which, as I think, you know not. Here is a letter
    Found in the pocket of the slain Roderigo,
    And here another. [*He shows papers.*] The one
       of them imports
    The death of Cassio to be undertook
360   By Roderigo.

OTHELLO

    O villain!

CASSIO

    Most heathenish and most gross!

LODOVICO

    Now here's another discontented paper,
    Found in his pocket, too; and this, it seems,
365   Roderigo meant t' have sent this damned villain;
    But that, belike, Iago in the interim
    Came in and satisfi'd him.

OTHELLO

    O thou pernicious caitiff!—
    How came you, Cassio, by that handkerchief
370   That was my wife's?

CASSIO

                 I found it in my chamber,
    And he himself confess'd but even now
    That there he dropp'd it for a special purpose
    Which wrought to his desire.

OTHELLO

375   O fool! fool! fool!

CASSIO

    There is besides in Roderigo's letter,
    How he upbraids Iago, that he made him
    Brave me upon the watch, whereon it came
    That I was cast. And even but now he spake,
380   After long seeming dead: Iago hurt him,
    Iago set him on.

LODOVICO

Sir, I'll try to explain what has happened,
since I don't believe you understand. I have a letter here,   355
which was found in the pocket of the slain Roderigo;
and here is another. One of them orders
that Cassio be killed
by Roderigo.   360

OTHELLO

Oh, you villain!

CASSIO

An unholy and horrible villain!

LODOVICO

And here's another disturbing letter,
which was found in his pocket too. It seems that this one
Roderigo meant to have sent to this damned villain,   365
but perhaps before it was delivered,
Iago spoke with him and convinced him.

OTHELLO

Oh, you despicable coward!
Cassio, how did you get that handkerchief
that belonged to my wife?   370

CASSIO

I found it in my room;
and he himself confessed just now
that he left it there deliberately
in order to carry out his plan.

OTHELLO

Oh, I am a fool! A fool! A fool!   375

CASSIO

Also in Roderigo's letter,
he angrily criticized Iago for making him
bait me while I was on guard duty, which led
to my dismissal. So even now he speaks,
long after he seemed to be dead. Iago ruined him;   380
Iago led him on.

LODOVICO [*to* OTHELLO]

You must forsake this room and go with us.
Your power and your command is taken off,
And Cassio rules in Cyprus. For this slave,
385 If there be any cunning cruelty
That can torment him much and hold him long,
It shall be his. You shall close prisoner rest,
Till that the nature of your fault be known
To the Venetian state.—Come, bring away.

OTHELLO

390 Soft you; a word or two before you go.
I have done the state some service, and they know 't.
No more of that. I pray you, in your letters,
When you shall these unlucky deeds relate,
Speak of me as I am; nothing **extenuate**,
395 Nor set down aught in malice. Then must you speak
Of one that lov'd not wisely but too well;
Of one not easily jealous, but being wrought,
Perplex'd in the extreme; of one whose hand,
Like the base Judean,* threw a pearl away
400 Richer than all his tribe; of one whose subdu'd eyes,
Albeit unused to the melting mood,
Drops tears as fast as the Arabian trees
Their medicinal gum. Set you down this;
And say besides, that in Aleppo once,
405 Where a **malignant** and a turban'd Turk
Beat a Venetian and traduc'd the state,
I took by th' throat the circumcised dog,
And smote him—thus. [*Stabs himself.*]

LODOVICO

O bloody period!

GRATIANO

410 All that's spoke is marr'd.

---

399 *the base Judean* a suggestion of Christian betrayal

LODOVICO (*to* OTHELLO)

You must leave this room and come with us.
Your authority and power have been taken away,
and Cassio is now ruler of Cyprus. As for this scoundrel,
whatever elaborate torture   385
can be devised to torment him a great deal and for a long time
will be used against him. You'll be kept a closely guarded
    prisoner
until the nature of your crimes is known
by the government of Venice. Come, let's go.

OTHELLO

But wait! Just a word or two before you go.   390
I have done some service for the state, and they know it.
But leave all that aside. I beg you, in your letters
telling of these unfortunate deeds,
speak of me as I am. Don't soften anything
or write anything out of hatred. You must describe me   395
as one who loved not wisely, but too much;
as one not easily made jealous, but, being manipulated,
became distracted in the extreme; as one whose hand,
like an ignorant Jew, threw a pearl away
worth more than all his people; as one whose humbled eyes,   400
not normally given to weeping,
let drop tears as fast as Arabian trees
drop their medicinal gum. Write all this;
and also tell how, in Aleppo once,
when a vicious Turk wearing a turban   405
attacked a Venetian and insulted the state,
I took the circumcised dog by the throat
and stabbed him—like this. (*He stabs himself.*)

LODOVICO

Oh, what a bloody end!

GRATIANO

Words can't describe it.   410

OTHELLO [*to* DESDEMONA]
I kiss'd thee ere I kill'd thee: no way but this,
Killing myself, to die upon a kiss.

[*Falls on the bed and dies.*]

CASSIO
This did I fear, but thought he had no weapon,
For he was great of heart.

LODOVICO [*to* IAGO]
415   O Spartan dog,*
More fell than anguish, hunger, or the sea!
Look on the tragic loading of this bed;
This is thy work.—The object poisons sight;
Let it be hid.—Gratiano, keep the house,
420 And seize upon the fortunes of the Moor,
For they succeed on you. [*to* CASSIO] To you, lord governor,
Remains the censure of this hellish villain;
The time, the place, the torture. O, enforce it!
Myself will straight aboard; and to the state
425 This heavy act with heavy heart relate.

[*Exeunt.*]

---

415 *Spartan dog* The dogs of Sparta were thought to have been very fierce.

OTHELLO (*to* DESDEMONA)

I kissed you before I killed you. Now this is the only way:
as I kill myself, I'll die with a kiss.

> OTHELLO *falls on the bed and dies.*

CASSIO

I was afraid of this—but I thought he had no weapon—
for he had a noble heart.

LODOVICO (*to* IAGO)

Oh, you Spartan dog, 415
more cruel than anguish, hunger, or the sea!
Look at the tragic victims on this bed.
This is your doing. This sight is too horrible to look at;
let it be hidden. Gratiano, you guard the house
and take possession of the Moor's property, 420
since you are the heir. (*to* CASSIO) Lord governor, it is up to you
to see that this hellish villain is punished.
Decide on the time, the place, and the means of torture—
> make sure it is enforced!
As for myself, I'll leave at once and report to the state
these sad acts with a sad heart. 425

> *Everyone exits.*

Act V Review

Discussion Questions

1. How does Iago intend to dispose of Cassio and Roderigo? Explain what actually transpires.

2. How does Iago take advantage of Bianca's entrance in Scene i?

3. When Othello first awakens Desdemona in Scene ii, he assures her that he won't kill her until she's repented her sins. What makes him change his mind?

4. Emilia asks Desdemona, "O, who hath done this deed?" Desdemona replies, "Nobody; I myself. Farewell!" Why does Desdemona lie with her dying breath?

5. In Scene ii, Othello says that the handkerchief was "an antique token / My father gave my mother." Back in Act III, Scene iv, he told Desdemona that an Egyptian charmer gave it to his mother. How do you explain this contradiction?

6. What role does Emilia play in Iago's downfall?

7. What is to be Iago's fate at the end of the play?

Literary Elements

1. Shakespeare is a master at using language to create **mood.** How does Othello's speech at the beginning of Act V, Scene ii, establish the mood for the rest of the play?

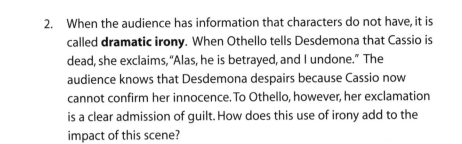

2. When the audience has information that characters do not have, it is called **dramatic irony**. When Othello tells Desdemona that Cassio is dead, she exclaims, "Alas, he is betrayed, and I undone." The audience knows that Desdemona despairs because Cassio now cannot confirm her innocence. To Othello, however, her exclamation is a clear admission of guilt. How does this use of irony add to the impact of this scene?

3. **Hyperbole** is an exaggeration or overstatement not meant to be taken literally. For example, after Othello has murdered Desdemona, he says that "she with Cassio hath the act of shame / A thousand times committed." What dramatic effect does such use of hyperbole contribute to the drama?

Writing Prompts

1. In the last scene, we learn that Roderigo wrote a letter to Iago that he never sent. In it, Roderigo describes how he was manipulated by Iago. Based on information in the play, write this letter, giving a strong sense of Roderigo's personality. You may write it in either Elizabethan or contemporary English.

2. Shakespeare often gave "dying speeches" to his characters. In Act V, Scene ii, we learn that Brabantio died of sorrow over his daughter's marriage. Write his last speech.

3. Imagine that Emilia survives at the end of the play. Write a monologue in which she addresses Iago, venting all her feelings about his treachery and her own unwitting complicity in his schemes. Write it in Elizabethan English and, if you like, in blank verse.

4. "Who can control his fate?" asks Othello in the play's final scene. It is a rhetorical question—one to which the answer is obvious. Othello is expressing his belief that *no one* can control his or her fate. Write a letter to Othello, expressing your agreement or disagreement with this point of view.

The Play in Review

Discussion and Analysis

1. Iago has eight soliloquies, while Othello has only three. Why do you think Shakespeare allows Iago to speak directly to the audience more often than Othello?

2. Critics describe Iago as an improvisationist—an actor who makes things up as he goes along. How does Iago continually modify his plots, making adjustments and taking advantage of changing circumstances?

3. As a Moor, Othello was almost certainly born and raised in the Islamic faith. But according to several references in the text, Othello has converted to Christianity. Why do you think Shakespeare portrays Othello as a Christian instead of a Muslim?

4. Some critics have been sharply critical of Desdemona's character. They point out that she deceives her father and breaks his heart, meddles in official matters by trying to help Cassio, lies about losing the handkerchief, and lies again with her dying breath. How do these actions make you feel about her character?

5. In Act V, Scene i, Iago says that Cassio "hath a daily beauty in his life / That makes me ugly. . . ." What do you think this comment suggests about Iago and his motives?

6. What role do you think Othello's race and ethnicity play in the unfolding of the drama?

Literary Elements

1. A **tragedy** is a serious work of literature that narrates the events leading to the downfall of a **tragic hero**, who is usually of noble birth and in almost every way displays noble qualities. His downfall is a result of a **tragic flaw** or fatal character weakness. How well does Othello fit this definition of a tragic hero?

2. Shakespeare's highly descriptive language often employs **figures of speech**. **Similes** are comparisons between two unlike things that use the words *like* or *as;* Iago uses a simile when he says that his jealousy of Othello "Doth, like a poisonous mineral, gnaw my inwards . . ." A **metaphor** is also a comparison between unlike things, but leaves out the words *like* or *as;* Iago is speaking metaphorically when he says that jealousy "is the green-eyed monster, which doth mock / The meat it feeds on." Look for examples of similes and metaphors in *Othello,* and explain how you think these comparisons add to the drama and meaning of the play.

3. **Conflict** is what creates tension and drama in a piece of writing. **External conflict** refers to a struggle between a character and an outside force such as nature or another individual. **Internal conflict** refers to a mental conflict within the individual. Find examples of both kinds of conflict in *Othello.*

4. The rich **diction**, or word choice, in *Othello* has provided English with well-known phrases and expressions—for example, "I will wear my heart upon my sleeve," or jealousy is a "green-eyed monster." Alone or with a partner, find other lines or phrases from the play that either sound familiar or quotable to you.

5. A work as complex as a Shakespeare play will have more than one **theme**. We've already considered the play's theme of the destructive effects of jealousy. Another theme in *Othello* (and many other Shakespeare plays) is the conflict between appearance and reality. For example, in the first scene of the play, Iago announces, "I am not what I am." Find as many other themes as you can in this play.

Writing Prompts

1. View at least one film or television version of *Othello*. It might be one of the following:
    - Orson Welles' 1952 movie version
    - The 1965 film of Laurence Olivier's stage portrayal of *Othello*
    - The 1981 BBC television production starring Anthony Hopkins
    - The 1995 movie version starring Laurence Fishburne and Kenneth Branagh
    - The 2001 movie *O*, in which the play is updated and reset in an American private school

    Write a review of the version you see, evaluating how successfully Shakespeare's tragedy has been adapted to the screen.

2. In the form of a short story, write a sequel to *Othello* involving all its surviving characters. Imagine that Iago escapes captivity and torture and unleashes more mischief.

3. Just what motivates Iago toward his acts of evil? Critics are very divided on this question. Iago mentions several motivations, including his being overlooked for promotion and his suspicion that his wife has been unfaithful with Othello and Cassio. Some critics feel that these motives are adequate to explain Iago's actions. Other critics think that Iago is purely evil and acts without any real motives at all; the motives he mentions are really just rationalizations. Write an essay about whether you think Iago is or isn't a realistically motivated character.

4. Pretend you are a Turkish spy in Cyprus. Write a report to your government describing events taking place on the island after the destruction of the Turkish fleet.

5. Write a story about one of Othello's adventures mentioned in his speech in Act I, Scene iii ("Her father loved me, oft invited me").

Multimodal and Group Activities

1. In a small group, pretend to be the casting directors for a new production of *Othello*. Begin by writing thumbnail sketches of the major characters. Then choose modern actors, thinking carefully about why an actor fits that choice. You may then design a playbill or poster advertising your production, using language and design that give the audience some idea of the way you will interpret your production of *Othello*.

2. Create a drawing or painting that shows the design of the handkerchief given by Othello to Desdemona.

3. Write and perform a comical skit in which Othello and Desdemona survive the last act of the play, and wind up going into therapy. Make as many references to the text as possible, while also using plenty of humor.

4. A storyboard is a layout of drawings used in moviemaking to show the sequence of shots in a scene. It looks a bit like a comic strip and is helpful for showing where to use close-ups, longshots, and unusual camera angles. Select a scene from *Othello* that you would like to see filmed, then create a storyboard showing what such a scene would look like.

5. In his final speech, Othello makes two extremely controversial assertions. He claims that he "loved not wisely, but too well," and that he was "not easily jealous." Some critics feel that Othello is justified in saying such things about himself; others feel that Othello is horribly self-deceived. Divide into two teams, affirmative and negative, and debate the following resolution:

   Resolved: Othello dies in a state of self-deception.

6. Pretend you are about to direct a stage production of *Othello*. Choose speeches and dialogue scenes to serve as audition pieces. Then conduct auditions among your fellow class members. Cast the play, then explain and justify your choices.

Shakespeare's Life

Many great authors can be imagined as living among the characters in their works. Historical records reveal how these writers spoke, felt, and thought. But Shakespeare is more mysterious. He never gave an interview or wrote an autobiography—not even one of his letters survives. What we know about his life can be told very briefly.

Shakespeare was born in April 1564. The exact date of his birth is unknown, but he was baptized on April 26 in the Stratford-upon-Avon church. His father, John, was a prominent local man who served as town chamberlain and mayor. Young William attended

grammar school in Stratford, where he would have learned Latin—a requirement for a professional career—and some Greek.

In 1582, William married Anne Hathaway. He was 18; she was 26. At the time of their marriage, Anne was already three months pregnant with their first daughter, Susanna. In 1585, the couple had twins, Judith and Hamnet. Hamnet died before reaching adulthood, leaving Shakespeare no male heir.

Even less is known about Shakespeare's life between 1585 and 1592. During that time, he moved to London and became an actor and playwright. He left his family behind in Stratford. Although he surely visited them occasionally, we have little evidence about what Shakespeare was like as a father and a husband.

Several of his early plays were written during this time, including *The Comedy of Errors*, *Titus Andronicus*, and the three parts of *Henry VI*. In those days, working in the theater was rather like acting in soap operas today—the results may be popular, but daytime series aren't recognized as serious art. In fact, many people were opposed to even allowing plays to be performed. Ministers warned their congregations of the dangers of going to plays.

But Shakespeare and his friends were lucky. Queen Elizabeth I loved plays. She protected acting companies from restrictive laws and gave them her permission to perform. Shakespeare wrote several plays to be performed for the queen, including *Twelfth Night*.

Queen Elizabeth I

After Elizabeth's death in 1603, Shakespeare's company became known as the King's Men. This group of actors performed for James I, who had ruled Scotland before becoming the King of England. Perhaps to thank James for his patronage, Shakespeare wrote *Macbeth*, which included two topics of strong interest to the king—Scottish royalty and witchcraft.

Unlike many theater people, Shakespeare actually earned a good living. By 1599, he was part owner of the Globe, one of the newest theaters in London. Such plays as *Othello*, *Hamlet*, and *King Lear* were first performed there.

In 1610 or 1611, Shakespeare moved back to the familiar surroundings of Stratford-upon-Avon. He was almost 50 years old, well past middle age by 17th-century standards. Over the years, he'd invested in property around Stratford, acquiring a comfortable estate and a family coat of arms.

But Shakespeare didn't give up writing. In 1611, his new play *The Tempest* was performed at court. In 1613, his play *Henry VIII* premiered. This performance was more dramatic than anyone expected. The stage directions called for a cannon to be fired when "King Henry" came on stage. The explosion set the stage on fire, and the entire theater burned to the ground.

Shakespeare died in 1616 at the age of 52. His gravestone carried this inscription:

> **Good friend for Jesus sake forbear**
> **To dig the dust enclosed here!**
> **Blest be the man that spares these stones,**
> **And curst be he that moves my bones.**

This little verse, so crude that it seems unlikely to be Shakespeare's, has intrigued countless scholars and biographers.

Anyone who loves Shakespeare's plays and poems wants to know more about their author. Was he a young man who loved Anne Whateley but was forced into a loveless marriage with another Anne? Did he teach school in Stratford, poach Sir Thomas Lucy's deer, or work for a lawyer in London? Who is the "dark lady" of his sonnets?

But perhaps we are fortunate in our ignorance. Orson Welles, who directed an all-black stage production of *Macbeth* in 1936, put it this way: "Luckily, we know almost nothing about Shakespeare . . . and that makes it so much easier to understand [his] works . . . It's an egocentric, romantic, 19th-century conception that the artist is more interesting and more important than his art."

In Shakespeare's world, there can be little question of which is truly important, the work or the author. Shakespeare rings up the curtain and then steps back into the wings, trusting the play to a cast of characters so stunningly vivid that they sometimes seem more real than life.

❈ ❈ ❈

Shakespeare's Theater

In Shakespeare's London, a day's entertainment often began with a favorite amusement, bearbaiting. A bear would be captured and chained to a stake inside a pit. A pack of dogs would be released, and they would attack the bear. Spectators placed bets on which would die first. Admission to these pits cost only a penny, so they were very popular with working-class Londoners.

The Swan Theatre in London, drawn in 1596, the only known contemporary image of an Elizabethan theater interior

After the bearbaiting was over, another penny purchased admission to a play. Each theater had its own company of actors, often supported by a nobleman or a member of the royal family. For part of his career, Shakespeare was a member of the Lord

Chamberlain's Men. After the death of Queen Elizabeth I, King James I became the patron of Shakespeare's company. The actors became known as the King's Men.

As part owner of the Globe Theatre, Shakespeare wrote plays, hired actors, and paid the bills. Since the Globe presented a new play every three weeks, Shakespeare and his actors had little time to rehearse or polish their productions. To complicate matters even more, most actors played more than one part in a play.

Boys played all the female roles. Most acting companies had three or four youths who were practically raised in the theater. They started acting as early as age seven and played female roles until they began shaving. Shakespeare had a favorite boy actor (probably named John Rice) who played

Richard Tarleton, Elizabethan actor famous for his clowning

Cleopatra and Lady Macbeth. Actresses would not become part of the English theater for another fifty years.

The audience crowded into the theater at about 2 p.m. The cheapest seats weren't seats at all but standing room in front of the stage. This area, known as the "pit," was occupied by "groundlings" or "penny knaves," who could be more trouble to the actors than they were worth. If the play was boring, the groundlings would throw rotten eggs or vegetables. They talked loudly to their friends, played cards, and even picked fights with each other. One theater was set on fire by audience members who didn't like the play.

The theater was open to the sky, so rain or snow presented a problem. However, the actors were partially protected by a roof known as the "heavens," and wealthier patrons sat in three stories of sheltered galleries that surrounded the pit and most of the main stage.

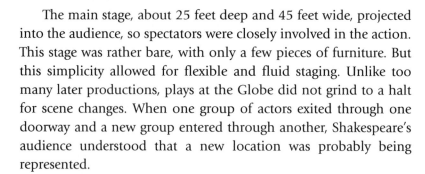

The main stage, about 25 feet deep and 45 feet wide, projected into the audience, so spectators were closely involved in the action. This stage was rather bare, with only a few pieces of furniture. But this simplicity allowed for flexible and fluid staging. Unlike too many later productions, plays at the Globe did not grind to a halt for scene changes. When one group of actors exited through one doorway and a new group entered through another, Shakespeare's audience understood that a new location was probably being represented.

Behind the main stage was the "tiring-house," where the actors changed costumes. Above the stage was a gallery that, when it wasn't occupied by musicians or wealthy patrons, could suggest any kind of high place—castle ramparts, a cliff, or a balcony.

Special effects were common. A trap door in the main stage allowed ghosts to appear. Even more spectacularly, supernatural beings could be lowered from above the stage. For added realism, actors hid bags of pig's blood and guts under their stage doublets. When pierced with a sword, the bags spilled out over the stage and produced a gory effect.

All these staging methods and design elements greatly appealed to Elizabethan audiences and made plays increasingly popular. By the time Shakespeare died in 1616, there were more than thirty theaters in and around London.

What would Shakespeare, so accustomed to the rough-and-tumble stagecraft of the Globe, think of the theaters where his plays are performed today? He would probably miss some of the vitality of the Globe. For centuries now, his plays have been most often performed on stages with a frame called the "proscenium arch," which cleanly separates the audience from the performers. This barrier tends to cast a peculiar shroud of privacy over his plays so that his characters do not seem to quite enter our world.

But with greater and greater frequency, Shakespeare's plays are being performed out-of-doors or in theaters with three- or four-sided stages. And a replica of the Globe Theatre itself opened in London in 1996, only about 200 yards from the site of the original.

The new Globe Theatre, London

This new Globe is an exciting laboratory where directors and actors can test ideas about Elizabethan staging. Their experiments may change our ideas about how Shakespeare's plays were performed and give new insights into their meaning.

✲ ✲ ✲

The Globe Theatre

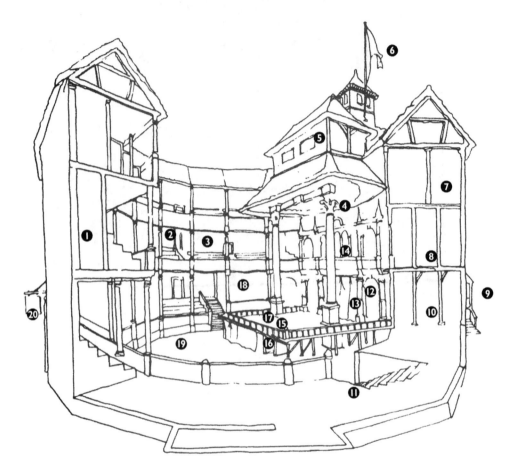

1 **Corridor** A passageway serving the middle gallery.

2 **Entrance** Point leading to the staircase and upper galleries.

3 **Middle Gallery** The seats here were higher priced.

4 **The Heavens** So identified by being painted with the zodiac signs.

5 **Hut** A storage area that also held a winch system for lowering characters to the stage.

6   **Flag** A white flag above the theater meant a show that day.

7   **Wardrobe** A storage area for costumes and props.

8   **Dressing Rooms** Rooms where actors were "attired" and awaited their cues.

9   **Tiring-House Door** The rear entrance or "stage door" for actors or privileged spectators.

10 **Tiring-House** Backstage area providing space for storage and costume changes.

11 **Stairs** Theatergoers reached the galleries by staircases enclosed by stairwells.

12 **Stage Doors** Doors opening into the Tiring-House.

13 **Inner Stage** A recessed playing area, often curtained off except as needed.

14 **Gallery** Located above the stage to house musicians or spectators.

15 **Trap Door** Leading to the Hell area, where a winch elevator was located.

16 **Hell** The area under the stage, used for ghostly comings and goings or for storage.

17 **Stage** Major playing area jutting into the Pit, creating a sense of intimacy.

18 **Lords Rooms** or private galleries. Six pennies let a viewer sit here, or sometimes on stage.

19 **The Pit** Sometimes referred to as "The Yard," where the "groundlings" watched.

20 **Main Entrance** Here the doorkeeper collected admission.

IMAGE CREDITS

Clipart.com: 4, 7, 8, 11, 352, 354, 355; Donald Cooper/Photostage: 145, 289;
© George E. Joseph: 6, 286; John Vickers Theatre: 19;
Library of Congress: 5, 351; ©Pawel Libera/CORBIS: 357;
Photofest: 16, 78, 81, 142, 218, 221